本书得到"厦门大学繁荣哲学社会科学专项资金"资助

赫斯顿、安吉洛和凯莉自传的新突破

江春兰　著

外国文学研究丛书

厦门大学出版社
XIAMEN UNIVERSITY PRESS
国家一级出版社
全国百佳图书出版单位

序

今年 5 月 28 日是美国黑人女作家玛雅·安吉洛逝世一周年。江春兰博士的专著《赫斯顿、安吉洛和凯莉自传的新突破》的出版，是对这位不平凡的黑人女作家的最好纪念。

《赫斯顿、安吉洛和凯莉自传的新突破》是以作者的博士学位论文为基础修订而成的。它涵盖了三位黑人女作家的自传，即左拉·尼尔·赫斯顿的《路上的尘迹》、玛雅·安吉洛的《我知道笼中鸟为何歌唱》和罗琳·凯莉的《黑冰》。这三部自传分别代表了 20 世纪 20 年代、40 年代和 90 年代美国黑人女性自传，展示了黑人女作家如何通过自传写作不懈地探索现代社会里黑人女性的身份和意义。尽管她们关注的重点不同，但她们共同继承了黑人女性自传的传统，修正了黑人女性在黑人男性自传笔下的软弱形象，并重新定义、重新命名黑人女性的自我身份和主体性。这个选题很有意义，对于深入研究美国现代文学，尤其是黑人文学具有重要的学术价值和理论创新意义。

美国黑人自传是美国黑人文学的组成部分。但 20 世纪前，大部分黑人自传都是黑人男性作家写的。比如弗莱德里克·道格拉斯的自传在美国文学史上影响很大。还有许多别的男性黑人的自传。但他们的传记往往没有充分书写黑人女性的生存状态，更常常忽视女性的力量。因此，美国黑人女作家的崛起成了美国文艺界的新鲜事。她们用自己的自传书写颠覆了黑人男性自传中对黑人女性形象的扭曲，揭示了女性在黑人社区和白人社会里不可取代的作用，引起了学术界的广泛关注。江春兰博士敏锐地发现了这个问题，选择赫斯顿、安吉洛和凯莉三人的自传作为她们的代表作，深入剖析她们的自传对美国黑人自传的新突破，揭示了黑人文学的新发展，为我国美国黑人文学研究的深化做出了重要的贡献。

专著注重语境—理论—文本的结合，采用对比的方法，深刻地揭示了赫斯顿、安吉洛和凯莉三人自传的共性和个性，展示了他们对美国黑人女性自传文学的独特贡献。

赫斯顿的《路上的尘迹》问世后遭遇许多负面评论，但她勇敢面对，坚持自己的文化观。她向白人读者和黑人读者展示黑人文化的丰富性、多样性以及活力。她用意指策略颠覆白人的文化霸权主义，将自传文本变成"言说者文本"。她的自传具有丰富的黑人口头文化传统和黑人民俗文化色彩。

安吉洛的系列自传有六部。专著重点选择了第一部《我知道笼中鸟为何歌唱》来评析。这部自传兼具黑人男性和女性自转的传统，表述了黑人的政治意识，描写了20世界30年代南方黑人姑娘玛雅. 安吉洛遭受各种种族歧视，失去了自由，犹如一只笼中鸟，后来她顽强抗争，成了一位坚强而独立的女性。自传文本富有戏剧性，涉及人类在困境中的痛苦和挣扎，具有普遍意义。

凯莉的《黑冰》则设想跨越种族界限的文化融合。她也没有忽略黑人奴隶制历史对黑人学生们造成的心理创伤。她认为通过耐心疏导，可帮助他们促进黑人文化与白人文化的融合。黑人文化已成为美国文化的一部分。黑人也不再是边缘人，而是美国人的合法成员。

专著还指出，三部黑人女性传记不仅继承了黑人传记传统的奴隶叙事，铭记黑人遭受歧视和迫害的历史，而且采用了不同的叙事策略，取得了良好的艺术效果，具有强烈的艺术魅力，在美国文学史上留下灿烂的一页。

《路上的尘迹》具有现代主义色彩。作者有意面对白人和黑人双重读者，叙述不确定性，文化内涵丰富，兼备混杂性特色。《我知道笼中鸟为何歌唱》则采用批判现实主义手法，以大量生动真实的细节描写展示小主人公的不幸遭遇、母性的力量和黑人社区的温暖等。作者还穿插使用嘲讽、幽默、自我戏仿等手法，使叙述更加生动感人。《黑冰》全新解读了黑人民间故事，从黑人传统文化中吸取力量，采用口述传统的手法，探讨跨越种族界限的可能性，提出新环境下两种文化融合的设想。

不仅如此，专著还指出：三部黑人女性传记作者都努力追寻黑人口述传统，但又各具特色。赫斯顿注重黑人修辞策略的"意指"和"言说性文本"。安吉洛遵循布鲁斯传统，叙述中略带抒情，笔调平易优美。凯莉则沿袭黑人口述故事传统，以此作为治愈黑人青少年心理创伤的良方。这些评析密切结合文本，有理有据，公正可信，令人感到专著的作者对三部黑人女性自转的深刻把握。

《赫斯顿、安吉洛和凯莉自传的新突破》的问世标志着江春兰博士学术道路的新起点，可喜可贺！作为一名高校教师，她既要教好书，育好人，又要搞科研，多出成果。要在繁忙的教学工作中挤时间坚持科研，刻苦钻研，大胆创新。古人云："良时正可用，行矣莫徒然"。今天，神州大地，春风浩荡。万人创业，万众创新已成热潮。形势催人奋进。我衷心地祝愿江春兰博士继续保持勤奋敬业、励志向前、与时俱进的精神，在美国黑人文学研究方面再谱新篇！

  是为序。

杨仁敬

2015 年 5 月

前　言

　　作为了解美国黑人生存状态最重要的文类，美国黑人自传在美国黑人文学史占据着举足轻重的位置。美国黑人作家在自传里猛烈抨击了奴隶制的残暴，讲述了他们为了摆脱奴役、争取自由而进行的坚持不懈的斗争，同时也探索了奴隶制对美国黑人造成的恶劣的社会和心理影响，揭示了现代社会里美国黑人仍然遭受种族歧视的现实。但是在20世纪之前，大部分黑人传记都是男性作家的作品。由于受到男权思想的影响，黑人女性对黑人男性作家来说只是可有可无的存在。所以黑人男性的传记并没有充分描述美国黑人女性真实的生存状态，更不用说展示黑人女性的力量了。直到黑人女性开始进行自传写作，利用这个武器重新进行自我定义，这种状况才开始改变。本书主要通过分析左拉·尼尔·赫斯顿、玛雅·安吉洛以及罗琳·凯莉的自传，探索黑人女性自传对美国黑人传记书写的新突破。

　　美国黑人自传拥有不同于白人自传的特点。奴隶叙事是美国黑人自传最早的形式，它为黑人自传的主题和形式设定了基本的模式。美国黑人自传最基本的特征是它所体现出来的政治意识：它肩负阶级的重任，反对奴隶制、争取黑人整个民族的解放是它的神圣使命。因此，在黑人自传里，自我只是整个黑人社区的组成部分，自我的声音和集体的声音往往融为一体。不过，虽然奴隶叙事为黑人传记设定了基本的模式，但是，美国黑人自传写作是一个不断修正传统的动态的过程，这是因为美国黑人在不同的历史阶段对于黑人自传中最基本的因素如自我、奴隶制以及自由等概念有新的阐释。同时，美国黑人女性也拿起自传写作这个武器书写自我，修正黑人女性在男性作家笔下的刻板形象。这些现象都体现了对黑人自传传统的修正和重新书写。

　　此外，黑人女性自传是黑人自传不可分割的一部分，也是黑人女性文学的重要组成部分。它宣称了黑人女性文学在美国文学，尤其是美国黑人文学中的地位，改变了黑人女性在文学领域的失语状态。黑人女性自传书写颠覆了黑人男性自传中被扭曲的黑人女性形象，是重新定义、重新命名黑人女性自我身份和主体性的重要途径。

　　黑人女性自传不仅继承黑人男性自传传统的一些因素，还创建了属于黑人女性自传独特的传统。一方面，黑人女性自传和男性自传一样，体现了黑人的政治意识。另一方面，黑人女性自传与黑人男性自传又有所不同：黑人男性作家在自传写作时把他们的成就归功于他们个人的能力和积极性；黑人女性作家则大力渲染女性之间非常牢固的纽带关系，颂扬女性母爱的伟大以及黑人女性之间无私的姐妹情谊。在黑人女性自传里，黑人女性不再是男性笔下柔弱无助的牺牲品；相反，黑人女性坚强、独立、乐观，是拥有尊严的人。她们是黑人社区的中流砥柱，不仅担负着养儿育女、教育后代的责任，还担负着传承黑人文化的使命。因为她们的存在，黑人的生活才拥有温暖和活力，黑人的口头文化传统才得以传承。同时，黑人女性自传又不同于白人女性自传，它对女性自传这个文类进行了一定的修正和补充，揭示了黑人女性的复杂命运。

赫斯顿、安吉洛和凯莉属于这一类的黑人女性自传作家。她们通过自传写作这个途径进行自我定义，自我命名，表达了对自由孜孜不倦的追求，以此丰富了对美国黑人生活经历的描述。这三部自传是三个不同历史时期黑人女性自传的代表作：赫斯顿的《路上的尘迹》是20世纪40年代黑人女性自传的代表，安吉洛的《我知道笼中鸟为何歌唱》代表了60年代末以后的黑人女性自传，凯莉的自传则是90年代后黑人女性自传的代表。20世纪90年代后，黑人女性仍然通过自传写作执着探索在现代社会里黑人女性的身份和意义，探索她们的前辈在自传中没有涉猎或者探索不够深入、还有待解决的各种问题。这三位作家的自传关注的焦点互不相同，但是从传承黑人女性自传传统的角度来看，她们是彼此相连、一脉相承的。

赫斯顿的自传《路上的尘迹》出版后，由于该作品从主题和形式上都颠覆了以往黑人自传的固有传统，负面的评论铺天盖地。事实上，作为一位投入的人类学家和充满激情的黑人民俗学家，赫斯顿热爱自己民族的文化。更重要的是，赫斯顿深谙黑人口头传统中最富有特色、最重要的修辞策略——意指。赫斯顿的自传面对的是双重读者，即处于中产阶层的白人读者和黑人读者。面临这双重读者，她采用意指叙事策略，试图对双重读者进行协调，和读者玩捉迷藏的游戏。笔者认为，意指策略是打开这部自传的钥匙。

赫斯顿真正的意图是：向读者展示黑人文化的丰富性、多样性和活力。赫斯顿深受其导师——著名人类学家弗朗兹·博厄斯的影响，树立了独特超前的文化观：认为文化具有流动性和混杂性，坚信文化没有高低贵贱之分。在收集黑人民俗文化的过程中，赫斯顿惊喜地发现，黑人文化并非是正在走向衰亡的文化；相反，黑人文化欣欣向荣，充满活力。对黑人文化了解得越多，研究得越多，她就越是为黑人文化的独特魅力所倾倒。

虽然赫斯顿和弗朗兹·法农不是属于同时代的人，但是赫斯顿的文化观却在法农的著作《黑皮肤，白面具》里得到了共鸣。在如何对待种族的问题上以及如何对待黑人受奴役的历史方面，二者表达了相似的态度。赫斯顿的自传表面上表达了无种族界限的思想，对于黑人的一些有关种族的观念进行质疑和解构。事实上，赫斯顿只是通过意指策略来对抗白人的文化霸权主义和文化帝国主义。通过意指策略以及其他口语传统叙事策略的使用，赫斯顿把她的自传文本变成了"言说者文本"，把她的家乡作为黑人文化的典型代表来描述。赫斯顿发现，文化的杂糅性是美国黑人文化的一大特征。

在安吉洛的系列自传中，她的第一部自传《我知道笼中鸟为何歌唱》被认为是黑人自传的典范：它一方面传承了奴隶叙事设定的黑人自传的模式，兼备黑人男性和女性自传的传统；另一方面，安吉洛的自传在一定程度上也超越了黑人自传的传统。

和其他典型的黑人自传一样，《我知道笼中鸟为何歌唱》也表达了黑人的政治意识，描述了20世纪30年代美国南方黑人女孩玛雅·安吉洛的成长经历，揭示了黑人在种族隔离制度下遭受到的各种歧视和面对这种制度的无能为力，探索如何挣脱强加在黑人身上的社会、经济以及其他各方面的枷锁，从而获得最终的自由。这本自传表现了黑人女孩小玛雅在当时的社会环境下犹如笼中之鸟一样失去自由的权利，但是作者强调的重点是小玛雅如何为生存而抗争，最终如何成功地摆脱了社会和心理的双重枷锁而成长为独立、自信的女性。这本自传是一段从牢笼走向自由的旅程，是一首追寻自由的颂歌。在自传里，安吉洛描述了黑人在种族隔离的制度下受尽歧视和磨难。面对这样的状况，玛雅从黑人丰富的社区文化中汲取了精神上的力量。在黑人社区里，女性是整个社区的灵魂人物，是整个社区赖以生存的精神力量，比如安吉洛的祖母亨德逊太太、母亲薇薇安以及福莱沃斯夫人等。正是在这些女性长辈的关怀下，饱受创伤的小玛雅成长为一位坚强、独立的女性。

同时，安吉洛在写作《我知道笼中鸟为何歌唱》的时候，有意识地把自传当作文学作品来创作，无论在主题还是表现手法上都取得了一定的突破。安吉洛跨体裁的系列自传是美国黑人自传书写的创新。在她的系列自传里，散文、游记、小说等多种体裁杂糅，现实主义与现代主义结合，史实与虚构结合，应用了许多小说写作的叙事技巧，比如有精心设计的场景、情节和主题，使用想象、嘲讽、幽默和自我戏仿等修辞手法，使文本更富有戏剧性、富有想象的张力，取得了意想不到的效果。此外，该自传讲述的是人类的普遍经历。不管读者是黑人或者白人，或者是其他肤色的人，都可以从中看到作为人类的一员在困境中的挣扎和痛苦、欢乐与悲伤、脆弱与坚强。正如安吉洛自己所说的，当她在叙述黑人的经历时，她也同时在关注整个人类的命运，关注人类如何忍受失败和挫折，如何在逆境中追求梦想，如何在艰难困苦中求生存。

凯莉的自传《黑冰》延续了赫斯顿自传中对于文化多样性的探索，提出了跨越种族界限进行文化融合的设想。在自传里，凯莉讲述了她作为第一批被圣保罗学校录取的黑人学生所遭遇的经历。凯莉着重描述了黑人奴隶制的历史对现代黑人的心灵造成的不可磨灭的创伤，给他们带来的沉重的心理负担。不过幸运的是，当凯莉回到圣保罗中学成为一名教师之后，她已经能够为那些遭遇同样处境的黑人学生提供指导，帮助他们平衡两种文化的冲突，以积极开放的心态面对两种文化的融合。霍米·巴巴的文化混杂性和间性协商理论可以提供理论基础，用于分析凯莉对于跨越种族界限进行文化融合的思想。

凯莉一方面从黑人传统，尤其是口头传统中获取力量，另一方面利用她作为黑人、作为一个边缘人的优势，探索在"间质空间"里的身份。她是一名教师，同时也是一名"跨界艺术家"，承担了融合两种文化的使命。黑人文化和白人文化互相影响、互相渗透，从而丰富了两种文化的内容。黑人文化因此也成了美国文化的重要组成部分。同样的，黑人不再只是边缘人，而是美国人的组成成员。笔者认为，作为黑人民俗学家的赫斯顿一定会同意并欣赏凯莉对那两个黑人民间故事的新的阐释，因为对于赫斯顿来说，那也是她一直想要实现的梦想。

在这三部自传里，作者采用了不同的叙事策略。笔者首先分析了主要的文学思潮对安吉洛和赫斯顿产生的影响：《我知道笼中鸟为何歌唱》表现了现实主义的色彩，《路上的尘迹》表现出了现代主义的特点。此外，《路上的尘迹》中的其他叙事技巧主要表现为不可靠性叙事、双重读者问题以及对黑人修辞策略"意指"的熟练应用。关于《我知道笼中鸟为何歌唱》，安吉洛的叙事视角也值得关注。笔者同时探讨了三部自传对于黑人口语传统的追寻：《我知道笼中鸟为何歌唱》的布鲁斯传统、《路上的尘迹》的言说者文本以及《黑冰》中民间故事的疗伤功能。

总之，这三部自传彼此不同，又相互联系，体现了美国黑人女性自传书写的突破。黑人女性自传在继承黑人自传的传统时，又以各自的方式对黑人自传进行了修正，以此丰富了黑人自传作为一个文类的内涵。自传写作为黑人女性提供了一个进行自由讲述的途径。

A Note on Abbreviations

Throughout this book, the following abbreviations are used to indicate the titles of the autobiographies of Hurston, Angelou and Cary.

Dust Tracks on a Road: DT

I Know Why the Caged Bird Sings: CB

Black Ice: BI

Gather Together in My Name: GTMN

Contents

Introduction

1. Hurston, Angelou and Cary's Lives and Works

Although the last decades of the 20th century saw the outpouring of the studies of American black autobiography, especially the studies of the earliest form of American black autobiography—the slave narratives, little research work was devoted to the study of American black women's autobiographies. Therefore, this book will explore American black women's autobiographies, mainly dwelling on Zora Neale Hurston's *Dust Tracks on a Road*, Maya Angelou's *I Known Why the Caged Bird Sings* and Lorene Cary's *Black Ice*. First of all, a general account will be given to the lives and works of Hurston, Angelou and Cary.

1.1 Hurston's Life and Works

Zora Neale Hurston (1891-1960), an African-American female author, folklorist, anthropologist, is regarded as the forerunner of African-American literature. She published four novels, more than 50 short stories, plays, and essays. All through her life, Hurston remained an enigmatic woman and was once considered by Mary Helen Washington as "a woman half in shadow."

According to Zora Hurston's autobiography *Dust Tracks on a Road*, she was born in Eatonville, Florida, but she didn't mention her birthday. However, birth records revealed that she was born in 1891 in Notasulga, Alabama. When she was three, her family moved to Eatonville, Florida, the first incorporated black town. Her father John Hurston was a Baptist preacher and the mayor of the town and her mother Lucie Potts was a school teacher. In Eatonville, Zora Hurston enjoyed a secure childhood, free from the inferior sense experienced by the Southern black Americans. The happy childhood there had a great influence on Hurston's whole life. But her happy life came to an end in 1904 when her mother died. Her father remarried almost immediately after her mother's death. Her father and stepmother didn't want to raise the children. As a result, Zora Hurston and her seven other siblings were dispersed to relatives and boarding schools. Zora was sent to a boarding school in Jacksonville, Florida, but was expelled because her father eventually stopped paying her tuition.

Though still a young girl, Zora Neale Hurston began her difficult life on her own in the American South. She later worked as a maid to support herself. In 1917, Hurston managed to attend Morgan Academy, graduating in 1918. As an eager student, she obtained the opportunity to go on with her study at Howard University in Washington, D.C., always working her way through school with odd jobs. At the university, she took courses in Spanish, English, Greek and public speaking, and earned an Associate's Degree in 1920. In 1921, she published her first short story in the college literary magazine, "The Stylus." In 1924, Hurston published "Drenched in Light," a story about a joyful child in Eatonville. The following year, she wrote a story, "Spunk" and a play, *Color Struck*, both of which won prizes in *Opportunity*'s literary contest. Thanks to her success in the contest, Hurston was able to become a member of the Harlem Renaissance. In 1925, she was offered a scholarship to Barnard College and became the sole black student in the college. Soon afterwards, Hurston studied anthropology under the noted anthropologist Franz Boas and conducted ethnographic research. She received her B.A. in anthropology in 1927. Hurston spent two years as a graduate student in anthropology at Columbia University.

In 1927, Hurston married a jazz musician Herbert Sheen, but they divorced four years later. In 1939, she married again, but the marriage ended after only seven months. In the following ten years, with the support from her patron, Mrs. Rufus Osgood Mason, Hurston devoted herself to observing, collecting and participating in the black culture of her hometown Florida, Georgia and Alabama. She reported on voodoo practices in Louisiana and Haiti and collected customs, dances and practices in Jamaica and the Bahamas. Her lifelong goal was to preserve the folk traditions and to create an original black literature.

In the anthropological field, Hurston published important works such as *Mules and Men* (1935) and *Tell My Horse* (1938). In 1930, she collaborated with Langston Hughes, writing *Mule Bone: A Comedy of Negro Life in Three Acts*, a play that was not published until 1991. As a novelist, Hurston published four novels: *Jonah's Gourd Vine* (1934), a story based on the life of her father, a blend of autobiography, folklore and fiction; *Their Eyes Were Watching God* (1937), written during her fieldwork in Haiti and considered as her masterpiece, a novel about a young woman Janie Crawford's search for love, self-identity and freedom; and *Moses, Man of the Mountain* (1939), a complex novel exploring the way into freedom; *Seraph on the Suwanee* (1948), a story notable principally for its focus on white characters (Butterworth 247-54).

At the request of her publisher, J.B. Lippincott, Hurston began in 1941 to work on her autobiography *Dust Tracks on a Road* (1942). The book is a controversial autobiography. Although the book was warmly welcomed by the white readers and was awarded the Anisfield-Wolf Book Award, it suffered lots of negative criticism, severely criticized especially by black intellectuals for her negligence of the race problem and her stance towards the whites.

Since the mid-1940s, Hurston seemed to be losing her voice especially after she was falsely charged for molesting a ten-year-old boy. Hurston was not able to recover from this scandal. She became more conservative and moved back to Florida, continued to write magazine articles and suffered from financial and medical difficulties. In 1959, Hurston had a stroke and entered a welfare home and died there on 28 January, 1960, buried in an unmarked grave. Zora Neale Hurston's books were out of print for more than three decades. The passionate author and anthropologist was forgotten until 1975, when the black writer and scholar Alice Walker wrote an article, "In Search of Zora Neale Hurston," which revived readers' interest in her works. Hurston was then recognized as the pioneer of Afro-American women's literature.

1.2 Maya Angelou's Life and Works

Maya Angelou (1928-2014), born Marguerite Ann Johnson in St. Louis, Missouri, on April 4, 1928, best known as an African-American author and poet, has published a series of six autobiographies, five books of essays, numerous books of poetry, and is credited with a long list of plays, movies, and television shows. Angelou has a rich and complicated life experience. She is not only a writer and poet, but also works as a dancer, a singer, an actor, a director and a journalist, a producer of plays, movies, and public television programs.

When Angelou was three, and her dear brother Bailey was four, they were sent back to Stamps, Arkansas by their divorced parents and were brought up by her grandmother Mrs. Henderson. Four years later, they were sent to St. Louis, living with their mother. But unfortunately, eight-year-old Maya was raped by her mother's boyfriend Mr. Freeman, who was later murdered probably by her maternal uncles. The rape experience caused a serious trauma for Maya, making her mute for a long time. She came back to Stamps, where she met Mrs. Flowers, who gave her courage to step out of her cage of muteness and taught her the power of words. When Angelou was 14, she moved with her brother to California, staying with their mother again. She studied in George Washington High School and at the same time learned dance and drama at the California Labor School. Angelou then struggled hard to become the first black female streetcar conductor in San Francisco. At the age of 17, she became a young single mother, giving birth to her son Guy. From the age 17 to 19, as a black single mother without job training or good education, she lived an extremely difficult life.

In 1951, Angelou married Enistasious (Tosh) Angelos, who was a Greek electrician and an aspiring musician. At that time, she continued to learn modern dances and began to form a dance team with her friend. After she ended her marriage with Angelos in 1954, Angelou began to dance professionally and toured Europe with the opera *Porgy and Bess* during the following two years. As a versatile artist, Angelou recorded her first album in 1957. In 1959, encouraged by the novelist James O. Killens, Angelou began to concentrate on her writing career. After she joined Harlem Writers Guild, she got acquainted with some major black authors including John Henrik Clarke, Paule Marshall, and Julian Mayfield. Influenced by the civil rights leader Dr. Martin Luther King, Jr., Angelou became the northern coordinator for Southern Christian Leadership Conference and began her anti-apartheid activism.

In 1961, Angelou moved to Cairo with her son, working as an associate editor for a newspaper. In 1962, they moved to Accra, Ghana. Unfortunately, her son was wounded in a car accident. As a result, Angelou stayed in Accra until 1965. During the time, she worked as an administrator at Ghana University and was actively involved in the African-American expatriate community. When Malcolm X visited there in the early 1960s, they became friends. In 1965, when Angelou returned to the U.S., she helped him build the Organization of Afro-American Unity. However, Malcolm X was assassinated shortly afterwards. In 1968, Angelou promised Martin Luther King to organize a march, but before she could carry out the plan, Martin Luther King was also assassinated. Both Malcolm X and Martin Luther King are not only the great leaders of the Civil Rights Movements, but also Angelou's close friends. Their assassinations were heavy blows to Angelou. In 1968, encouraged by her friend James Baldwin and challenged by the Random House editor Robert Loomis, she accepted the challenge to write her first autobiography *I Know Why the Caged Bird Sings*.

In 1973, Angelou married Welsh carpenter Paul du Feu, but the marriage ended in 1981. In the next ten years, she made great achievements. Since the 1990s, Angelou has actively taken part in giving lectures. In 2002, Angelou accomplished her last autobiography *A Song Flung Up to Heaven*. As for her personal life, besides her son Guy, Angelou has one grandson, and two young great-grandchildren, and a large group of friends and extended family.

Angelou is best known for her series of autobiographies, which focus on her childhood and early adult experiences. They include *I Know Why the Caged Bird Sings* (1969), up to 1944; *Gather Together in My Name* (1974), 1944-1948; *Singin' and Swingin' and Gettin' Merry Like Christmas* (1976), 1949-1955; *The Heart of a Woman* (1981), 1957-1962; *All God's Children Need Traveling Shoes* (1986), 1962-1965 and *A Song Flung Up to Heaven* (2002), 1965-1968. Angelou won a National Book Award nomination for her first autobiography *I Know Why the Caged Bird Sings* (1969), which tells of her first seventeen years. The book is her most highly-acclaimed autobiography and has won her international recognition.

Besides, Angelou is also an outstanding poet. Her poetry *Just Give Me a Cool Drink of Water 'Fore I Diiie* (1971) gained her a Pulitzer Prize nomination. Other books of poetry include *Oh Pray My Wings Are Gonna Fit Me Well* (1975), *And Still I Rise* (1978) and *Shaker, Why Don't You Sing!* (1983). Angelou's most famous poem was "On the Pulse of Morning," which she recited at the inauguration of President Bill Clinton in 1993. Reviewer Elsie B. Washington called Angelou "the black woman's poet laureate."

As one of the most honored American writers, Angelou has been granted numerous awards and more than 30 honorary degrees. She was awarded the National Medal of Arts in 2000, the Lincoln Medal in 2008, and the Presidential Medal of Freedom in 2011.

Angelou's books have often received mixed reviews. Her first autobiography *I Know Why the Caged Bird Sings* has been negatively criticized by many parents and schools due to "the depictions of lesbianism, premarital cohabitation, pornography, and violence." In spite of the criticism, *I Know Why the Caged Bird Sings* is still regarded as one of the most important African American autobiographies. Angelou is highly respected as a spokesperson of American black people and women, and her works have been considered a defense for American black culture. Both her autobiographies and poetry center on such themes as racism, identity, family, seeking freedom, etc. According to Stefanie K. Dunning, Angelou's autobiographies and poems show that "the personal is political and that the events that shape and inform an individual life are often related to large political movements and events that affect an entire community" (60).

1.3 Lorene Cary's Life and Works

Lorene Cary (1956-) was born on November 29, 1956 in Philadelphia, Pennsylvania. She is regarded as a highly-respected African-American author, professor and social activist. Cary's father was a science teacher, while her mother was a beautician. At the age of 14, a neighbor first told Cary of the very prestigious St. Paul's School in Concord, New Hampshire. It was told that the formerly all-white college-preparatory boarding school had recently gone coed and was interested in finding black girls to attend it. Fortunately, in March, 1972, Cary was admitted to the elite St. Paul's, where she underwent painful psychological experiences, which inspired her to write her bestseller *Black Ice* (1991). As one of the first black students to study at St. Paul's, Cary was forced to confront the problem of identity.

In 1974, Cary graduated from St. Paul's School and attended the University of Pennsylvania. With excellent academic records, she was offered a Thouron Fellowship for British-U.S. student exchange. Cary decided to enroll in Sussex University, where she received a master's degree of arts in Victorian literature. In 1979, she received her MA degree from the University of Pennsylvania. Besides, Cary has also received several honorary doctorates from Colby College, Chestnut Hill College and some other colleges.

Cary started her writing career as an apprentice for *Time* in 1980 and then as an associate editor at *TV Guide*. She worked for other major magazines such as *Time* and *Newsweek*. Cary also freelanced for *American Visions*, *Essence*, *Mirabella*, and *The Philadelphia Inquirer Sunday Magazine*. In 1983, Cary was married and settled into her career as a writer.

Cary's masterpiece is her memoir *Black Ice* (1991), which won her national recognition as a writer. *Black Ice* has certainly been Cary's most acclaimed work. According to the American Library Association, *Black Ice* ranked as one of the Notable Books in 1992. In 1995, Cary finished her first novel—*The Price of a Child*, a story about how a slave woman sought freedom via the Underground Railroad and built a new life. The novel gained her much praise throughout the literary world. In 1998, she published her second novel, *Pride: A Novel*, a story about the life of four contemporary black middle-class women. In 2005, Cary's first young adult book *Free! Great Escapes on the Underground Railroad* was published. It was Cary's collection of 12 tales about slaves seeking freedom. Meanwhile, Cary also wrote the script for the videos. In 2011, Cary published her third novel *If Sons, Then Heirs*, a story dealing with the complicated themes of family, race, and the relationship between the present and the past.

In 1998, Cary founded Art Sanctuary in North Philadelphia, a nonprofit organization that invites and encourages artists to appreciate the power of black art, to draw inspiration from the inner city and to produce excellent African-American arts, lectures and performances. Each year, thousands of people participate in the arts education programs in urban Philadelphia. Art Sanctuary offers the artists an opportunity to hold an annual African-American arts festival.

Cary received the 1998 Provost's Award for Distinguished Teaching and is now a senior lecturer teaching creative writing at the University of Pennsylvania. She enjoys a happy family life and has two daughters, a son, and two grandchildren.

2. Criticism on African-American Autobiographies in the United States and China

According to James Olney, American black writing was barely mentioned as literature until recently (15), there is no wonder that American black autobiography has not aroused attention until the 1940s. In 1946, Marion Wilson Starling presented her Ph.D. dissertation: *The Slave Narrative: Its Place in American History*, the first extensive book to examine the slave narratives, which inspired scholars to study early black writings. In 1948, Rebecca Chalmers Barton published *Witness for Freedom: Negro Americans in Autobiography*, which is regarded by William L. Andrews as the first major critical analysis of American black autobiography. In the book, Barton anticipates "an accelerating militancy in modern black autobiography" (Andrews, "African American Autobiography Criticism: Retrospect and Prospect" 196). Owing to the influence of the Civil Rights Movement, the Feminism Movement and the Black Arts Movement, the 1960s witnessed the wave of interest in American black writing, including black autobiography. Numerous black autobiographies were published.

Since the 1970s, literary critics have showed great interest in the study of black autobiography, especially in the effect of the slave narratives on the development of American black autobiography. As a result, many books about the study of slave narratives were published. In 1974, Stephen Butterfield published his book *Black Autobiography in America*, the most comprehensive literary history of black autobiography, in which he gives a cogent analysis about 50 black autobiographies published between 1831 and 1972, dividing the history of black autobiography into three periods: the slave-narrative period (1831-1895), the period of search (1901-1961) and the period of rebirth (since 1961). In the first period, he analyzes the rhetorical devices of slave narratives such as point of view, irony, parody and language, examining the white influence on the slave narratives. Fredrick Douglass's *The Narrative* and *The Life and Times of Frederick Douglass* are given detailed analyses. In the second period, he focuses on the examination of a new consciousness and sense of identity. In the third period, he dwells on the new radicalism and the revolutionary self represented in the autobiographies. (Andrews 199) The year of 1974 witnessed another important critical book about American black autobiography, Sidonie Smith's *Where I'm Bound*: *Patterns of Slavery and Freedom in Black American Autobiography* (1974). In the book, she examines the slave narratives and finds in them a communal pattern of escaping from the enslaving community and pursuing a chance to break into a community in which the autobiographer is allowed to express himself fully. She makes an analysis of the autobiographies of Cleaver, Horace Cayton, Claude Brown and Maya Angelou, and finds that the subsequent autobiographies also revoice the pattern of flight and seeking freedom. In the book, Smith reexamines the meaning of freedom. Robert B. Stepto's *From Behind the Veil*: *A Study of Afro-American Narrative* (1979) emphasizes the black autobiographers' quest for literacy and freedom. Stepto classifies the slave narratives into four types, examines the influence of the slave narratives on modern African-American narratives and analyzes how modern black narratives revoice and answer the call of the slave narratives. *Afro-American Literature*: *The Reconstruction of Instruction* edited by Dexter Fisher and Robert B. Stepto (1979) and *Witnessing Slavery*: *The Development of Ante-bellum Slave Narratives* (1979) by Frances Smith Foster are also important works about the study of slave narratives.

Meanwhile, there are also important essays which dwell on American black autobiography studies such as Elizabeth Schultz's "To be Black and Blue: The Blues Genre in Black American Autobiography" (1975), Albert E. Stone's

"After Black Boy and Dust of Dawn: Patterns in Recent Black Autobiography" (1978), Paul John Eakin's "Malcolm X and the Limits of Autobiography" (1976), Houston A. Baker, Jr.'s "The Problem of Being: Some Reflections on Black Autobiography" (1975), etc.

In the 1980s, the criticism on black autobiography continued to center on slave narratives, especially on the antebellum slave narratives. Charles T. Davis and Henry Louis Gates Jr. edited *The Slave's Narrative* (1985), collecting critical essays about slave narratives from the perspective of historical analysis. An introduction and a bibliography of black narratives from 1760 to 1865 are included in the book. In 1988, the second edition of Marion Wilson Starling's *The Slave Narrative: Its Place in American History* was published. On the other hand, the 1980s saw the shift of American black autobiography criticism focus on the study of the formal, stylistic and rhetorical richness of black autobiography as a narrative tradition. For example, John Sekora and Darwin T. Turner edited the book *The Art of the Slave Narrative: Original Essays in Criticism and Theory* (1982), focusing on the rhetorical devices such as form, metaphor and point of view, etc. Deborah E. McDowell and Arnold Rampersad edited the book *Slavery and the Literary Imagination* (1989). In 1986, William L. Andrews published his book *To Tell a Free Story: The First Century of Afro-American Autobiography*, 1760-1865. He regards the writing of autobiography as a vehicle of self-liberating. The history of American black autobiography is considered as the history of "free storytelling." He focuses on the rhetorical devices that the narrators use to represent their way of self-liberating. In addition, there are two literary books of great importance: Houston A. Baker's *Blues, Ideology, and Afro-American Literature* (1984) and Henry Louis Gates's *The Signifying Monkey* (1988). In *Blues, Ideology, and Afro-American Literature*, Baker points out the relationship between the blues and American social and literary history, viewing the blues voice as a way of expression in black culture and how it is represented in black writing. In Gates's *The Signifying Monkey*, he points out the cultural practice of signifyin(g) is the "trope of tropes" in black oral tradition, and examines how black writers such as Richard Wright, Ralph Ellison, Zora Hurston and Ishmael Reed use the trope in their writings.

In William L. Andrews' article "African American Autobiography Criticism: Retrospect and Prospect," he summarizes the main features of the criticism of American black autobiography in the 1990s. Firstly, critics viewed the genre of autobiography from a fresh perspective: viewing American black autobiography "as a site of formal revisionism and the free play of signification" (Andrews 208). Andrew's article "Toward a Poetics of Afro-American Autobiography" points out the necessity of considering "the inevitable revision of tradition that has occurred in the past and that continues to occur today" (87) and the necessity of the study of postbellum slave narratives such as Booker T. Washington's *Up From Slavery*. Secondly, American black women's autobiography should deserve more critical attention. Finally, Andrews points out "the comparative studies of the pan-African dimensions of this genre" should be another direction of studies on American black autobiography.

However, despite numerous books on American black autobiography, most of them focus on the study of American black male autobiographers. The study of American black women's autobiographies is mostly ignored. Only a few critics began to show their interest, among whom Joanne M. Braxton is prominent. Braxton views the tradition of American black autobiography from a fresh feminist perspective, expanding the study of the genre by including American black women's autobiography as an important part of American black autobiography. She published her book *Black Women Writing Autobiography*: *A Tradition within a Tradition* in 1989, exploring the communal themes and archetypal images in modern American black women's autobiographies that echo the thematic concerns of slave narratives and spiritual autobiographies. Besides, there are some important articles examining American black women's autobiographies such as Mary Burgher's "Images of Self and Race in the Autobiographies of Black Women," Regina Blackburn's "In Search of the Black Female Self: African-American Women's Autobiographies and Ethnicity" (1980), Elizabeth Fox-Genovese's "To Write My Self—The Autobiographies of Afro-American Women" and "My Statue, My Self: Autobiographical Writing of Afro-American Women," Selwyn R. Cudjoe's "Maya Angelou: The Autobiographical Statement Updated," Susan Stanford Friedman's "Women's Autobiographical Selves: Theory and Practice," bell hooks' "Revolutionary Black Women: Making Ourselves Subject," George E. Kent's "Maya Angelou's *I Know Why the Caged Bird Sings* and Black Autobiographical Tradition," Nellie Y. McKay's "Reflections on Black Women Writers: Revising the Literary Canon" and "The Narrative Self: Race, Politics, and Culture in Black American Women's Autobiography," Sidonie Anne Smith and Julia Watson's "Introduction: Situating Subjectivity in Women's Autobiographical Practices," and so on.

In China, recent years have seen the increasing interest in American autobiography studies, and there are some articles about the study of autobiography: Yang Zhengrun's "On Confession and the Autobiography" (2002), Zhao Baisheng's "Three Constituents of Fact in Autobiographical Narratives" (2001), Yang Jincai's "American Autobiography in the 19th Century and Self-Representation" and Wang Chenjun's "An Account of and Comment on Autobiographic Theory Research in the West" (2006), etc. Chinese readers and critics have also shown great interest in African-American novels such as Toni Morrison's *The Bluest Eye*, *Beloved*, *Jazz* and *Paradise*, Zora Hurston's *Their Eyes Were Watching God*, Alice Walker's *The Color Purple*, etc.

However, little attention is given to the study of American black autobiography. There are only a few essays published in the major critical journals. For example, Professor Jin Li's "Subversive Narrative Strategy in Harriet Jacobs's *Incidents in the Life of a Slave Girl*" (2002), Xi Chuanjin's "A Review of the Poetics of Afro-American Autobiography" (2005), Tang Youmin's "Postmodernist Study of Slave Narrative—Review of Williams L. Andrews' *To Tell a Free Story*" (2010). In Zhou Chun's doctoral dissertation *A Study of Black Feminist Criticism in America* and Wang Shuqin's doctoral dissertation *A Study on Black Feminist Literature Criticism in America*, they have both given a brief introduction to the importance of American black women's autobiographical writing.

Xu Dejin's doctoral dissertation *Towards a Contextualized Narratology of African American Autobiography* is an important book dealing with the narratology of American black autobiography. He takes a narratological-ideological approach to black autobiography, trying to establish a narratological framework of autobiography and illustrate the narrative strategies in the autobiographies of Frederick Douglass, Richard Wright, Zora Neale Hurston, Maya Angelou, Booker T. Washington and W. E. B. Du Bois. He published his essays "Contemporary African American Autobiography Studies: Retrospect and Prospect" (2005) and "Narratology of Autobiography" (2004).

As for Maya Angelou, there are some articles such as Liu Zhifang's "Race Discourse and the Construction of Identity in the Cage—Analysis of Maya Angelou's Autobiography *I Know Why the Caged Bird Sings*" (2006), Guo Zhetao's "The Race and Gender in Maya Angelou's Poems," Bao Lili's "On Maya Angelou's *I Know Why the Caged Bird Sings*" (2006), Yu Xiaodan's "The Lily in the Cliff Is Blossoming in the Hopeless Situation—An Analysis on Maya Angelou's Autobiographical Novels." Most of the essays review the book from the perspective of identity-building.

Although Hurston's novels, especially *Their Eyes Were Watching God*, have aroused the great interest of Chinese readers and critics, there are few introductions and critical concerns about her autobiography *Dust Tracks on a Road*. The main literary criticism is Chen Xilin's *Study on Hurston* (2005), in which there is a chapter discussing hcr autobiography. The important essays about *Dust Tracks on a Road* include Chen Xilin's "On Z. N. Hurston's *Dust Tracks on a Road*" (2004) and Zhang Huifang's "Perfect Combination of 'Ideal Self' and 'Real Self'—Reading *Dust Tracks on a Road* by Hurston." Wang Lianxiang's M. A. thesis makes a comparative study of Hurston and Angelou, "Naratorial Commentary and Race Consciousness: A Comparative Study of *Dust Tracks on a Road* and *I Know Why the Caged Bird Sings*" (2007). As for Lorene Cary's autobiography *Black Ice*, there is not any review about it in China.

Considering the lack of adequate systematic research on black women's autobiography, I choose to explore how American black women's autobiographies construct their own literary tradition by inheriting the tradition of American black autobiography and how black women's autobiographies differ from the black male autobiographies. In this book, I mainly focus on the autobiographies of Maya Angelou, Zora Neale Hurston and Lorene Cary, as the representative autobiographies of their respective times.

3. The Theoretical Framework and Structure of the Book

American Black autobiography, a special genre for African Americans to define their identity, is different from other autobiographies and has its unique characteristics. In this book, I will use the autobiography theories of Philippe Lejeune, Paul John Eakin, Estelle C. Jelinek, Leigh Gilmore and James Olney to illustrate the features of the genre of autobiography. More importantly, I will apply the theories of African American autobiography of Stephen Butterfield, William L. Andrews, Sidonie Ann Smith and Joanne Braxton, etc. to analyze the values and traits of American black autobiography. The narrative theories of Houston Baker and Henry Louis Gates will be employed to explore the narrative strategies of black autobiography. Concerning the black female autobiography, I will use the post-colonial feminist critics such as bell hooks, Nellie MacKay, Christian Barbara, etc. to make an analysis of the specific conditions of American black women. I will resort to the theories of the post-colonial critics such as Homi K. Bhabha and Frantz Fanon to elucidate black culture.

In 1956, the French critic Georges Gusdorf published his article "Conditions and Limits of Autobiography," which is regarded as the starting point of contemporary autobiographical theory. Gusdorf is the forerunner of autobiographical studies "for his cogent articulation of the theoretical foundations of a formerly marginalized genre of writing" (Friedman 72). According to Gusdorf, the precondition of autobiography is his concept of individualistic self, "a conscious awareness of the singularity of each individual life" (qtd. in Friedman 72). Gusdorf states that the autobiographer can resort to the autobiographical writing "to reveal a coherent individual self" and claim his subjectivity. He asserts that "Autobiography properly speaking assumes the task of reconstructing the unity of a life across time" (qtd. in Tidwell 32), and "The author of an autobiography gives himself the job of narrating his own history: what he sets out to do is to reassemble the scattered elements of this individual life and to regroup them in a comprehensive sketch" (qtd. in Tidwell 32). Gusdorf contends that autobiography has an existential function and "it recomposes and interprets a life in its totality" (qtd. in Popkin 25). However, the deconstructionist literary theorist Paul de Man denied "the effort to classify autobiography as a literary genre" and questioned Gusdorf's theory, thinking that autobiographical texts "could not in any event communicate 'reliable self-knowledge' " (qtd. in Popkin 26). Besides, his assertion that autobiography is a phenomenon unique to European civilization is also attacked by some critics who are influenced by deconstructionism and feminism, and those who question the existence of a humanist and essentialist self (Popkin 26).

Trying to lay a firm foundation for the autobiography genre, the French scholar Philippe Lejeune proposed his concept of "the autobiographical pact," a contract between author and reader, arguing that in autobiography, the author, narrator and protagonist must be the same person, and that in autobiography, autobiographers "explicitly commit themselves not to some impossible historical exactitude but rather to the sincere effort to come to terms with and understand their own lives. The formal mark of this commitment to autobiographical discourse is the identity posited among author, narrator, and protagonist, who share the same name" (Eakin 24). According to Lejeune, autobiography is a genre of "telling the truth about the self, constituting the self as complete subject" (qtd. in Eakin 24), believing that autobiography is "a retrospective prose narrative produced by a real person concerning his own experience, focusing on his personal life, in particular on the development of his personality" (qtd. in Tidwell 32).

In the 1970s and 1980s, the criticism on autobiography focused on the relationship between fact and fiction. Paul John Eakin, one of the most influential American scholars studying autobiography, points out that "in the last twenty years, the pervasive initiative had been to establish autobiography as an imaginative art, with special emphasis on its fictions. This shift in perspective from fact to fiction has been accompanied by the poststructuralist critique of the concept of the self (autobiography's principal referent) and of the referential possibilities of language" (qtd. in Popkin 27). In terms of the relationship between fact and fiction, Eakin views it in his own perspective that "the autobiographical truth is not a fixed but an evolving content in an intricate process of self-discovery and self-creation, and further, […] the self that is the center of all autobiographical narrative is necessarily a fictive structure" (qtd. in Popkin 28).

In defining the concept of self, James Olney emphasizes the importance of the metaphor of self in his book *Metaphor of Self* (1972). Jelinek summarizes James Olney's idea that "all autobiography is a process, neither a form nor a content. It is neither fiction nor history, but each man's metaphor of his self—the predetermined self-image that shapes both the content and form of his life and his life study" (Jelinek 3). For James Olney, "the key element in any autobiographical text was the master metaphor chosen by the author to present his or her life, metaphor being by definition a departure from literal reality" (Popkin 28).

Meanwhile, some feminist critics began to examine American women's autobiographies from the perspective of feminism. For example, in 1986, Estelle C. Jelinek published her book *The Tradition of Women's Autobiography: From Antiquity to the Present*. In 1994, Leigh Gilmore published her book *Autobiographics—A Feminist Theory of Woman's Self-Representation*. Their studies of women's autobiography offer us a site to reexamine the significance of autobiographical writing as a way of women's self-definition and liberation.

By analyzing the women's autobiographies in Britain and America, Estelle C. Jelinek draws the conclusion that women's autobiographies "demonstrate the continuation of a discrete women's autobiographical tradition, a literary tradition of their own" (xv). Jelinek points out different traditions of men and women's autobiographies. Unlike male autobiographers, women autobiographers dwell on personal subjects: family, close friends and domestic activities, but "not the professional, philosophical, or historical events that are more often the subjects of men's autobiographies" (xiii). Unlike men who often create "the self-confident, one-dimensional self-image," women often describe "a multidimensional, fragmented self-image colored by a sense of inadequacy and alienation, of being outsiders or 'others'; they feel the need for authentication, to prove their self-worth" (xiii). Meanwhile, paradoxically, women autobiographers "project self-confidence and a positive sense of accomplishment in having overcome many obstacles to their success—whether it be personal or professional" (xiii). Jelinek also points out that the style of women's autobiographies "is integral with such a paradoxical self-image: episodic and anecdotal, nonchronological and disjunctive" (xiii).

Leigh Gilmore argues in her book *Autobiographics—A Feminist Theory of Woman's Self-Representation* that the genre of autobiography affords the autobiographers in a marginal social status a way to articulate their voice. As she puts it, "In the context of these important feminist insights, we could argue that first-person, nonfictional narrative offers voice to historically silenced and marginalized persons who penetrate the labyrinths of history and language to possess… the engendering matrix of textual selfhood: the autobiographical *I*" (63). She asserts that "even in the narrowest and most ambivalent sense, writing an autobiography can be a political act because it asserts a right to speak rather than to be spoken for" (40). She uses the term "autobiographics" to illustrate her understanding of the genre autobiography, to describe those elements of self-representation that "mark a location in a text where self-invention, self-discovery, and self-representation emerge within the technologies of autobiography—namely, those legalistic, literary, social, and ecclesiastical discourse of truth and identity through which the subject of autobiography is produced" (42). She asserts that "an exploration of a text's autobiographics allows us to recognize that the *I* is multiply coded in a range of discourses: it is the site of multiple solicitations, multiple markings of 'identity,' multiple figurations of agency" (Gilmore 42).

Some post-colonial feminists point out the characteristics of women's autobiographies. For example, Sidonie Smith states that "women who attempt traditional autobiography are forced to blend two stories. They must at once support and further the individualistic sense of self constructed by male culture and mold that sense of self to their experiences as women" (Tidwell 32-33). According to Smith, autobiography is then "an assertion of arrival and embeddedness in the phallic order" (Tidwell 33).

Jeremy D. Popkin regards autobiography "as one of the vehicles through which hierarchies of domination can be challenged" (27). This is true with African-American autobiography, which is regarded by Cudjoe as "the quintessential… literary genre for capturing the deep cadences of the Afro-American being, in which deepest aspirations are revealed and evolution and development under impact of slavery and modern-day United States capitalism is traced" (Cudjoe 272-73). Many black critics examine the genre and propose their literary theories, among whom Stephen Butterfield, William L. Andrews, Sidonie Ann Smith and Joanne Braxton are the influential ones. Stephen Butterfield's *Black Autobiography in America* (1974) and Sidonie Smith's *Where I'm Bound: Patterns of Slavery and Freedom in Black American Autobiography* (1974) are predominant literary books.

In *Black Autobiography in America*, Butterfield makes a comprehensive analysis of the autobiographers between 1830 and 1972, classifying Black autobiography into three periods: the slave narrative period (1831-1895), the period of search (1901-1961) and the period of rebirth (since 1961). Butterfield defines the genre of autobiography as living in "the two worlds of history and literature, objective fact and subjective awareness" (1). As he points out, by autobiographical writing, "the autobiographer examines, interprets, and creates the importance of his life" (Butterfield 1). The important ideas in the book are as follows. Firstly, Butterfield emphasizes political awareness, believing that the high quality of black writing should be a function of the "black viewpoint," which means "a sharper awareness of social relationships, acquired through having to direct constant attention to the social relationship of color" (154). To serve political consciousness, he gives a new definition of "self" in black autobiography. Butterfield argues that the self in black autobiography is different from the Western self in white autobiography. He considers the autobiographical form as "one of the ways that black Americans have asserted their right to live and grow" (3). In black autobiography, "the self belongs to the people, and the people find a voice in the self" (3). He regards "the unity of the personal and the mass voice" as "a dominant tradition" of black autobiography (3). Secondly, black autobiography is greatly influenced by its earliest form—the slave narratives, which have set basic thematic and structural patterns for black autobiography. Butterfield argues that the traditional themes in black autobiography include "the identity crisis, the alienation, the restless movement, and the views on education, knowledge, and resistance" (155).

Sidonie Smith explores the patterns that influence the plots of ten black autobiographies, examining the patterns of slavery and freedom in black American autobiography. Her understanding of slavery and freedom is somewhat different from that of Butterfield. She points out the prototypal thematic and structural patterns set by the slave narratives that recur in subsequent black autobiographies. In the book, by analyzing the autobiographies by Wright, Cleaver, Angelou, Cayton and Brown, Smith attempts to give a new explanation of the concepts of imprisonment and freedom. The blacks are always in the process of escaping imprisonment and seeking freedom. For the blacks, the North is not the place of freedom any more. Rather, no place in America is a place of freedom for them, so the blacks are always in the state of ceaseless wandering. The meaning of running is ambiguous: on the one hand, "running becomes a new form of imprisonment; on the other hand, exile can be positive if it becomes the means to freedom and not an end in itself. The alternative to geographical freedom becomes the discovery of spiritual freedom" (75). So Smith draws the conclusion that "the ultimate place of freedom lies within the self, which alone must be content to create its own 'free' consciousness" (75). Meanwhile, she also views the act of writing autobiography as a way of liberating oneself and achieving personal freedom (180).

William L. Andrews tries to establish a poetics of Afro-American autobiography in his article "Toward a Poetics of Afro-American Autobiography." Andrews points out the necessity to think seriously about two questions simultaneously concerning the criticism of the Afro-American genre: "What does it mean?" and "How does it work?" (81). He asserts that "the study of black autobiography can be *its own* discipline" (80). Critics should not only study what black autobiography tells us, but also study it "as a *form* of oral and written expression" (80). Andrews points out that Butterfield's *Black Autobiography in America* and Sidonie Smith's *Where I'm Bound* set a standard and canon for the criticism of black autobiography. Both of them emphasize the profound influence of the slave narratives on subsequent autobiographies. The slave narratives have set both thematic and structural patterns for black autobiography. However, Andrews points out the weakness of Butterfield's conclusion about the tradition for ignoring "the more fundamental canon-formation question of how any historian of black autobiography should define representativeness in the genre and what significance he or she should assign to unrepresentative expression" (83). Andrews argues for the importance of revision of the tradition of black autobiography: "A poetics of Afro-American autobiography must take into

17

account the inevitable revision of traditions that has occurred in the past and that continues to occur today" (87). He regards the dynamic principle in the history of Black autobiography as "the *revising*, not the canonizing, of traditions, and even texts" (87). He points out two major principles of Afro-American autobiography: firstly, "revision… signifies formal renewal where black autobiography is concerned" (88); secondly, the phenomenon of "free storytelling" is the "overarching or underlying motif in Afro-American autobiography" (89). He emphasizes his firm conviction that "freedom is not just the theme but the *sign* of Afro-American autobiography" (89). By writing autobiography, black people wish "to demonstrate one's freedom in and through oral or written storytelling" (89). Critics like Houston Baker and Henry Louis Gates have developed their theories to analyze how black autobiographers "tell freedom," "not just tell about freedom" (90).

In this book, I will use Baker's blues theory and Gates' theory about signifyin(g) to analyze the narrative strategies of American black women's autobiographies. William L. Andrews summarizes Baker's blues theory as follows: "Baker homes in on [the] 'blues moment' in Afro-American discourse when the 'trained' voice translates into metaphorical and formal terms the 'unrestrained mobility and unlimited freedom' of the railroad, the focal and aural symbol of black vernacular expression in this country. To read and hear the blues in this extended fashion is to suggest that freedom plays through Afro-American narrative in ways hitherto unimagined" (Andrews, "Toward a Poetics of Afro-American Autobiography" 90).

Henry Louis Gates' book *The Signifying Monkey—A Theory of Afro-American Literary Criticism* argues that "Signifyin(g) is the black trope of tropes, the figure for black rhetorical figures" (51). This idea represents his understanding of "the value assigned to Signifyin(g) by the members of the Afro-American speech community" (51). As Gate states, "the Signifying Monkey is the figure of a black rhetoric in the Afro-American speech community. He exists to embody the figures of speech characteristic to the black vernacular. He is the principle of self-consciousness in the black vernacular, the meta-figure itself" (53). The Signifying Monkey "exists not primarily as a character in a narrative but rather as a vehicle for narration itself" (62). Gates points out that "the black rhetorical tropes, subsumed under Signifyin(g), would include marking, loud-talking, testifying, calling out (of one's name), sounding, rapping, playing the dozens, and so on" (52). While analyzing Hurston's novel *Their Eyes Were Watching*

God, Gates defines it as the speakerly text, "a text whose rhetorical strategy is designed to represent an oral literary tradition, designed 'to emulate the phonetic, grammatical, and lexical patterns of actual speech and produce the illusion of oral narration" (Gates, *The Signifying Monkey* 181). I will use the concept of "the speakerly text" to analyze Hurston's autobiography *Dust Tracks on a Road*.

While illustrating the narrative strategies of the autobiographies of Hurston and Angelou, I will also resort to the autobiography narrative theories, in particular the concepts of unreliability, readership, and narrative perspective to analyze the autobiographical texts. I will mainly use the theories of contextualized narratology of African American autobiography developed by Xu Dejin to analyze the narrative perspective in Angelou's *I Know Why the Caged Bird Sings*, and the unreliability and dual readership in Hurston's *Dust Tracks on a Road*.

When analyzing Hurston's cultural view, I employ the post-colonial theory of Frantz Fanon. I make a comparison between Fanon's idea about race and culture with that of Hurston. In the book *Black Skin, White Masks*, he uses psychoanalytical theory to analyze the psyche of black people in a white world. He points out the divided self-perception of the blacks is mainly caused by their inferiority complex caused by the trauma of the history of slavery. To combat the oppression of black people against white dominant society, the blacks have to struggle for cultural and political autonomy. He points out the fact that "white civilization and European culture have forced an existential deviation on the Negro" and that "what is often called the black soul is a white man's artifact" (Fanon 6). He advocates that black people should not become the slaves of the prison of their past. He points out the importance of taking actions to create a bright future.

Homi Bhabha's concepts of cultural hybridity, liminal negotiation of cultural difference, and third space lay the theoretical foundation for my discussion about Lorene Cary's *Black Ice*, which explores the possibility of crossing the racial dividing line. Homi Bhabha, an influential Indian-American post-colonial theorist, proposed the important concept of cultural hybridity. In his work *The Location of Culture*, Bhabha explores the possibility of "liminal negotiation": "it is in the emergence of the interstices—the overlap and displacement of domains of difference—that the intersubjective and collective experiences of *nationess*, community interest, or cultural value are negotiated" (Bhabha 2). According to Bhabha, "the social articulation of difference, from the minority perspective, is a complex, on-going negotiation that seeks to authorize cultural hybridities that emerge in moments of historical transformation" (Bhabha, *The Location of Culture* 2). Paul Meredith concludes that "Bhabha posits hybridity as such a form of liminal or in-between space, where the 'cutting edge of translation and negotiation' (Bhabha 1996) occurs and which he terms the *third space*" (Meredith 2). Bhabha argues that by stepping into this third space, we "may open the way to conceptualizing an international culture, based not on exoticism or multi-culturalism of the diversity of cultures, but on the inscription and articulation of culture's hybridity" (Bhabha, "Cultural Diversity and Cultural Differences" 209).

Having elaborated the theoretical framework of the book, I will dwell on its structure. It is composed of an introduction, five chapters and a conclusion. First of all, a brief introduction is given to the lives and works of Hurston, Angelou and Cary, the criticism on American black autobiographies in the United States and China, and the theoretical framework and structure of this book.

Chapter One explores the role of black autobiography in American literature. I trace the development of American black autobiography from the 18th century to the end of the 20th century. Then the characteristics of black autobiography, in particular the traits and values of American black women's autobiographies, will also be analyzed. The blacks use autobiographical writing as a vehicle to claim black identities, a way to assert their right to live. The slave narratives as the earliest form of black autobiography have exerted a profound influence on the development of this genre, setting certain thematic and structural patterns for subsequent black autobiographies. Firstly, one of the most striking characteristics of American black autobiography lies in its political consciousness—assuming the responsibility of uttering both the personal and collective voice of fighting for freedom. Secondly, black people use the weapon of knowledge, language and writing to fight against oppression, because obtaining knowledge would enable them to engage in persuasive discourses to create their self-identity. Narrative discourses afford the blacks "a means of survival, control and empowerment" (Davis 40). Thirdly, black autobiography undergoes the revising process. Black women's autobiographies share the above-mentioned fundamental characteristics of American black autobiography. However, American black women's autobiography has its own unique values and traits. It helps black women construct their unique literary tradition and claim their status in African American literature. The autobiographical writing affords black women an instrument to revise the stereotyped images of American black women, to redefine their subjectivity and to serve as the guide of other black women. American black women's autobiography differs from black male autobiography in that women put more emphasis on their intimate relationships with others, such as female bonding, motherhood, sisterhood, and on the importance of the family. In the chapter, I also examine the difference between autobiographies written by white women and black women in the United States. The problem of readership in American black women's autobiography is also analyzed. In the end, I give a general account of the autobiographies by Hurston, Angelou and Cary, the critical opinions they have received from the literary critics and my comments on them.

In Chapter Two, I use the approach of cultural analysis to elaborate Hurston's *Dust Tracks on a Road* as a cultural autobiography. Hurston's autobiography is harshly criticized because of its subversion of the tradition of American black autobiography both in content and form and because of its avoiding the racial problem. I will try to make a cultural analysis to offer a new angle to read the text. Influenced by her mentor Frantz Boas, Hurston develops her view of cultural fluidity and hybridity. Based on her cultural view, she serves as the cultural interpreter to represent the richness and diversity and vitality of black culture. Hurston's cultural ideas and her attitude toward race and history are similar to the ideas expressed in Frantz Fanon's *Black Skin, White Masks*. Hurston's cultural view has transcended that of her contemporaries.

Chapter Three analyzes Angelou's serial autobiographies, especially her first one *I Know Why the Caged Bird Sings*. I will focus on Angelou's inheritance from American black autobiography tradition and her surpassing over the tradition of autobiography. As a paradigm of black autobiography, Angelou inherits the thematic tradition of black autobiography, dealing with the traditional themes such as seeking freedom, emphasizing the power of words, female bonding, the roles of women in nurturing the children and passing on black culture. In the autobiography, Angelou combines the voice of personal self-discovery with the voice of the whole community. She reveals the sufferings of both the community and her personal painful experiences as a black girl. Meanwhile, she discovers the power of the community and gains her strength from it. Angelou's autobiography has transcended the tradition of American black autobiography in that she writes it as literature and succeeds in achieving the universal meaning in her autobiographies.

Chapter Four explores Lorene Cary's *Black Ice* and examines Cary's perplexing and ambiguous situation when she studied in the white-dominant school of St. Paul's. When still a student in St. Paul's, she was painful because of her psychological experience of isolation, alienation and her puzzle about racial loyalty. However, fifteen years later when she worked as a teacher in the school, she seemed to have found the way out not only for herself but also for the black students in St. Paul's by serving as "a crossover artist." She explores the possibility of crossing the racial dividing line, trying to integrate black culture into American culture. Bhabha's theory of cultural hybridity and third space will be used to explore Cary's effort to enrich both black and white cultures.

In Chapter Five, I explore the narrative strategies in the three autobiographies, mainly focusing on realism, narrative perspective and the blues aesthetics in *I Know Why the Caged Bird Sings*; modernism, unreliability, readership and the use of the oral tradition of signifyin(g) in *Dust Tracks on a Road* and the function of storytelling in *Black Ice*.

In Conclusion, the interrelationship among the three autobiographies is analyzed and it concludes that American black women use autobiographical writing to claim their positive black female self, to shoulder their responsibility of revising the literary canon so as to make contributions to the flourishing of American black women's literature.

Chapter One

The Role of Black Autobiography in American Literature

1.1 American Black Autobiography: Now and Then

1.1.1 The Development of American Black Autobiographies

The genre of autobiography, as "one of the most democratic forms of writing in Western culture" (Gunzenhauser 77), stems from the need "to construct a unique self, an identity that is clear and clearly differentiated from all others" (Balée 92). The autobiographers "have used the form to reflect on what it means to be human, to live in society, to be educated, to find a vocation, to develop principles and live accordingly" (Gunzenhauser 77). The first full-length example of the genre was *Confessions* written by Augustine in the 4th century. In Augustine's *Confessions*, he depicted his life experiences aiming to set a model example as a servant of God for the Christians. In Enlightenment Europe the genre of autobiography proliferated. With the emergence of rationalism, autobiographers begin to focus more on themselves as individuals. Autobiography is a genre where the changing cultural conceptions of the self can be fully embodied (Gunzenhauser 75-76).

In America, the genre of autobiography plays an important role in building a national identity. In the "Introduction to *The Norton Book of American Autobiography*" by Jay Parini, autobiography is considered as "the essential American form of expression." In some sense, "autobiographies 'invent' America" (Balée 92). During the first several hundred years, most autobiographers reflected their personal lives and attempted to construct their identities in response to external pressures such as wars, severe weathers, pestilence, the experience of religious oppression, slavery and immigration. Jonathan Edwards, a Puritan, wrote the most important spiritual autobiography of the 18th century. The most influential memoir of the 18th century is *The Autobiography of Benjamin Franklin* (1770-1791), a pragmatic one in which Franklin reveals how a man shaped by his time and circumstances achieved success. In the 19th century, a prominent transcendental autobiography was Henry David Thoreau's *Walden*, opposing the destruction of the American wilderness. An important subgenre of American autobiography in the 19th century was the slave narratives, which describe how the black people struggle against the oppression of the white so as to construct a self. In the first several decades of the 20th century, autobiographers still focused on the influence of the external forces on their lives and sense of identity. The outer forces included historical events such as the Great Depression, the two world wars, the influence of industry and technology, and so on. Such works of great writers include those thinly disguised autobiographical fiction and coming-of-age autobiographies written by Eugene O'Neill, Gertrude Stein, F. Scott Fitzgerald, and Ernest Hemingway. But since the 1950s, American autobiographers have shifted their attention from outside forces to inner landscapes such as forces from within the family. Mary McCarthy's *Memories of a Catholic Girlhood* is an example. In the 1960s, the tell-all-about-how-my-family-shaped-me autobiographies and the drug-drenched memoir made another attempt to explore self-identity. In the following two decades, the autobiographical writing of ill health became a way to achieve identity. However, in the 21st century, American autobiography depicts the fragmentation of both national and self-identity (Balée 92-104).

In American literature, black writing has always been neglected by white dominant culture. As James Olney notes, "until fairly recently, black writing in general was barely mentioned as literature—if mentioned at all it was usually in some other context—and until very recently, [black] autobiography received much the same treatment" (*Metaphor of Self* 15). However, nowadays, black writings including black autobiography deserve attention from American literary critics. In fact, black autobiography has become an important cultural form of expression of black literature and an indispensable part of American literature. Selwyn R. Cudjoe argues that "the Afro-American autobiographical statement is the most Afro-American of all Afro-American literary pursuits" (272). Since the 18th century, American black autobiography has become a vehicle for black people to express their "minority status in a white-dominated nation, chattel slavery until the civil war, and ongoing economic and social repression" (Dudley 23). The black autobiography is "one of the ways that black Americans have asserted their right to live and grow," and "a bid for freedom, a beak of hope cracking the shell of slavery and exploitation" (Butterfield 3).

Slave narratives, the earliest form of black autobiography, are considered as the roots of African-American autobiographies. They describe the physical and spiritual journeys from slavery to freedom. Black autobiographers write slave narratives to challenge white hegemony, to "fight their battle against chattel slavery and to engage in the search for political and psychological freedom for all black people" (McKay, "The Narrative Self: Race, Politics, and Culture in Black American Women's Autobiography" 96). Slave narratives written from the mid-18th to the mid-20th century have a wide range of formal, linguistic, and geographical diversity (Meer 814).

According to the research for her dissertation in 1946, Marion Wilson Straling found 6 006 slave narratives written between 1703 and 1944, including books and brief testimonies found in judicial records, journals and newsletters, among which about one hundred slave narratives were published as books or pamphlets between 1760 and 1865, and about another one hundred after the Civil War. The slave narrative has exerted a great influence on African American literature. The genre achieved immense popularity and reached its height during the antebellum period, from 1836 to 1861 (Scott 105).

One of the most important slave narratives in the 18th century is *The Interesting Narrative of the Life of Olaudah Equiano,* or *Gustavus Vassa, the African* (1789), which served as a prototype for many of the later fugitive slave narratives. Among the most influential narratives are *A Narrative of the Adventures and Escape of Moses Roper from American Slavery* (1837), *Narrative of the Life of Frederick Douglass, An American Slave* (1845), Douglass's two later versions of his autobiography—*My Bondage and My Freedom* (1855) and *The Life and Times of Frederick Douglass* (1881), *Narrative of William Wells Brown, A Fugitive Slave* (1847), Solomon Northrup's *Twelve Years a Slave* (1853), and Josiah Henson's second autobiography—*Truth Stranger than Fiction*: *Father Henson's Story of His Own Life* (1858), *Incidents in the Life of a Slave Girl* (1861) by Harriet Jacob. There are also some slave narratives describing an adventurous escape such as the *Narrative of Henry Box Brown, Who Escaped from Slavery in a Box Three Feet Long, Two Wide, and Two and a Half High* (1849), and *Running a Thousand Miles for Freedom;* or, *the Escape of William and Ellen Craft from Slavery* (1860) (Scott 106-07).

After the Civil War, America stepped into the era of Reconstruction. Slavery was abolished, but "Jim Crow" laws assured racial segregation, and the blacks' status was legalized as second-class citizens. Ida B. Wells-Barnett, a journalist, lecturer, publisher, civil rights activist, wrote her autobiography *Crusade for Justice* (1928) after she retired. In this autobiography, the author chronicles her "tireless efforts to combat lynching, inferior segregated schools, economic oppression, and limits on opportunities for women" (Dudley 24).

Since the slave narratives are believed to be the roots of black autobiography, they have aroused the intense interest of critics. Therefore, lots of books, essays and articles have been devoted to the notable genre of slave narratives. William L. Andrews writes in "Toward a Poetics of Afro-American Autobiography": "I can think of no other genre of Afro-American literature whose earliest history has been more extensively studied than autobiography" (78). However, according to William L. Andrews, when people talk about the slave narratives, most of them invariably refer to the antebellum slave narratives.

William L. Andrews observes that the slave narratives continue to play a dominant role in African-American autobiography for 70 years, from the end of the Civil War to the Great Depression in the 1930s. But the autobiographies during this period have been almost entirely ignored or they have not been seriously considered by literary scholars. In fact, during this period, there were important autobiographies such as the success story of William Wells Brown's *My Southern Home* (1881), John Mercer Langston's *From the Virginia Plantation to the National Capitol; or, the First and Only Negro Representative in Congress from the Old Dominion* (1894), Booker T. Washington's *Up From Slavery* (1901), a typical success story, James Weldon Johnson's *Along This Way: The Autobiography of James Weldon Johnson* (1933), a story full of optimism.

Among them the most famous and popular one is Washington's *Up From Slavery* (1901), a classic black version of a story about the American Dream. Washington believed that with self help, people could go from poverty to success. In the story, Washington described his birth in slavery, his efforts to receive education, and above all, his great success as the first leader of the Tuskegee Normal and Industrial Institute. Washington stressed that African Americans could also succeed financially by learning trades, saving money and buying land. He strongly believed that when whites recognized black people's worthiness, black people could also obtain their civil rights. Washington's autobiography was immensely popular among the whites, but critics did not give full consideration about its value. Butterfield did not comment on the book in his *Black Autobiography in America*, while Sidonie Smith was not comfortable with Washington's way of self-presentation, doubting whether Washington's recognition of the standards of the dominant socioeconomic order of his day was a way to reject his own black identity and heritage, although Smith devoted one chapter to Washington's *Up from Slavery* in her *Where I'm Bound: Patterns of Slavery and Freedom in Black American Autobiography.*

Like Washington's *Up From Slavery*, these post-bellum slave narratives are not seriously considered by scholars partly because there were changes in the image of slavery. Some postbellum ex-slaves did not portray slavery as harshly as their antebellum predecessors. These autobiographies can be regarded as the origins of middle-class black autobiography in the United States. The autobiographers were optimistic and devoted themselves to the pursuit of the American Dream. They did not describe much about the misery and cruelty they had confronted in the past. Instead, they wrote with enthusiasm about how they managed to become a member of the middle class, a status they were eager to achieve in spite of the prejudice and oppression that black people have to continue to face even after emancipation. This type of success story can be dated back to the tradition of Benjamin Franklin's autobiography. It seems that the autobiographers believed in the mainstream values such as the American Dream, which contradicted with the traditional ideological values and paradigm of the antebellum slave narratives. Andrews advised that the shifts should be regarded as "indicative of a revision of the paradigm, literally, a looking back again at the assumptions on which fundamental parameters of the tradition, such as the concepts of selfhood, freedom, and slavery, had been based" ("Toward a Poetics of Afro-American Autobiography" 87).

In the 1930s and 1940s, the noteworthy black autobiographies were written mostly by the professional writers of the Harlem Renaissance, the "New Negro Movement" that spanned in the 1920s and 1930s, when the black arts flowered. Among them are *Darkwater: Voices From Within the Veil* (1920) by W. E. B. Du Bois, *A Long Way from Home* (1937) by Claude McKay, *Dusk of Dawn: An Essay Toward an Autobiography of a Race Concept* (1940) by W. E. B. Du Bois and *The Big Sea* (1940) by Langston Hughes. The anthropologist and author Zora Neale Hurston wrote her controversial autobiography *Dust Tracks on a Road* (1942). In the 1940s, the most influential African American autobiography is Richard

Wright's *Black Boy* (1945), a description of the artist's coming of age. Both the theme and structure of *Black Boy* belong to the genre of the slave narrative. David L. Dudley regards it as "a model of autobiographical self-fashioning." Stephen Butterfield wrote in his *Black Autobiography in America*:

> Richard Wright's *Black Boy* is the autobiography most worth reading of all the works of its kind in American literature, whether black or white. It has the tough, pure beauty of a desert cactus, squeezing life energy from the dry sand, rich in water beneath the protective spines, putting forth roots, flowers, seeds and curiously shaped stalks in a land of death and buzzards. (155)

He believes that the qualities that make *Black Boy* great are the ones that appear in the slave narratives. What's more, when writing the autobiography, Richard Wright skillfully uses fictional techniques to satisfy his own demand for autobiographical writing.

Since the end of the Civil War, African Americans have struggled for the full recognition of rights. But even in the 1950s and the 1960s, African Americans still suffered severe racial discrimination, which resulted in the Civil Rights Movement. African Americans underwent the most dynamic periods of social interaction and change in U.S. history. The social movement had a deep influence on African American autobiographies. Claude Brown's *Manchild in the Promised Land* (1965) depicted the bleak and blighted black lives. Other autobiographies include W. E. B. Du Bois' *The Autobiography of W. E. Burghardt Du Bois* (1968), *Die, Nigger, Die* (1969) by H. Rap Brown, *Seize the Time* (1970) by Bobby Seale, *Soledad Brother* by George Jackson, and *Search for the New Land* by Julius Lester. The most important African American autobiography in the 1960s was *The Autobiography of Malcolm X* (1965), which used approximately the same form of the slave narrative. These autobiographies described the terrible economic and social conditions black Americans confronted and black people's aggressive stance toward the white-dominated society. Butterfield thinks these autobiographies all "construct identities on revolutionary terms" (Butterfield 222).

Since the last decades of the 20th century, black women writers have produced some important autobiographies, such as Anne Moody's *Coming of Age in Mississippi* (1968), Maya Angelou's multi-volume autobiographies among which the most famous one is *I Know Why the Caged Bird Sings* (1969), and Audre Lorde's *Zami: A New Spelling of My Name* (1982). Anne Moody describes the unbearable tensions as a black woman when she was involved in the Civil Rights Movement in the south. Angelou's and Lorde's autobiographies are representative works of black women's narratives in the 1970s and 1980s, which dwell on issues about women's harsh conditions in a white-dominated and male-dominated world, exploring some problems relevant to women such as family relationships, sexual abuse, lesbianism, and so on (Dudley 24).

The 1990s witnessed the outpouring of some memoirs written by black women writers such as Lorene Cary's *Black Ice*, Rebecca Walker's *Black, White, and Jewish*: *Autobiography of Shifting Self*, Debra J. Dickenson's *An American Story*, Asha Bandele's *The Prisoner's Wife*, Catherine E. McKinley's *The Book of Sarahs*: *A Family in Parts*, Yolanda Young's *On Our Way to Beautiful*, and Natasha Tarpley's *Three Generations of Black Women*, and so on. Meri Nana-Ama Danquah edited the book *Shaking the Tree*, *A Collection of New Fiction and Memoir by Black Women*, which includes the above-mentioned works. *Shaking the Tree* "offers the literature of twenty-three young black women writers whose voices are among those defining this new era of contemporary American literature" (Danquah xv-xvi). In those autobiographies, the women writers explore the themes of love, alienation, displacement and isolation, and describe "the tragedies and triumphs of contemporary black women in their struggle to negotiate a sense of individual identity beyond the limited scope of gender and race" (Danquah, the back cover of the book).

1.1.2 The Characteristics of American Black Autobiographies

1.1.2.1 The Political Consciousness of American Black Autobiographies

Butterfield claims that "the appeal of black autobiographies is in their political awareness" (3). In my opinion, political consciousness is the most important feature of black autobiographies. Unlike white autobiographies which follow the confessional mode and focus on individualism and on the reflections on the autobiographers' personal lives and values, black autobiographies, as a vehicle to articulate the voice of the marginalized blacks, shoulder the responsibility of exposing the brutality of slavery, fighting against the oppression and exploitation imposed on the blacks by the whites, asserting the black people's right to live equally in the world and fighting for their liberation from the prison of slavery and oppression. Selwyn R. Cudjoe argues that "the entire social development of

Afro-Americans has been conditioned by their struggle to liberate themselves from the crippling social and psychological effects of the dominant ideology and culture. To a large degree, this struggle manifested itself in the literature of Afro-American peoples, particularly in the autobiography" (273). Therefore, black autobiographical writing is not only a way of reflecting one's personal life, but more importantly, a weapon of fighting against the atrocity of slavery and other various forms of oppression suffered by the blacks even after slavery was abolished. When writing autobiographies, most of the black autobiographers will reckon with their communal responsibility of participating in the cause of liberation of their race. Its political awareness and responsibility determines that in black autobiography, the self is not the self expressed in white autobiographies, and the self of black autobiography is not an individual self, but a member of the whole black community. As Butterfield states, "the self belongs to the people, and the people find a voice in the self" (3). The unity of the self and the community is always a dominant tradition in black autobiography. In the process of freeing themselves from various forms of enslavement, literacy is regarded as a crucial weapon to seek for freedom. By acquiring knowledge, black slaves find a path to their freedom. By learning to read and write, the slaves have gained keen insights into the source of their sufferings, knowing what should be done to change their destiny. Keenly aware of the power of language, black autobiographers use the instrument of the autobiographical act to tell the world about the violence and atrocity imposed on them by the whites, and to seek sympathy and support from the abolitionists, including some white men and women, and simultaneously, encourage their black compatriots to join in their communal cause of liberating their race. Black autobiography, as a result, has become a self-liberating discourse.

The emphasis on the political consciousness of black autobiography is a tradition inherited from its earliest form—the slave narrative. Butterfield argues that the slave narrative is "an instrument of political struggle" and its ultimate goal is "to create public sentiment in favor of the abolitionist cause" (131). The slave narrative, especially the antebellum slave narrative, is the foundation of black autobiography. The slave narratives are so influential because they establish certain prototypal thematic and structural patterns for subsequent black autobiographies. Just as William L. Andrews stated, Afro-American autobiography has five canonical texts: Douglass's 1845 *Narrative*, Washington's *Up From Slavery*, Wright's *Black Boy*, *The Autobiography of Malcolm X*, and Maya Angelou's *I Know Why the Caged Bird Sings*. They are considered to be canonical mainly because "they all have been compared and interpreted as major evolutions of the slave narrative, a tradition epitomized by Douglass's 1845 *Narrative*, which is the central text in Afro-American autobiography studies today" (Andrews, "Toward a Poetics of Afro-American Autobiography" 81). I will elucidate the prototypal patterns set by the slave narrative by centering on the three aspects: seeking for freedom, combining the voice of the self and that of the collective, and considering literacy as a weapon of questing for freedom.

In general, slave narrators tell their personal stories, describing the harsh living conditions of slaves, the cruelty of the slave owners, the severe oppression they suffered in slavery, their awareness to fight against the hostile environment, their eagerness for freedom, and their victory in escaping from slavery and gaining freedom at last. Therefore, fighting against slavery and calling for its abolition, seeking for freedom and fighting for an identity remain a thematic matrix in the slave narratives. The slave narratives' concerns about "the fetters of mankind and the yearning of all living things for freedom" (Bontemps xviii) become the themes intrinsic to subsequent black autobiography. Sidonie Smith observes that black autobiographies follow the prototypal patterns of the slave narratives:

> The ex-slave narrated the story of his successful break into a community that allowed authentic self-expression and fulfillment in a social role: his achievement of a "place" within society. He also narrated the story of his radical break away from an enslaving community that forbade him authentic selfhood by foisting a false identity upon him: his continual flight to a "place" outside society. (*Where I'm Bound* ix)

These patterns recur again and again in succeeding generations of black autobiographers. David L. Dudley adds that "after the legal abolition of slavery, later black writers would carry on the slave narrator's crusade by calling for an end to the 'slavery' of segregation laws, economic exploitation, unequal justice, and the curtailment of civil rights" (23).

To fight against the fetters of enslavement, the black people never forget that they are not isolated individuals, but members of the whole group. Not surprisingly, in black autobiography, "the individual and the community are not polarities; there is a community of fundamental identification between 'I' and 'We' within any single autobiography in spite of differences in autobiographical modes and in the autobiographers' visions" (Schultz 81). Stephen Butterfield discusses how black people integrate their racial identities into their individual life stories:

> The "self" of black autobiography… is not an individual with a private career, but a soldier in a long, historic march toward Canaan. The self is conceived as a member of an oppressed social group, with ties and responsibilities to the other members. It is a conscious political identity, drawing sustenance from the past experience of the group, giving back the iron of its endurance fashioned into armor and weapons for the use of the next generation of fighters. (Butterfield 2-3)

According to Selwyn R. Cudjoe, black autobiography "is bereft of excessive subjectivism and mindless egotism and presents the Afro-American as reflecting a much more impersonal condition" (280). As a result, "the autobiographical statement emerges as a public rather than a private gesture, me-ism gives way to our-ism and superficial concerns with the individual subject (individualism) give way to the collective subjection of the group" (280). Therefore, the black autobiography "is meant to serve the group rather than to glorify the individual's exploits. The concerns of the collective predominate and one's personal experiences are presumed to be the closest approximation of the group's experiences" (Cudjoe 280).

In the process of questing for freedom, the black people find that literacy is an important weapon of pursuing freedom and fighting against slavery. European intellectuals have long held the view that having a written language is the main symbol of being human, being mentally and culturally superior humans. In their opinion, the black people is an inferior race in that they are illiterate and uncivilized people. In order to rule the slaves, slave owners did not allow them to learn to read and write. Even though the black slaves didn't obtain the chance to learn to read and write, many of them were fully aware of the importance of literacy and the link between literacy and freedom. In the slave narrative, "the acquisition of literacy is the precondition for the slave's decision to revolt against his enslavement, and literacy becomes the first step toward mental as well as physical freedom" (Scott 107). In fact, a number of black narrators described vividly the process of struggling for a chance to get education despite the prohibitions from the slave owners. A case in point is the following words from the *Narrative of the Life of Frederick Douglass, An American Slave* (1845): "These words sank deep into my heart, stirred up sentiments within that lay slumbering, and called into existence an entirely new train of thought. It was a new and special revelation, explaining dark and mysterious things, with which my youthful understanding had struggled, but struggled in vain." (50)

In fact, the slave narrative is "a self-conscious refutation of the European charge that blacks could not write" (Scott 107). David L. Dudley also argues that "slave narrators also epitomize the impulse of African Americans to 'write themselves into existence.' Because literacy was considered a mark of humanity, these narratives were their authors' bid to be recognized as fellow human beings with the same abilities, emotional lives, and aspirations as other Americans" (23). The direct relationship between literacy and freedom remains a theme in the later works of black autobiography such as Maya Angelou's *I know Why the Cage Bird Sings* (1970). The theme is also embodied in contemporary black female autobiographies such as Lorene Cary's *Black Ice*, Rebecca Walker's *Black, White, and Jewish*: *Autobiography of Shifting Self* and Debra J. Dickenson's *An American Story*.

Therefore, in their autobiographies, the blacks who manage to receive education use the language to express their unique sufferings as a race and their eagerness for acquiring their subjectivity. In some sense, the writing of autobiographies became a weapon for them to "negotiate their way out of the condition of enslavement as well as a means of expressing the intensity with which they experienced their violation and denigration as individual subjects" (Cudjoe 279). As Cudjoe puts it, "as an expression and signification of his/her experience, the autobiographical statement became an extension of the word, that strange ritual through which the complex consciousness and historical unfolding of a people revealed itself" (282).

Having illustrated the primary thematic patterns set by the slave narrative, I will briefly introduce its basic structure. Since black autobiographical writing is a crucial part of the anti-slavery argument, so in order to obtain the sympathy of their white northern readers, acquire the support from white abolitionists, and persuade them to join the antislavery cause, slave narrators attached much importance to the authenticity of their works, trying to portray themselves as objective and representative witness of southern slavery. Selwyn R. Cudjoe states that "from its inception, the Afro-American autobiography has been subjected to the question of how authentic a statement it has been and whether or not the Afro-American had the ability or the capacity to make such a statement" (274). Therefore, the slave narratives bear some common formulaic features of structures. Generally speaking, the title page asserted that the narrative was written by the slave himself or dedicated to a friend. To make it more convincing, some authenticating documents were attached before or after the narratives. The documents were written by prominent white citizens and editors who promised readers that the fugitive slaves are people of good character and are trustworthy, and that the slave narrators have not exaggerated the brutality of slavery (Scott 106-07). Bell hooks analyzes the purpose of the emphasis on authenticity,

> Slave autobiographies worked to convey as accurately as possible the true story of slavery as experienced and interpreted by slaves, without apology or exaggeration. The emphasis on truth had a twofold purpose, the presentation of reliable sources, and most importantly, the creation of a radical discourse on slavery that served as a corrective and a challenge to the dominant culture's hegemonic perspective. ("Writing the Subject: Reading *The Color Purple*" 464)

Most of the slave narratives begin with the description of their unknown conditions about their date of birth and parentage. Then the precarious and dehumanizing aspects of slavery are bombarded, including the plots about how the slaves are brutally beaten, how they are sold at auction, and how they are miserably separated from their relatives. Then the narrators recount a life turning point which leads to the awakening consciousness of fighting for freedom. Detailed descriptions are offered about the specific planning of escaping from the slave owners. But the details of escaping are not described so as not to compromise those who have helped them. The antebellum slave narratives generally describe the journey from the south to the north, from rural areas to urban cities, and from slavery to freedom. The ending of the slave narratives describes the fact that the narrators finally succeed in running to the northern states or Canada, and the former slaves adopt new names to symbolize that they are longing to begin a completely new life (Scott 106-07). In fact, many black autobiographies in succeeding generations have echoed the basic structure of the slave narratives.

1.1.2.2 The Revising and Renewal of Traditions in Black Autobiography

As has been stated above, the slave narratives, especially the antebellum slave narratives, set the main thematic and structural patterns of black autobiography. Critics have written numerous books to dwell upon the significant role that antebellum narratives play in establishing the tradition of black autobiography. However, as William L. Andrews points out, the post-bellum black autobiographies underwent significant and revolutionary revisions in response to the new challenges that black people confronted after the Civil War. Black autobiographical writing is a dynamic process of revising its traditions. Andrews states that "revising does not necessarily mean a deviation from historical truth," and "the history of Afro-American autobiography has evolved through a rhythm of revisionary renewals of certain powerful myths and images of the past in response to the changing realities of the present" ("A Poetics of Afro-American Autobiography" 87). I will explore the process of revising the canon of black autobiography from the following perspectives.

Firstly, according to Andrews, "between 1865 and 1930, some of the defining parameters of the Afro-American autobiography—such as the image of slavery and the idea of heroic selfhood—underwent subtle but extremely significant revision" (85). Some black autobiographers did not focus on the horrors of slavery and shifted their interest in describing how they achieved success despite the racial discrimination and oppression that still existed even after slavery was abolished. As Frances Smith Foster writes in his *Witness Slavery* (1979),

> From the Reconstruction period on, a number of autobiographical writings of ex-slaves … did not dwell upon the horrors of their writers' past conditions of servitude but were instead cheerleading exercises to urge continued opportunities for integration of blacks into American society… Their descriptions of slavery were mild and offered as "historical" evidence only. (qtd. in Andrews 86)

Those autobiographies can be classified as the middle-class black autobiographies, in which the autobiographers narrated their success stories, trying to prove that they were intelligent enough and capable of realizing the American Dream. In the process of pursuing their dreams, they freed themselves from the past and acquired freedom they had been questing for all the time. A good case in point is Washington's *Up From Slavery*, a classical black version of the American Dream. There are other success stories such as William Wells Brown's *My Southern Home* (1881) and Weldon Johnson's *Along This Way*: *The Autobiography of James Weldon Johnson* (1933). Those autobiographers' identification with the American mainstream values did not conform to the traditional ideological values and paradigm of the antebellum slave narratives. But confronting the new circumstances in the new era, some black people have gained new insights into "the fundamental parameters of the tradition, such as the concepts of selfhood, freedom, and slavery" (Andrews 87). They had a new understanding of these concepts and gradually revised the canon of black autobiography. For example, in antebellum slave narratives, the word "freedom" meant freedom from slavery, but later its meaning varied. As Elizabeth Schultz observes, in Washington's *Up From Slavery*, the word means freedom to fight for a prominent place in the middle class, "in W. E. B. Du Bois' *Autobiography* (1968), as in Angela Davis's *Autobiography*, it is freedom from capitalistic oppression; in Malcolm X's *Autobiography* (1964) it is freedom from the illusion of white supremacy and toward the development of a powerful black community" (83).

The revising and renewal of traditions in black autobiography are also embodied in the same autobiographers' different autobiographies. For example, Frederick Douglass wrote three autobiographies: *Narrative of the Life of Frederick Douglass*, *An American Slave* (1845), *My Bondage and My Freedom* (1855) and *The Life and Times of Frederick Douglass* (1881). Readers will find the discrepancies and contradictions between Douglass's three narratives. In some sense, Douglass's narratives written later can be regarded as the revision of his previous ones. Nellie Y. McKay points out that "Douglass was less interested in documenting facts than in employing rhetorical strategies that enabled him to replace the erroneous identity that dominant culture had bestowed on him with an 'equally fictitious,' 'stolid black self' " ("Race, Gender, and Cultural Context in Zora Neale Hurston's *Dust Tracks on a Road*" 180). Similarly, William Wells Brown also wrote two autobiographies: *Narrative of William Wells Brown*, *A Fugitive Slave* (1847) and *My Southern Home* (1881). There also exist some contradictory statements about himself and his understanding of the concept of slavery between those two narratives. The latter autobiography can also be veiwed as the revised text of the first one. As Andrews points out, "the dynamic principle… in the history of Afro-American autobiography is the revising, not the canonizing, of traditions, and even texts" ("Toward a Poetics of Afro-American Autobiography" 87).

Another important aspect of the revisionary tradition is embodied in black women's autobiographies. Black women use autobiographical writing as an instrument to debunk the negative stereotyped images described in black male autobiographies as vulnerable and helpless victims, and to describe themselves as strong, courageous and dignified human beings. In addition, black women's autobiographies have revised the tradition of women's autobiography, showing the difference between black women's autobiography and white women's autobiography. According to McKay, "the slave narratives written by slave women are especially important for their revisionist elements in relationship to the narratives of ex-slave men and the American female experience in the autobiographical accounts of white women" ("Reflections on Black Women Writers: Revising the Literary Canon" 154). The representative works of such black women's autobiographies are Harriet Jacobs's *Incidents in the Life of a Slave Girl* (1861), which "deconstructs the meaning of the female slave experience in relationship to that of her male counterpart and the white world around her" (McKay, "Reflections on Black Women Writers: Revising the Literary Canon" 154). Hurston, while writing her autobiography, subverts the conventional patterns of black autobiography even more fiercely and shifts her focus on black folk culture. In modern times, black women autobiographers are now employing various rhetorical devices to explore more complicated and diverse black women's experiences, examining more candidly such issues as family relationships, sexual abuse and even lesbianism, etc. Black women's autobiographical writing is an instrument for them to revise the images imposed on them, to express themselves freely and to add a new dimension to the tradition of black autobiography. In conclusion, by breaking away from the conventional patterns of black autobiography, both black men and women use autobiographical writing as a way of "free storytelling" (Andrews 89) and a way of revising and reconstructing the traditions of black autobiography. As William L. Andrews states, black autobiography becomes "a revisionistic instrument in the hands of its greatest practitioners. It urges the revision of the myths and ideals of America's culture-defining scriptures while it demands new insight of white readers to recognize the ways in which [black] autobiography had become a mode of Afro-American scripture" (*To Tell a Free Story*: *The First One Hundred Years of Afro-American Autobiography* 14).

1.2 The Values and Traits of American Black Women's Autobiographies

1.2.1 The Values of American Black Women's Autobiographies

Since the 19th century, black women have used autobiographical writing as a means to reflect their particular experiences and claim their subjectivity. Classic examples of black women's autobiographies are as follows: Harriet Jacobs's *Incidents in the Life of a Slave Girl* (1861), Sojourner Truth's *The Narrative of Sojourner Truth* (1878), Zora Neale Hurston's *Dust Tracks on a Road* (1942), Daisy Lee Bates's *The Long Shadow Litttle Rock* (1962), Anne Moody's *Coming of Age in Mississippi* (1968), Maya Angelou's *I Know Why the Caged Bird Sings* (1969), Ida B. Wells-Barnett's *Crusade for Justice*: *The Autobiography of Ida B. Wells* (1970), Shirley Chisholm's *Unsought and Unbossed* (1970), Nikki Giovanni's *Gemini* (1971), Gwendolyn Brooks' *Report from Part One* (1972), Angela Davis's *The Autobiography of Angela Davis* (1974), Anne Moody's popular autobiography *Coming of Age in Mississippi*, poet and novelist Audre Lorde's *Zami*: *A New Spelling of My Name* (1982), Lorene Cary's *Black Ice* (1991), Rebecca Walker's *Black, White, and Jewish*: *Autobiography of Shifting Self* (2000), Debra J. Dickenson's *An American Story*, Asha Bandele's *The Prisoner's Wife*. Those works are the treasures of black women's autobiographies. In their narratives, the writers inform the readers of "the intensity, complexity, and diversity of the experience of black women from their own point of view" (Christian 16). I will then illustrate the value of black women's autobiographies: serving as a vehicle of claiming black women's identity, contributing to the foundation of black women's literary tradition and its significance in giving guidance to other black women.

1.2.1.1 A Means to Subvert Stereotyped American Black Women's Images and Claim Black Women's Subjectivity

The slave narrative genre is dominated by male narrators and male experiences. According to Lynn Orilla Scott, only 12 percent of slave narratives are written by female blacks. However, in the thousands of early black male autobiographies, black women's violation and degradation remained largely ignored and seldom discussed, because their lives were considered to be meaningless. In the male Afro-American autobiographies, there is no statement about the values of black women. This absence and negligence lasted well into the contemporary era (Cudjoe 273-74). Because of their marginal social status, black women become invisible and mute, and lose the opportunity to define themselves. Joanne M. Braxton states that "as black American women…we have been as invisible to the dominant culture as rain; we have been knowers, but we have not been known. The paradox is central to what I suggest we call the Afro-American experience" (*Black Women Writing Autobiography—A Tradition Within a Tradition* 1). Bell hooks considers black women's status as "others": "As a group, black women are in an unusual position in this society, for not only are we collectively at the bottom of the occupational ladder, but our overall social status is lower than that of any other group. Occupying such a position, we bear the brunt of sexist, racist, and classist oppression" (*Feminist Theory: from Margin to Center* 14). Hooks protests that "as 'objects,' we remain unequals, inferiors" (12). In such a social status, black women don't have the opportunity to articulate their own voice. Mae Gwendolyn Henderson states that "it is not that black women, in the past, have had nothing to say, but rather that they have had no say. The absence of black female voices has allowed others to inscribe, or write, and ascribe to, or read, them" (24). As a result, in both white and black literature, the writers created certain types of stereotyped images of black women. According to Patricia Hill Collins, the black women's images can be classified into four types: mammies, matriarchs, irresponsible mothers and prostitutes (Wang 106). Barbara Christian states:

> Until the 1940s, black women in both Anglo- and Afro-American literature have been assigned stereotyped roles—their images being a context for some other major dilemma or problem the society cannot resolve. Throughout the novels of the slavery and reconstruction periods, Anglo-American literature, particularly southern white literature, fashioned an image of the black woman intended to further create submission, conflict between the black man and woman. (Christian 2)

According to Barbara Christian, the mammy figure is the most prominent black female figure in southern white literature, which is in sharp contrast with the ideal white woman. The mammy figure is described as "black in color, fat, nurturing, religious, kind, above all strong, and… enduring" (2). Her identity mainly derives from the nurturing service, so she is an all embracing figure, and she herself needs or demands little. In contrast, the white woman is considered to "be frail, alabaster white, incapable of doing hard work, shimmering with the beauty of fragile crystal" (2). In white literature, the writers emphasizes the strong and gross physical aspects of black women, while white women are described as the fragile images who need protection. For the whites who practice hegemonism, the sharp contrast of white and black women's images reveals the most ideal relationship

39

between the owners and slaves. Meanwhile, the sharp contrast of white and black images in physical appearance also reveals the standards of beauty imposed on the black people. Even both black men and women unconsciously agree with the whites that the whites are beautiful in appearance, while black women are born to be ugly. The ideas have become part of the consciousness of the black people. That is why they have the strong sense of inferiority and self-hatred. The extreme negative effect on the black people has been revealed in Toni Morrison's *The Bluest Eye* and Maya Angelou's *I Know Why the Caged Bird Sings*.

The other images of the American black women in southern white literature are the concubines, prostitutes, and the conjure women. In the discourse of the whites, in order to strengthen their domination, the writers create these stereotyped black women images and distort the fact. Their recurring description of these negative images has exerted negative effects on the psychology and consciousness of black women. Wang Shuqin states in her Ph.D. dissertation:

> By using the tool of the stereotyped images, the oppressors will easily defeat the oppressed and prevent them from expressing their own ideas, depriving them of their dignity and confidence. When there is no way for black women to express and define themselves, they will internalize the distorted images imposed on them into the source of their self-definition and self-identity. And the internalized self-identity will conversely strengthen the oppression of dominant cultural discourse, so that it becomes part of the source of the oppression… The dominant culture objectifies the black women so thoroughly that black women themselves become the accomplice of their oppressors. (Wang 111-12, translated by myself)

Alice Walker's *The Third Life of Grange Copeland* and Toni Morrison's *The Bluest Eye* both reveal that the black communities have deeply internalized racist stereotypes that radically affect their definition of woman and man. In both novels, the tragic fate of the heroines is in part caused by the black communities, because "in these novels it is not only that an individual heroine accepts the sexist and racist definitions of herself, but that the entire black community, men and women, accept this construct—resulting in the destruction of many black women" (Christian 178).

While white discourses mainly describe the stereotyped female images of mammies, concubines and conjure women, black literature mainly depicts the image of the tragic mulatta (Christian 3). Christian argues that "the tragic mulatta theme reveals the conflict of values that blacks faced as a conquered people" (Christian 3). Christian adds that as the vehicle for cultural transference, the mulatta woman's destiny is tragic because of the alienation and plight she confronts. For the white masters, the mulatta is the child of a slave woman; for the white mistresses, she is the evidence of their husbands' promiscuity; for the slave mother, she is a child who cannot even be brought up by herself; for the slave man, the mulatta child represents his powerlessness. Therefore, in every sense, the mulatta is an alienated existence. In literature, writers often choose the mulatta woman rather than the mulatta man as the image to project the argument. The stereotyped image of the mulatta can be found in the works of many black writers such as *Cane* (1923) by Jean Toomer and *Passing* (1929) by Nella Larson (Christian 4).

According to Christian, in Afro-American literature the description of the images of black women is also influenced by the values of dominant white culture, which reveals the omniscient power of cultural colonization. The case is true even with the works of the prominent black male writers including Richard Wright, James Baldwin, Chester Himes and Ralph Ellison. Richard Wright created female images such as Bessie in *Native Son*, his grandmother and mother in his autobiography *Black Boy*. These women just play the role of a slightly outlined mama or as painful, long-suffering and fanatically religious women. In Ellison's *Invisible Man*, the black woman is again depicted as the stereotyped mammy, who disappeared from the novel after she fulfilled her task as a mammy. In Chester Himes' works such as *Pinktoes*, women are portrayed as the sex kitten, the image created and used for sex. In Baldwin's novels, though women play more diverse roles, they are not perceptive and vivid images, either. As is stated above, it is ironic that the women images created even by the black literary giants almost accord with the stereotyped images of the black women created by white dominant discourse (Christian 15).

In the American poetry of the 1960s, there occurred a different stereotype— the idealized black women's image for the sake of advocating nationhood. Propelled by the Civil Rights Movement and the Black Arts Movement, black women are often admired as Queens and Mothers of the universe, and become the "symbolic holders of the moral condition of blacks in much of the nationalist poetry" (Christian 16). However, no matter whether black women are depicted as stereotyped suffering mammies, sex kittens, lazy and evil women, or as idealized Queens or Mothers of the universe, there is no denying that black men are deeply influenced by the patriarchal ideology and have unconsciously internalized the criteria set by the whites.

Barbara Christian criticizes the distortion of black women in both white discourses and black literature, asserting that stereotype is "the very opposite of humanness," "a byproduct of racism" and "one of the vehicles through which racism tries to reduce the human being to a nonhuman level" (16). Since the stereotyped images of black women do not embody the real complicated conditions of black women, it is necessary and urgent that the black woman herself should "illuminate her own situation, reflect on her own identity and growth, her relationship to men, children, society, history, and philosophy as she had experienced it" (Christian 16). Just as Audre Lorde states, "for black women as well as black men, it is axiomatic that if we do not define ourselves for ourselves, we will be defined by others—for their use and to our detriment" (45). Fortunately, black women have also come to realize that they can use writing as a means to define themselves as the subject. The feminist Helene Cixous dwells on the important role of writing to women. In "The Laugh of the Medusa," she states that writing is

> an act that will…be marked by woman's seizing the occasion to speak, hence her shattering entry into history, which has always been based on her suppression. To write and thus to forge for herself the antilogos weapon. To become at will the taker and initiator, for her own right, in every symbolic system, in every political process. It is time for women to start scoring their feats in written and oral language. (Cixous 351)

Therefore, discourse becomes a weapon to fight against oppression and a tool to claim their identity. For black women, the most important form of writing is the genre of autobiography. As the earliest form of autobiographical writing, the slave narrative becomes the earliest important tool for black women's self-definition and representation of their subjectivity, revealing "how humans under extreme subjugation locate her personal and political identities by inventing and engaging in persuasive discourse" (Davis 40). Olga Idriss Davis argues that

> the slave narrative genre afforded black women, for the first time in American history, a chance to declare their presence by rhetorically stating, 'I am here.' This symbolic expression of claiming self…begins the momentum for creating an oppositional discourse that identified black women as thinkers, creators and namers of themselves in an attempt to

confront dominant discourses that mythologized their existences as breeding sows. (Davis 40)

In their narratives, black women narrators record their real life experiences, express their true feelings and refute the distorted images in white dominant discourse and black male discourse. They announce to the whole world their inhuman sufferings under the sexist, racist, and classist oppression. In their autobiographical writing, they prove to the world their existence and their efforts to change the fate of black women as a whole group. In the process of writing they are the subject. As Toni Morrison says, "we are the subjects of our own narrative, witnesses and participants in our own experience, and, in no way coincidentally, in the experience of those with whom we have come in contact. We are not, in fact, 'other.' We are choices" (Morrison 31-32).

In the autobiographies, black women writers subvert the negative and stereotyped portrayal imposed on them by the dominant and racist society and create completely new characters in their slave narratives, novels and poems. Barbara Christian examines the revision of the distorted stereotyped black women's images in the works written by black women themselves:

> The image of the tragic mulatta no longer dominates the literature and is replaced by a diversity of physical and psychological types. The role of mammy is carefully and continually moved from the level of stereotype to that of a living human being with her own desires and needs. The relationship between black men and women is also scrutinized, often in less generic and more particular terms, with special emphasis placed on the societal forces that strain marriage. (Christian 16)

In American black female autobiographies, black women are not described as the stereotyped images any more. Instead, they are projected as "thinkers, feelers, human beings, not only used by others, but as conscious beings" (Christian 16). A case in point is the image of mammy. In the mythology of Africa, mammy is an important figure, but it is distorted by the white dominant culture. The image of mammy depicted in black women's narratives is completely different from that in white literature. The mammy image in black women's narratives is not the symbolic holder of the white dominant discourse, rather, she is a living human being with her own dignity, feeling, desires, needs, and her own love and hatred. She is not the obedient slave. Instead, she is trying to fight against her owners and her destiny in an active and cunning way.

1.2.1.2 Contributing to the Building of Black Women's Literary Tradition

Owing to the black people's marginal status in the white dominant culture, black writing was not considered seriously by critics and scholars. Considering the doubly marginalized status of black women, no wonder black women's autobiography did not arouse the interest of critics. James Olney states that "women writers have not always been given due consideration as makers of literature" ("Autobiography and the Cultural Moment: A Thematic, Historical, and Bibliographical Introduction" 15). Fox-Genovese argues that "the common discourse has treated black writing, especially the writing of black women: shamefully, outrageously, contemptuously, and silently" ("My Statue, My Self: Autobiographical Writing of Afro-American Women" 183). In fact, all the black women writers, including the black women autobiographers, not only narrate their personal stories and experiences, but also express the untold histories of black Americans. In her article "Histories, Communities and Sometimes Utopia," Susan Willis argues that black women are in a better position to grasp history as a concrete experience for the following reasons. Firstly, black women writers have keen interest in their mothers' and grandmothers' generations, which enables them to gain more knowledge about the past. Secondly, from the economic and historical perspective, history is defined by the mode of labor. As is known to all, the history of black women is the history of a labor force, because black women have gained firsthand knowledge of slavery, sharecropping, and domestic and wage labor. (Willis 3-13) Just as Susan Willis states, "as workers, they have sustained their families; as mothers, they have borne the oral histories from their grandmothers to their children. For all these reasons, today's black women writers understand history both as period and as process" (7). Therefore, autobiographical writing, owing to its emphasis on authenticity, performs an important function in expressing and representing American history and makes contributions to building black women's literary tradition.

In the latter part of the 20th century, many black feminist critics made great efforts to construct the literary tradition of black women. For example, the American author and feminist Alice Walker wrote her famous work *In Search of Our Mothers' Gardens* (1967). In this collection of essays, Alice Walker traces the umbilical thread linking black writers, values women's culture and strength, and celebrates black women's legacy of creativity in art. She tells how she discovered the importance of Zora Neale Hurston and her collections of black folklore in the essay "Looking for Zora" and regarded Hurston as the forerunner of black women's literature. In this book, Alice Walker coins the expression "womanist prose", explores the "womanist" tradition of African American women which is handed down from generation to generation. In this book, Alice Walker argues that one of black women's main achievements in art lies in the aesthetic representation embodied in everyday life. Meanwhile, she also explores the oral tradition of black women as a way of rhetoric expression.

When trying to construct the special and unique literary tradition of black women writers, black feminist critics find the important roles of black women's autobiography which is an indispensable part of their studies. They examined the development of black women's autobiographies, pointing out that as the earliest form of black women's writing, black women's autobiographies have changed the muteness of, and earned a place for, black women in American literature. Bell hooks argues that "with the publication of slave autobiographies, oppressed African-American slaves moved from object to subject, from silence into speech, creating a revolutionary literature—one that changed the nature and direction of African-American history; that laid the groundwork for the development of a distinct African-American literary tradition" ("Writing the Subject: Reading *The Color Purple*" 464). As part of slave narratives, women's slave narratives also contribute to the development of black literary tradition.

Of course, many prominent African-American women's novels and poetry, whose directions have in part been shaped and influenced by women's slave narratives, also vividly reflect the complicated and diverse experiences of black women, such as Paule Marshall's novel *Browngirl, Brownstones* (1959), Nikki Giovanni's books of poetry *Black Feeling, Black Talk, Black Judgement, Re: Creation*, and *My House*, Zora Nearle Hurston's *Their Eyes Were Watching God*, Toni Morrison's *The Bluest Eye* (1970), *Sula* (1974), *Beloved* (1987), Alice Walker's *The Color Purple*, Maya Angelou's poetry. They are all evidence of black women's self-definition. The writers depict black women's stories from political, cultural, historical and philosophical points of view. The diversity of the black women's experiences in America are vividly embodied in their works.

1.2.1.3 American Black Women's Autobiography's Guiding Significance in Reality

What's more, black women's autobiographies play a vital role in reality and offer guidance for other black women, encouraging them to quest for their subjectivity. According to Audre Lorde, "the development of self-defined black women, ready to explore and pursue our power and interests within our communities, is a vital component in the war for black liberation" (45). Bell hooks believes that black women's autobiographies "represent our reality in the interest of promoting monolithic notions of black female experience or celebrating how wonderfully we have managed to overcome oppression" ("Revolutionary Black Women: Making Ourselves Subject" 232). Bell hooks argues that the genre of black women's autobiography has gained a privileged place in black literary history in terms of its great significance in giving guidance to other black women. She writes:

> As a literature of resistance, confessional narratives by black folks were didactic. More than any other genre of writing, the production of honest confessional narratives by black women who are struggling to be self-actualized and to become radical subjects are needed as guides, as texts that affirm our fellowship with one another…Even as the number of novels published by black women increases, this writing cannot be either a substitute for theory or for autobiographical narrative. Radical black women need to tell our stories; we cannot document our experience enough. Works like *Lemon Swamp*…enable readers to understand the complexity and diversity of black female experience. (232-33)

1.2.2 The Traits of American Black Women's Autobiographies

Black women's autobiographies not only share some elements of the tradition of black autobiography and women's autobiography, but also bear some unique characteristics of their own.

1.2.2.1 The Political Consciousness in American Black Women's Autobiographies

In their autobiographies, black women depict their personal experiences and sufferings in the context of a white supremacist patriarchal society. They have different experiences and their destiny varies from each other owing to their different personalities and attitudes toward life. In spite of the differences, black women's autobiographies share some elements of the tradition of black autobiographies. Black women's autobiographies, like all autobiographies, also undertake the responsibility of expressing their political awareness of fighting against slavery and other various forms of enslavement for liberation, integrating their individual experiences with the fate of their collective community, especially with the voice of the black women as a group. According to Nellie Y. McKay, black autobiographers use the autobiographical act to challenge "white hegemony," "to fight battle against chattel slavery and to engage in the search for political and psychological freedom for all black people" ("The Narrative Self: Race, Politics, and Culture in Black American Women's Autobiography" 96-97). Similarly, writing autobiography is a tool for black women to reveal the atrocity of slavery and other forms of enslavement in the white dominant society, and to record their unremitting pursuit of both political and psychological freedom.

In black women's autobiographies, the black writers examine their personal experiences, describe what the system of slavery and other forms of enslavement have done to them and reveal the inhuman sufferings they have experienced. However, the poor living conditions of black women are much more complicated than that depicted in the black male autobiographies. In fact, the sufferings of black women are not the simple mathematical addition of the dual oppression of race and gender (McKay, "Race, Gender, and Cultural Context in Zora Neale Hurston's *Dust Tracks on a Road*" 176). Fox-Genovese points out that the integrity of black women "derives not from the general categories of race or sex, but from the historical experience of being black and female in a specific society at a specific moment and over succeeding generations" ("My Statue, My Self: Autobiographical Writing of Afro-American Women" 179).

In the female slave narratives, they disclose their unknown condition under the "black male sexism, white female racism and white patriarchal authority" (McKay, "The Narrative Self: Race, Politics, and Culture in Black American Women's Autobiography" 97). They describe the special horrors of slavery for women and the sexual exploitation of female slaves. Harriet Jacobs's autobiography *Incidents in the Life of a Slave Girl* portrays the institution of slavery as a violation of womanhood. Fox-Genovese points out that Jacobs "not merely asserts but demonstrates that if slavery is bad for men, it is worse for women...she specifically relates the horrors of slavery for women to assault upon female chastity and conjugal domesticity" ("My Statue, My Self: Autobiographical Writing of Afro-American Women" 189). Zora Neale Hurston uses the mule image to symbolize the burdens of triple oppression imposed on black women. In her autobiographical novel *Their Eyes Were Watching God*, Hurston "reveals the extent to which the black community—or black men—have embraced the gender conventions of white bourgeois society. Black men seek to transfer their burdens to black women by forcing those women into domestic corsets" (Fox-Genovese, "My Statue, My Self: Autobiographical Writing of Afro-American Women" 196).

According to Regina Blackburn, autobiographical writing is an instrument for black women to define "the black female self in black terms from a black perspective" (147). But "that self originated from a source other than the alienated self within the dominant culture" (McKay, "Race, Gender, and Cultural Context in Zora Neale Hurston's *Dust Tracks on a Road*" 176). The image of the self comes from, in the terms of Friedman, "the merging of the individual with a collective group identity" (176). To illustrate the blending of personal and collective voice, bell hooks says, "One important aspect of the slave narrative as revolutionary text was the insistence that the plight of the individual narrator be linked to the oppressed plight of all black people so as to arouse support for organized political effort for social changes." ("Writing the Subject: Reading *The Color Purple*" 465) Therefore, not surprisingly, like the black male autobiographers, black women autobiographers attach more importance to community identification. For black women, individuals cannot be separated from the whole black community. As a result, black women's autobiographies not only articulate their individual voices, but also reflect the sufferings and the brave struggles of the black women as a whole. In fact, black women's autobiographies "constitute a running commentary on the collective experience of black women in the United States" (Fox-Genovese, "My Statue, My Self: Autobiographical Writing of Afro-American Women" 184). Black women's autobiographical writings "bear witness to a collective experience—to black powers of survival and creativity as well as to white oppression" (184).

Their autobiographies are not only the reflection of their individual experiences, but also the recording and embodiment of the collective consciousness of black women. There exists the conscious political nature in black women's autobiographies as well as in all black autobiographies. Just as Stephen Butterfield states, in black autobiographies, "the self is conceived as a member of an oppressed social group, with ties and responsibilities to the other members" (3). Joanne M. Braxton writes about the combination of personal voice and the voice of the group, "like the blues singer, the autobiographer incorporates communal values into the performance of the autobiographical act, sometimes rising to function as the 'point of consciousness' of the people" (*Black Women Writing Autobiography—A Tradition Within a Tradition* 5). Susan Stanford Friedman also analyzes the importance of group identification, which repeatedly surfaces in women's and minority groups' autobiographies. According to Friedman, "community identity permits the rejection of historically diminishing images of self imposed by the dominant culture; it allows marginalized individuals to embrace alternative selves constructed from positive (and more authentic) images of their own creation" (McKay, "Race, Gender, and Cultural Context in Zora Neale Hurston's *Dust Tracks on a Road*" 175).

1.2.2.2 The Difference Between American Black Male and Female Autobiographies

Although black male and female autobiographies share the common racial experiences and other elements of Afro-American tradition, there exist evident differences between the two subgenres.

In black male autobiographies, the male narrators depict their successful escape and emphasize their personal bravery and strength. They emphasize how they gain literacy and knowledge with much difficulty, which lead them to the road of freedom. As David L. Dudley states,

> Male slave narrators often presented themselves as successful American men within a tradition established by Benjamin Franklin's *Autobiography*. Drawing upon another archetype, these authors present themselves as self-sufficient heroes who escape slavery and run to freedom alone. Thus they claim a place among the mythic company of American frontiersmen, rugged individuals living free from society's laws. (23)

Accepting the white patriarchal ideological ideas, they owe much of their success to their own strong mind and remarkable ability. They seldom reflect the roles of black women in their lives. In their narratives, slave women are depicted as completely helpless victims who can do nothing to rebel against their masters but endure their miserable fate. There is no way for slave women to protect themselves, not to mention define themselves. Therefore, by only reading male autobiographies, readers cannot learn more knowledge about the diverse black women's experiences, which are in fact greatly different from the descriptions by black male narrators.

In sharp contrast, black women's autobiographies tell quite another story, with its own distinctiveness and characteristics. Black women describe women's images which form a sharp contrast with those in male autobiographies. The black female narrator "brilliantly deconstructs the meaning of the female slave experience in relationship to that of her male counterpart and the white world around her" (McKay, "Reflections on Black Women Writers: Revising the Literary Canon" 154). As Lynn Orilla Scott states, "while enslaved women are portrayed as passive victims of sexual exploitation in narratives written by men, women narrators portray themselves as active and heroic agents in the struggle for freedom" (108). In their own accounts, black women do depict their experiences as the victims of the atrocities of slavery, victims of sexual exploitation, rape and seduction, but priority is given to the delineation of the positive aspects of their image. They depict themselves not just as the oppressed victims, but rather complicated human beings with dignity, strength, confidence, love, hope, courage and rebellious spirit as well. Many slave women don't escape from their plantations not because they are willing to live an inhuman life, not because they are lacking in the courage to seek freedom, but because they choose to give up the opportunities to escape for the security of their children. For example, in *Incidents in the Life of a Slave Girl* (1861), Harriet Jacobs describes how she abandoned the chance to seek freedom in order to protect her children. Unlike black men, black women attach much more importance to the family relationships and to child nurturing. In her book *Black Women Writing Autobiography—A Tradition Within a Tradition*, Braxton examines the main literary traditions that are unique in the black women's autobiographies. In Braxton's point of view, the importance of family, female bonding, the nurturing and self-sacrificing qualities of the heroines remain one of the literary traditions that recurs again and again in the black female autobiographies. In the view of Braxton, the traditional themes of black American women's autobiographies include "the importance of family, the nurturing of and rearing of one's children, as well as the quest for self sufficiency, self-reliance, personal dignity and self-definition" (*Black Women Writing Autobiography* 184).

Celebrating motherhood and emphasizing female bonding remain an important tradition of black female autobiographies. The black women autobiographers show respect and love to their black female elders, including their grandmothers, mothers and other intimate female relatives, who play the model roles in their life, giving them immense love, power and strength. These female elders are depicted as strong both physically and mentally, deeply active in the religious activities in church, as pious guardians of the values of black communities. And more importantly, they take on the responsibility of teaching the children the survival skills in the difficult condition. Elizabeth Fox-Genovese agrees that

> Black women's autobiographies abound with evidence of or references to the love that black female autobiographers felt for and felt from their female elders: mothers, aunts, grandmothers. For the most part, those female elders are represented as rural in identification and origin, if not always in current location; immersed in folk communities; deeply religious; and the privileged custodians of the values and, especially, of the highest standards of their people. They are not necessarily literate... ("My Statue, My Self: Autobiographical Writing of Afro-American Women" 185)

Braxton categorizes those women as "outraged mother", an image that appears repeatedly in Afro-American history and literary tradition. Citing Linda Brent in *Incidents in the Life of a Slave Girl* as an example, Braxton views the "outraged mother" as

> an ignorant creature, degraded by a system that has brutalized her from childhood; but she has a mother's instinct, and is capable of feeling a mother's agonies. The archetypal outraged mother travels alone through the darkness to impart a sense of identity and "bolongingness" to her child. She sacrifices and improvises to create the vehicles necessary for the survival of flesh and spirit. (Braxton, *Black Women Writing Autobiography—A Tradition Within a Tradition* 21)

Braxton furthers her argument that "it is a distinct feature of the outraged mother that she sacrifices opportunities to escape without her children. Linda is motivated by an overwhelming concern for the freedom and literacy of her children, a concern that is not apparent in the narratives of questing male slaves" (33). Braxton analyzes some other women slave narratives such as Susie King Taylor's *Reminiscences of My Life in Camp: With the U.S. 33D Colored Troops Late S.C. Volunteers* (1902), Elizabeth Keckley's *Behind the Scenes, or, Thirty Years a Slave and Four Years in the White House* (1968), Maya Angelou's *I Know Why the*

Caged Bird Sings (1969). In these autobiographies, Taylor, Keckley, Angelou's Momma Mrs. Henderson are all images of the "outraged mother," taking all the risks to protect their children and grandchildren.

Besides, black women autobiographers emphasize the function of sisterhood on the way to freedom. Unlike black men who ascribe their success to their individual initiative and intelligence as heroic loners, black women attribute their success in seeking freedom to the efforts made by all the people who have helped them, including the other black men, the other black women, even the white women who provided help to them. As Nellie Y. McKay notes, "black women's slave narratives pay tribute to the roles that women play as models and inspiration in their struggle to rise above oppression. The 'sisterhood' of black women... were already well documented in the black female slave narrative tradition" ("Reflections on Black Women Writers: Revising the Literary Canon" 154). For example, it was with the help of a number of women that Jacobs could manage to escape safely. As McKay argues, the most significant contribution that slave narratives such as Harriet Jacobs's *Incidents in the Life of a Slave Girl* have made to history is "its identification of the existence of and effectiveness of a woman's community in which black and white, slave and free women sometimes joined forces to thwart the brutal plans of masters against helpless slave women" (154). Susan Stanford Friedman argues that "women's sense of collective identity... can also be a source of strength and transformation" (75). In Harriet Jacobs's *Incidents in the Life of a Slave Girl*, as Braxton observes, "the heroine celebrates the cooperation of all people, slave and free, who make her freedom possible. She celebrates her liberation and her children's as the fruit of a collective effort, not an individual one" (*Black Women Writing Autobiography—A Tradition Within a Tradition* 19-20).

In conclusion, black women's emphasis on motherhood and sisterhood enables them to acquire more support, warmth and strength in the process of questing for their freedom and well-being.

1.2.2.3 The Difference Between American Black Women's Autobiographies and White Women's Autobiographies

The main difference between American black women's autobiographies and white women's autobiographies from the perspective of gender relationships lies in the following two aspects: firstly, white women autobiographers follow the domestic tradition and the confessional mode, focusing on the examination of their personal experiences and their searching for the soul (Fox-Genovese, "My Statue, My Self: Autobiographical Writing of Afro-American Women" 184), while black women's personal experiences are only part of the black women's experiences as a group; secondly, white women reveal themselves as "the others," who suffer gender discrimination in the patriarchal society. Black autobiographers also demonstrate their identity as "the others," but its meaning is far more complicated than that for white women.

Fox-Genovese argues that "for white American women, the self comes wrapped in gender, or rather, gender constitutes the invisible, seamless wrapping of the self" (187), so they self-consciously write autobiographies from the perspective as women, "as the representatives of a gender" (187). They have never questioned their identity as women, but know well that they are regarded as the "second sex," so they describe the gender discrimination imposed on them by the patriarchal society. Confronted with the hegemony from males, white women often describe "a multidimensional, fragmented self-image colored by a sense of inadequacy and alienation, of being outsiders or 'others'; they feel the need for authentication, to prove their self-worth" (Jelinek xiii). In their writing, they question "the attributes of or limitations on their gender" (Fox-Genovese, "My Statue, My Self: Autobiographical Writing of Afro-American Women" 187) and fight against the constraints imposed on them by the patriarchal society. Fox-Genovese argues that "white women largely accepted the limitations of their sphere, sometimes turning the limitations to their advantage, and wrote either as representatives of its values, or for its other members, or both" (186).

Comparatively speaking, the condition of Afro-American women autobiographers is much more complicated. As Fox-Genovese states, "Afro-American women have written of themselves as persons and as women under special conditions of colonization. In this respect, their writings cry out for comparison with those of white women" (186). Black women, like white women, suffer hegemonism from males. In addition, they have to confront the complicated triple oppression from "black male sexism, white female racism and white patriarchal authority" (McKay, "The Narrative Self: Race, Politics, and Culture in Black American Women's Autobiography" 97). To a degree, black women are not regarded as women in the real sense, just as Sojourner Truth declared: "Ar'n't I a woman?" Sojourner Truth points out that "black slave women had suffered the pain of childbirth and the sorrow of losing children and had labored like men. Were they or were they not women?" (Fox-Genovese, "My Statue, My Self:

Autobiographical Writing of Afro-American Women" 188). Fox-Genovese argues that "the experience of Afro-American women has left them simultaneously alienated from and bound to the dominant models [the hegemony of the gender system] in ways that sharply differentiate their experience from that of white women" (188). The reason is that "slavery bequeathed to Afro-American women a double view of gender relations that fully exposed the artificial or problematic aspects of gender identification. Slavery stripped black men of the social attributes of manhood in general and fatherhood in particular. As a result, black women had no satisfactory social definition of themselves as women" (188). Therefore, when constructing their narratives, black women writers have to deal with the complicated interrelationship between racist, sexist and classist oppressions in the white dominant society.

However, black women's autobiographies and white women's autobiographies share something in common: both of them bear one of the traits of women's autobiography, which is illustrated by Jelinek as the embodiment of the sense of being outsiders and the positive sense of self-confidence and self-fulfillment (Jelinek xiii). Both black and white women autobiographers depict a sense of inadequacy and alienation as marginal people in the society on the one hand; and on the other hand, they emphasize their optimism and self-confidence in overcoming obstacles.

1.2.2.4 Problem of Readership in American Black Women's Autobiographies

In her article "My Statue, My Self: Autobiographical Writing of Afro-American Women," Elizabeth Fox-Genovese analyzes the problem of readers for black female autobiographies. Like all other autobiographies, black women's autobiographies have to take the problem of readers into consideration. They should keep in mind who are their audience. As Fox-Genovese states, "black female autobiographers confront the problem [of readers] in especially acute form—or so their texts suggest" (185). Black female autobiographies, like all black autobiographies, attach importance to their conscious political nature. Just as Stephen Butterfield declares, "the appeal of black autobiographies is in their political awareness…their knowledge of oppression and discovery of ways to cope with that experience, and their sense of…communal responsibility" (3). Nellie Y. McKay notes that before the 19th century, "part of the aim of Afro-American autobiography was to persuade white men and women that people of color were just as human as white people and deserving of humane treatment" ("Race, Gender and Cultural Context in Zora Neale Hurston's *Dust Tracks on a Road*" 179). As a result, black female autobiographers write not only for the purpose of self-representation, but also for the cause of seeking freedom for all black people, especially for black women. Therefore, there is no wonder that in their minds, their self-representation is addressed to the northern white women, especially white middle-class abolitionists or potential abolitionists. When analyzing Harriet Jacobs's *Incidents in the Life of a Slave Girl* and Harriet Wilson's *Our Nig*, Fox-Genovese argues that both Jacobs and Wilson tried to arouse the interest of the white female readers and that "in both cases, the professed reason for seeking the interest was to instruct white women in the special horrors of slavery for women and the ways in which the tentacles of slavery reached into the interstices of northern society" (185). According to Fox-Genovese, the targeted readers for the subsequent black female autobiographers are "those who might influence the course of public events, might pay money for their books, or might authenticate them as authors" (185-86).

However, we should keep in mind that black female autobiographers did not identify themselves with the Northern white women readers. On the one hand, they sought to gain sympathy and support from the white women; on the other hand, they harbored very complicated feelings and deep bitterness toward the white women. Nellie Y. McKay points out in the black female slave tradition, there exists the peculiarity of relations between black and white women. ("Reflections on Black Women Writers: Revising the Literary Canon" 154) The main reason maybe lies in white women's racism toward black women. Actually, because of their racism, they did not welcome black women into "the sisterhood of womanhood" (Fox-Genovese, "My Statue, My Self: Autobiographical Writing of Afro-American Women" 189). Bell hooks points out black women's social status which "is lower than that of any other group" (*Feminist Theory: From Margin to Center* 14). Even white feminists make black women the "objects" of their privileged discourse on race. Bell hooks states that "white women may be victimized by sexism, but racism enables them to act as exploiters and oppressors of black people" (15). She says: "When I participated in feminist groups, I found that white women adopted a condescending attitude towards me and other non-white participants…They did not see us as equals. They did not treat us as equals" (11).

Fox-Genovese points out that black female autobiographers, such as

Sojourner Truth, often counterposed the self "I" and "woman" in their hostile challenge to their white audience. "The tension at the heart of black women's autobiography derives in large part from the chasm between an autobiographer's intuitive sense of herself and her attitude toward her probable readers. Imagined readers shape the ways in which an autobiographer constructs the narrative of her life." ("My Statue, My Self: Autobiographical Writing of Afro-American Women" 189) Maybe that is part of the reason why black female autobiographers didn't follow the white women's confessional mode of writing autobiographies. Because of their complex and contradictory attitudes toward their imagined white readers, "black women's autobiographies seem torn between exhibitionism and secrecy, between self-display and self-concealment" (184). A case in point is the readership problem in Hurston's *Dust Tracks on a Road*.

Since most slaves were deprived of the right to learn to read and write, before the 19th century, few women autobiographers wrote for black women themselves. Changes took place recently. With the explosion and popularity of the works of professional black writers such as Toni Morrison, Alice Walker and Lorde Audre, black women writers tend to write not only for white readers, but also for black male intellectuals and for other black women, especially for younger women, for daughters so that they will follow the instructions expressed in their works. (Fox-Genovese, "My Statue, My Self: Autobiographical Writing of Afro-American Women" 185-86) Just as bell hooks points out, by reading black women's autobiographies, the other black women will realize that "I need not feel isolated if I know that there are other comrades with similar experiences. I learn from their strategies of resistance and from their recording of mistakes" ("Revolutionary Black Women: Making Ourselves Subject" 233). Nellie Y. McKay also observes that "today's black writer addresses a sophisticated multiracial audience through a text that lends itself to multiple levels of reading" ("Race, Gender, and Cultural Context in Zora Neale Hurston's *Dust Tracks on a Road*" 179).

1.2.2.5 Black Women Autobiographers' Different Attitudes Towards Their Lives

Because black women are confronted with special conditions of colonization, they have to find out ways to change their life conditions. That is why so many black women seize every opportunity to write about their unique experiences, not only for self-definition, but also for the cause of liberating all the black men and women. Writing autobiographies became a weapon to fight against slavery and seek for freedom. Black women autobiographers actively took part in the political activities on behalf of the black community. This is a tradition of black women writers. "Many black women continued in the tradition of autobiography centered upon their overt political activities on behalf of the black community into the late 20th century." (McKay, "Race, Gender, and Cultural Context in Zora Neale Hurston's *Dust Tracks on a Road*" 178)

In the process of constructing their identity, black women use multiple strategies in their narratives. McKay states that "whatever their strategies of self-construction, active resistance to oppression of all kinds has been at the center of the history of black women's lives in this country from slavery to the present time" ("The Narrative Self: Race, Politics, and Culture in Black American Women's Autobiography"105). Most of the black women autobiographers represent their optimism, strength and hope in their works, such as Harriet Jacobs, Harriet Wilson, Ida B. Wells, Zora Neale Hurston, Maya Angelou, Era Bell Thompson, etc. All of them were brave fighters, who were at war with the hostile outside world in their attempt to seek freedom and achieve their integrity as a human being. For example, Fox-Genovese argues that "where Jacobs warred with slavery, Hurston warred with a dominant bourgeois culture in which she sought acceptance as an equal. No less than Jacobs, Hurston warred with the legacy of slavery for black women" ("My Statue, My Self: Autobiographical Writing of Afro-American Women" 197-98).

Nellie McKay listed some ex-slave women's narratives which are equally confirming in their assertion of the positive identity of their authors. Among them are Elizabeth Keckley, Susie King Taylor, Amanda Berry Smith, all of whom "wrote not only to expose the evils that had been done to them, but also to demonstrate their abilities to gain physical and psychological liberty by transcending those evils" ("Reflections on Black Women Writers: Revising the Literary Canon" 156).

While most of the black female autobiographers express their strength and optimism in their representation of the individual and collective identity, a few other black female writers express pessimism in the struggle against the hostile environment. For example, unlike Maya Angelou who celebrated the heritage of the black community, Anne Moody elaborated her bitterness and pessimism in her *Coming of Age in Mississippi* (1968), with "her idealism having faded when the majority of poor Mississippi Blacks whose rights she has defended will neither support her nor register to vote" (McPherson 127). Dismayed at the discouraging reality, Moody felt puzzled and wondered whether what she did was worthwhile. "Unlike Angelou, whose innocence is somehow renewed with each bitter or bittersweet experience, by the end of *Coming of Age*, Moody is stripped of both innocence and faith." (McPherson 127)

Another female writer deserving our attention is Ann Petry, a journalist and short-story writer, who published her best-known work *The Street* (1943). Though neglected for a long time, she was rediscovered by readers with the republication of *The Street* in 1983. In this novel, she created a passive and pessimistic heroine, defeated by the hostile environment. Unlike most black women's heroines, she didn't seek help from the community of black women, which remains an important group offering strength and hope for black women (McKay, "Reflections on Black Women Writers: Revising the Literary Canon" 159-60). In spite of the few exceptions, however, McKay argues that

> black women have told their own stories both as a way of self-confirmation and a means of correcting the erroneous white and male record of their inner reality. Black women writers project a dynamic 'I' into the canon, one that makes more complete the reality of the multi-faceted American experience. (161)

Most black women's autobiographies represent the courage, strength and optimism of black women in their struggle against enslavement and pursuit of freedom. Angelou's serial autobiographies are representatives of such black women's autobiographies full of celebration of women's triumphs and optimism for the future. The contemporary black women autobiographers are expanding their exploration of all aspects of black women's experiences, including their setbacks and sufferings as well as their courage and power in overcoming the obstacles in their lives.

1.3 The Autobiographies by Hurston, Angelou and Cary

Among the black women autobiographers, Hurston, Angelou and Cary are the important representatives of three different generations. Hurston's *Dust Tracks on a Road* is a representative of women's autobiographies in the 1940s, when the black women used the weapon of autobiographical writing to define their self-sufficiency and wholeness rather than the identity as the stereotyped victims of the white dominant cultures. Maya Angelou's *I Know Why The Caged Bird Sings* is a typical woman's autobiography immediately after the Civil Rights Movement, when the black writers emphasized the close relationship between autobiographical writing and political consciousness. I take Cary's *Black Ice* as the major autobiography of the newest generation of black women since the 1990s, who are trying to negotiate their sense of identity and freedom beyond the limitations of gender and race.

1.3.1 Zora Neale Hurston and Her Autobiography

Zora Neale Hurston published *Dust Tracks on a Road* in 1942. This controversial autobiography aroused negative remarks although it gained the recognition from white readers and was awarded the Anisfield-Wolf Award. It was bitterly criticized by her black peers. The reasons mainly lie in the fact that Hurston steers her autobiography away from the traditions of black autobiographies both in content and form. Like most of the black autobiographies, Hurston began to tell the stories of her childhood she spent in her hometown Eatonville. But after describing emotionally her mother's death, she told just briefly her difficult experiences as a child without protection from family, her experience of working as a maid, her returning to school and then seizing the opportunity to get education in Howard University. She gave lots of detailed descriptions about her work as an anthropologist under the guidance of the famous anthropologist Frantz Boas. In the latter part of the autobiography, Hurston totally deserted the chronological narration about her personal life. Rather, she arranged her autobiography thematically into a few topics such as the race problem, love, religion, etc., and dwelt on her opinions about those topics.

Hurston's peculiar way to write her autobiography, her concealment about her personal life and her ambiguous attitudes toward racial problems irritated many readers, especially black intellectuals. Not surprisingly, the autobiography received negative and harsh criticism from her contemporary critics. Harold Preece calls the book "the tragedy of a gifted, sensitive mind, eaten up by an egocentrism fed on the patronizing admiration of the dominant white world" (Hemenway, *Zora Neale Hurston—A Literary Biography* 289). Hemenway regards *Dust Tracks on a Road* as "a discomforting book" which harms her reputation (Hemenway, *Zora Neale Hurston—A Literary Biography* 276). Alice

Walker says in her forward to Robert Hemenway's biography: "For me, the most unfortunate thing Zora ever wrote is her autobiography" (xvii). Fox-Genovese also points out that "Hurston's autobiography singularly lacks any convincing picture of her own feelings" (194) and "refuses to attribute any significance to race" (195). So, most of the evaluations of the autobiography dwell on Hurston's contradictory ideas and her negligence of racial problems.

In the next part, I will analyze *Dust Tracks on a Road* as a cultural autobiography by analyzing the influence of her cultural view and the black oral tradition on her autobiographical writing. Unlike the black male autobiographers such as Richard Wright, who follow the protest mode, Hurston embodies her identification with the black people by serving as an interpreter and translator of black folk culture and representing the vitality and diversity of black folk culture rather than focusing on the negative effects of slavery on the black people.

1.3.2 Maya Angelou and Her Autobiographies

Maya Angelou is famous for her six serial autobiographies, including *I Know Why the Caged Bird Sings* (1969), up to 1944 (age 17); *Gather Together in My Name* (1974), 1944-1948; *Singin' and Swingin' and Gettin' Merry Like Christmas* (1976), 1949-1955; *The Heart of a Woman* (1981), 1957-1962; *All God's Children Need Traveling Shoes* (1986), 1962-1965; *A Song Flung Up to Heaven* (2002), 1965-1968. In the six-volume autobiography, Angelou delineates her rich life experiences and personal growth as a black woman, a mother and an artist. She describes the difficult situations confronted by a black female as "tripartite crossfire of masculine prejudice, white illogical hate and Black lack of power" (Duran 36). Confronted with such a hostile environment, Angelou refuses to become the victim but struggles to be a strong-minded warrior who keeps seeking self-fulfillment.

The first volume of Angelou's autobiography *I Know Why the Caged Bird Sings* recounts the coming-of-age experiences of Marguerite Johnson from the age of 3 to 16 as an insecure black girl in rural Arkansas in the 1930s and in California in the 1940s. The stories include episodes such as her abandonment by her parents, the deep love and mutual trust between Angelou and her brother Bailey, her witness to the deep-rooted southern racism, her Momma's protection of the two children, her traumatic experience of being raped by her mother's lover and its traumatic influence on her later life, her interest in the beauty of language and reading encouraged by Mrs. Flowers, her success in becoming the first black streetcar conductor at the age of 15, and her pregnancy and becoming a mother at the age of 16, giving birth to her son Guy Johnson.

Gather Together in My Name (1974) describes Angelou's life from the age of 16 to 19 after her son Guy was born, revealing how the young woman struggles courageously as a single mother to provide security and love for her son. She once worked as a cook, waitress, dancer, clothing seller, restaurant manager, even as a prostitute and madam, realizing how difficult it is to survive for a black woman. *Singin' and Swingin' and Gettin' Merry Like Christmas* (1976) describes her experiences of getting married and divorced, seeking a career in show business, giving a detailed description about her stage debut, her international tour of *Porgy and Bess*, which made her known to the world. *The Heart of a Woman* (1981) describes the formative years of her exciting life: how she becomes a writer and an activist. Angelou becomes mature and enjoys her own creativity and success, examining the roles of being a woman and a mother. In *All God's Children Need Traveling Shoes* (1986), Angelou describes her experiences as an expatriate in Ghana, celebrating the sensuousness of Africa, exploring what it means to be an African American (Duran 36-37; Dunning 60-62). *A Song Flung Up to Heaven* (2002) is the final installment of Maya Angelou's series of autobiographies. This book tells about Angelou's experiences from 1965 to 1968. It begins with her coming back to America after leaving Ghana, depicting her grief after the assassinations of Malcolm X and Dr. Martin Luther King Junior. All of those events led her to accept the editor Robert Loomis's invitation who challenged Angelou to write her autobiography as literature. That's how Angelou began to write *I Know Why the Caged Bird Sings*. In this book, Angelou examined her entire life rather than only focusing on one specific period (Dunning 62).

Cudjoe states that through these self-explorations, "Angelou presents a powerful, authentic, and profound signification of Afro-American life and the changing concerns of the Afro-American woman in her quest for personal autonomy, understanding, and love…It is a celebration of the struggle, survival, and existence of Afro-American people" (285). Among Angelou's six serial autobiographies, the first one *I Know Why the Caged Bird Sings* has been regarded as the most valuable and has received praises from all the critics. James Olney states that "if black autobiography is a paradigm, the history of Maya Angelou's *I Know Why the Caged Bird Sings* is a paradigm of a paradigm" ("Autobiography and the Cultural Moment: A Thematic, Historical, and Bibliographical

Introduction" 15). In fact, many critics analyze Angelou's autobiographies, especially her first one *I Know Why the Caged Bird Sings*. The prominent critical works include D. A. McPherson's *Order out of Chaos*: *The Autobiographical Works of Maya Angelou* (1990), *Maya Angelou's I Know Why the Caged Bird Sings* edited by Joanne M. Braxton (1999), *Maya Angelou's I Know Why the Caged Bird Sings* edited by Harold Bloom (1998) and *Critical Insights*: *I Know Why the Caged Bird Sings* edited by Mildred R. Mickle (2009). Most of the critical essays in these books dwell on Angelou's autobiography about its thematic concerns and its relationship with the tradition of black autobiography.

In this book, I will mainly explore Angelou's first autobiography *I Know Why the Caged Bird Sings*. I will analyze the autobiography from the following perspectives. Firstly, I regard it as an inheritance of the tradition of black autobiography in that it shares the patterns of slave narratives both in themes and form. Secondly, the autobiography is a combination of the personal voice and the group voice. As Fox-Genovese states, "the account of the black woman's self cannot be divorced from the history of that self or the history of the people among whom it took shape" (198). Besides, I will also illustrate the transcendence of Angelou's *I Know Why the Caged Bird Sings* over the traditional black autobiography.

1.3.3 Lorene Cary and Her Autobiography *Black Ice*

In *Black Ice*, Cary describes her experience in St. Paul's School as a black girl. In 1972, Cary was offered the opportunity to become a scholarship student in St. Paul's School where only white and male students were admitted in the past. As one of the first black students and one of the first girls of the school, she had to confront unexpected challenges and threw herself into the new life passionately. However, gradually she found herself trapped in a difficult and ambiguous position. She seemed to be suspicious of everything around her. She wondered whether she was only one of the black students who were part of the liberal experiment, whether she should trust her teachers, how she would get along with the white students and black students, and how she could retain her racial loyalty. Besides, she found herself estranged from her family and the black community that she had been loving. Cary expressed her double role as a black student in the white dominant culture. Seventeen years later, Cary became a trustee in St. Paul's School, facing those black students who faced the same problems as she once did in her school days. Cary recalled those school days with a fresh eye and gave them new meaning.

Since its publication, the book has aroused critics' keen interest and got positive remarks. Arnold Rampersad views it as "probably the most beautifully written and the most moving African-American autobiographical narrative since Maya Angelou's *I Know Why the Caged Bird Sings*." Houston Bakes states that it is "a journey into selfhood that resonates with sober reflection, intelligent passion, and joyous love." *Washington Post Book World* considers it

> a genuinely remarkable book that takes its place alongside those by Wright [and] Maya Angelou...by a writer of singular grace, wit and self-knowledge. (qtd. in Cary, the back cover of *Black Ice*)

Exploration will be given to a new quest for identity in *Black Ice*. Cary is particularly confused about her identity as a black student in St. Paul's School. In her school days, she placed herself in a dilemma, not knowing what place she should take towards her identity both as a member of the black community and a member of St. Paul's School where the dominant culture is white culture. With time passing, however, Cary examines the possibility of crossing the racial divide, exploring her identity not only as a member of the black people, but also as a member of the American people, which her predecessors such as Hurston and Angelou did not achieve. The concepts of Homi K. Bhabha's cultural hybridity and liminal negotiation of cultural difference will be used to analyze Cary's exploration of the possibility of crossing the racial dividing line.

Chapter Two

Hurston's *Dust Tracks on a Road* as a Cultural Autobiography

2.1 Truth and Fiction in Hurston's *Dust Tracks on a Road*

When Hurston wrote her autobiography *Dust Tracks on a Road*, she was a prominent black female writer. Her five important books had been published, including her three novels *Jonah's Gourd Vine* (1934), *The Eyes Were Watching God* (1937), *Moses, Man of the Mountain* (1939), and her two folklore collections *Mules and Men* (1935) and *Tell My Horse*: *Voodoo and Life in Haiti and Jamaica* (1938). At the request of her publisher J. B. Lippincott, Hurston reluctantly wrote her autobiography and published the book in 1942. The book was a commercial success and was welcomed by many white readers. Some influential newspapers and magazines gave favorable reviews. However, at the same time, negative criticism poured out to her from many other readers, especially from her contemporary black literati. The main reason lies in Hurston's ambiguous attitude towards the relationship between truth and fiction in her autobiography.

According to Philippe Lejeune's "the autobiographical pact", there is a referential pact between the author and the reader, which implies the author's promise about the sincerity and truth of the autobiographical narrative. For Lejeune, autobiography is "a retrospective prose narrative produced by a real person concerning his own experience, focusing on his personal life, in particular on the development of his personality" (qtd. in Tidwell 32). In the autobiography, the author will be devoted to "telling the truth about the self, constituting the self as complete subject" (qtd. in Eakin 24). But Hurston does not obey the rules of the autobiographical pact. In her autobiography, some aspects about Hurston's personal life have proved to be fictitious, including her birthplace, her birth date, her marriage status, etc.

Jelinek points out most critics' expectations or assumptions about a good or ideal autobiography:

> Critics by and large still have certain expectations of a 'good' autobiography. It must center exclusively or mostly on their authors, not on others; otherwise, it becomes memoir or reminiscence. It should be representative of its times, a mirror of the predominant zeitgeist. The autobiographer should be self-aware, a seeker after self-knowledge. He must aim to explore, not to exhort. His autobiography should be an effort to give meaning to some personal mythos. (4)

For such a shining star in literature as Hurston, readers, especially black intellectuals, would expect to read her autobiography as a recording of her struggles as a black woman against the social oppression and racial discrimination to achieve the great success as a writer. However, to readers' disappointment, Hurston didn't satisfy their expectations in any sense. In effect, Hurston briefly mentioned her writing career with only several pages. Besides, what annoys readers most is the self-concealment, evasiveness, the lack of disclosure of her personal life. Claudine Raynaud argues that "if every autobiography oscillates between what Hugh J. Silverman sees as a truth discourse (discourse de verite) and a tendency towards fiction (diffusion dans le fictionne), Zora Neale Hurston's text is irresistibly drawn to the second pole" (Raynaud 112). When commenting on the problems of Hurston's autobiography, McKay states that "today's critics find it frustrating and wanting in its lack of self-disclosure, and they disparage its silences, evasions, and distortions, its deliberate suppression of the author's personal history" ("The Autobiographies of Zora Neale Hurston and Gwendolyn Brooks: Alternative Versions of the Black Female Self" 266).

In *Dust Tracks on a Road*, Hurston introduced herself to be born in Eatonville, Florida. In fact, Hurston was born in Notasulga, Alabama on January 7, 1891. Her family moved to Eatonville, Florida when she was at the age of three. As for her birth date, Hurston deliberately wished to hide the truth. As Hurston's biographer Robert E. Hemenway states, "Hurston was deliberately ambiguous about her birth date during her life time, variously citing 1898,1899, 1900,1901,1902,1903,1910 on public documents" ("Introduction," *Dust Tracks on a Road* xi). However, according to the 1900 census records for Eatonville, Florida, Zora Neale Hurston was born on January 7, 1891 (x-xi). Why did Hurston deliberately disguise her real birth date? Did she just wish to be regarded as young as possible? Did she wish to keep the life of the ten-year gap secret to the public? Her deception about her real birth date and her real age still remains a mystery. Readers feel disappointed and even annoyed at her misrepresentation of the date of birth, because the lie which was consistent through her lifetime "confuses the historical context in which the events of her life occurred" (McKay, "Race, Gender, and Cultural Context in Zora Neale Hurston's *Dust Tracks on a Road*" 179).

Besides, Hurston did not tell the real condition of her marriages, either. She just gave a brief description about her first marriage without even mentioning the name of her husband. She did not mention anything about her second marriage. When describing the topic "love," Hurston only gave some generalized comments on it without connecting it to her personal experiences of love. It is hard to imagine that in a female autobiography, important issues such as love and marriage would occupy such an insignificant place in Hurston's life narrative. As a successful writer at that time, she only wrote an eight-page chapter about her writing career. As for the most important black literary movement—the Harlem Renaissance, she only wrote a paragraph. She didn't mention the effect of the Great Depression of the 1930s or other political events, either ("Introduction," *Dust Tracks on a Road* x).

In the autobiography, Hurston managed to distract readers' attention from her personal life and thus created a world with the confusion of truth and fiction. As a result, her real self and her real attempt to write the autobiography seemed to be hidden behind the veil of truth and fiction. So, what does Hurston want to tell the readers behind the veil of truth and fiction?

2.2 Subverting the Conventional Patterns of Black Autobiography

Hurston's *Dust Tracks on a Road* is negatively criticized by black readers not only because of its deliberate deception about her private life, but also partly because of her subversion of the genre of black autobiography. Unlike most of the black male and female autobiographers, just as McKay notes, Hurston "stepped outside of the boundaries of conventional patterns in black autobiography" both in form and content. ("The Autobiographies of Zora Neale Hurston and Gwendolyn

Brooks: Alternative Versions of the Black Female Self" 264) and "Hurston was the first black woman writer to venture on the uncertain path of creating the self outside of the group framework in which black autobiography had existed since the late 18th century" (266).

2.1.1 Subverting the Themes of American Black Autobiography

The most important characteristic of American black autobiography is its political consciousness. The autobiography as a genre becomes a weapon for black people to reveal to the world the evils of slavery and the racial injustice and oppression imposed on them by the white dominant society so that black people's condition will change for the better. The black writers know well that a black individual is only part of the group and should take on the responsibility of fighting against "a political, social and economical system that treated them in ways that violated the premises on which it was founded" (McKay, "The Autobiographies of Zora Neale Hurston and Gwendolyn Brooks: Alternative Versions of the Black Female Self" 264). According to McKay, "the most common types of the Afro-American autobiography are the confessional/conversion narratives and the overt historical/political documents of individual struggle and triumph over racial and sexual oppression" (267). W. E. B. Du Bois also illustrates the importance of the racial problem. He argues that "the content rather than form of my writing was to me of prime importance…I knew the Negro problem and this is more important to me than literary form" (Stone 32). As for black women's writings, black feminist critics even consider them "as personal testimony to oppression, thus emphasizing experience at the expense of text" (Fox-Genovese, "My Statue, My Self: Autobiographical Writing of Afro-American Women" 178). Therefore, for black autobiographers, including men and women writers, making contributions to solving "the Negro problem" is the mission and the responsibility for their people that should never be forgotten. Such a conclusion can be made by examining black male and female autobiographies, the former exemplified by Richard Wright's *Black Boy*, Claude Brown's *Manchild in the Promised Land* (1965), *The Autobiography of Malcolm X*, the latter including Angela Davis's *Angela Davis: An Autobiography*, Sojourner Truth's *The Narrative of Sojourner Truth*, Anne Moody's *Coming of Age in Mississippi*, Mary Church Terrell's *A Colored Woman in a White World*, etc. Following the conventional patterns of black autobiography, regarding racial problems as the focus of their autobiographies, these writers have made great contributions to the acquiring of liberation and equal rights of black people.

However, in this respect, Hurston makes an exception. Contrary to the expectations of the audience, Hurston did not tell a story about how a young black woman struggled hard to achieve her literary success as a prominent black woman in the society which would not provide opportunities for the blacks, let alone a black woman, an artist, neither did Hurston denounce the destructive effects of the evil slavery on black people or the injustice and oppression black people continued to suffer even after slavery had been abolished. What's worse, Hurston even made some startling statements about the racial problem such as "I was and am thoroughly sick of the subject [the race problem]," and "My interest lies in what makes a man or a woman do such and so regardless of his color" (Hemenway, "Introduction," *Dust Tracks on a Road* xxiv). As a result, Hurston's contemporaries complained that Hurston's autobiography "not only failed to contribute positively to the ongoing struggle against racism, but had a counterproductive effect on it" (McKay, "The Autobiographies of Zora Neale Hurston and Gwendolyn Brooks: Alternative Versions of the Black Female Self" 266). Born in Eatonville, Florida, an all-black town governed by the black people themselves, Hurston did not experience the segregation of the South. Not surprisingly, about the legacy of slavery, she wrote, "I have no personal memory of those times, and no responsibility for them" (*DT* 329). As for racial solidarity which had played a vital role for the black people in quest for freedom, she wrote, "Negroes are just like anybody else. Some soar. Some plod ahead. Some just make a mess and step back in it—like the rest of America and the world. So Racial Solidarity is a fiction and always will be" (*DT* 235). "None of the Race clichés meant anything any more. I began to laugh at both white and black who claimed special blessings on the basis of race" (*DT* 329). When the black civil rights activists were fighting for the equal rights for the black people, Hurston said: "There is no *The Negro* here" (*DT* 327).

Hurston's "rejecting the [race] 'problem' as the central issue of the life and writing" (McKay, "The Autobiographies of Zora Neale Hurston and Gwendolyn Brooks: Alternative Versions of the Black Female Self" 267) provoked the wrath of black nationalists, who denounced her as a racial accommodationist. She was reckoned to be flattering the white patrons and readers in order to acquire their support and "get money from white folks" although some black writers "were often themselves totally supported" by white patrons (Alice Walker, xvi).

Hurston, the author of *Their Eyes Were Watching God*, the anthropologist writing *Mules and Men*, immerses herself in the culture of her people and loves black folk culture. How can such a devotee of the culture of her people be politically accommodationist? How can such a person write a book just for flattering her white patrons and for the sake of money? I totally agree with McKay's argument that "those evaluators disturbed by its evidently accommodationist politics have failed to apprehend the politics of its author's identification with southern black culture and the linguistic strategies by which black women writers have affirmed their literary autonomy even at the expense of literal authenticity" (Andrews, "African-American Autobiography Criticism: Retrospect and Prospect" 209). Hurston's ostensibly disturbing attitudes towards race and other political issues are actually the embodiment of "what Barbara Johnson refers to as Hurston's strategies rather than her truths" (McKay, "Race, Gender, and Cultural Context in Zora Neale Hurston's *Dust Tracks on a Road*" 180). McKay argues that Hurston "chose to explore the personal self through verbal constructions that do not fit the models in the tradition" ("The Autobiographies of Zora Neale Hurston and Gwendolyn Brooks: Alternative Versions of the Black Female Self" 264). Hurston's use of verbal strategies will be analyzed in Chapter Five.

2.1.2 Subverting the Traditional Gender Roles as a Woman

Hurston not only rejected the depiction of her identity as a victim of racial group oppression, she also resisted restrictive gender roles. In most of the black male autobiographies, women are described as the passive suffering victims of the slavery system. Although most black female autobiographers revised the negative stereotyped female images, depicting the black women as human beings with strength, dignity and hope, black women are still exposed to the triple oppression of race, gender and class. The black women narrators depicted themselves as brave warriors fighting against the institutions which deny both racial equality and women's achievements. To a degree, the values of black female autobiographies lie in the fact they have offered model examples for other black women to follow, which in fact is also what the readers expect to find in Hurston's autobiography. However, to their disappointment, Hurston refused to tell such a success story about a black woman struggling against the hostile imprisonment. On the contrary, she depicted a mischievous and adventurous young black woman transcending both race and gender limitations. Just as she subverted the concept of race, Hurston subverted the traditional role as a woman as well.

Since childhood, she liked to play with boys rather than girls because "I discovered that I was extra strong by playing with other girls near my age… Everything was all right, however, when I played with boys" (*DT* 39), although "in my family it was not ladylike for girls to play with boys…I used to wonder what was wrong with playing with boys" (*DT* 40). When her father asked her what Christmas gift she wanted, she asked for "a fine black riding horse with white leather saddle and bridles" (*DT* 38), which shocked and horrified her father, "a saddle horse!... It's a sin and a shame!... my young lady; you ain't white" (*DT* 38). What frightened her father was not the horse itself, but the way his daughter behaved. Hurston behaved as if she was a white and a man, not a black girl. Since her father would not buy her a saddle horse, she made up one for herself. "No one around me knew how often I rode my prancing horse, nor the things I saw in far places" (*DT* 39). Her eagerness to see the outside world was satisfied in her own imagination.

Hurston's perspective of gender was positively influenced by her mother Lucy Ann Potts. Lucy was physically weak but strong in character and will. Just as she chose to marry John Hurston decisively even without the permission of her parents, she dealt with the relationship with her husband and children in her own way. Unlike her husband, rather than suppressing children's spirits, she encouraged them to "jump at de sun," to breathe the air of freedom and take advantage of their imagination. For Zora Hurston, her special daughter, she created a free environment for her personal development. She was patient enough to listen to Zora's creative stories made up by herself. The harmonious and intimate relationship between Hurston and her mother remained a source of power through all her life. In this respect, Hurston observes the convention of black women's autobiography. Just as Friedman observes, "the mother-daughter relationship remains central to the ongoing process of female individuation" (77). Her mother's encouragement helped Hurston to transcend the limitations of gender. As Raynaud argues: "She sees her life and her gender...as having marked her more than her race alone. Such a vision accounts, no doubt…for her feminism" (133). Hurston's feminist idea has been reflected in her portrayal of herself, her mother and some other powerful black women such as Big Sweet, Hurston's bodyguard when she collected folklores in Polk County.

Therefore, Hurston's depiction of gender roles does not belong to the conventional modes of black autobiographies, which might also incur negative reviews from critics.

2.1.3 Subverting the Structure of American Black Autobiography

As has been stated in the first chapter, in the black autobiographies of the 19th and 20th centuries, there were prefaces written by white people to authenticate the Afro-American authors, promising to the readers that the stories told by the black narrators were true. The proof document was provided even in the works of Richard Wright (McKay, "The Autobiographies of Zora Neale Hurston and Gwendolyn Brooks: Alternative Versions of the Black Female Self" 277). This is one of the common formulaic features of structures of black autobiographies. However, in Hurston's autobiography, there was no such proof document to authenticate her text as true stories. By deviating from the earlier black autobiography tradition, Hurston implied that her real personal life did not conform to the account in her autobiography. In this way, she shattered "the boundaries of previous forms of black self-representation" (McKay, "Race, Gender, and Cultural Context in Zora Neale Hurston's *Dust Tracks on a Road*" 180). In her autobiography, she just selected some materials that would establish the "statue" of the "self" she liked (McKay, "Race, Gender, and Cultural Context in Zora Neale Hurston's *Dust Tracks on a Road*" 180). As Fox-Genovese argues, Hurston identifies the problematic relation between her private self and her self-representation: "I did not know then, as I know now, that people are prone to build a statue of the kind of person that it pleases them to be" ("My Statue, My Self: Autobiographical Writing of Afro-American Women" 176).

Influenced by the antebellum slave narratives, most of the black autobiographers describe chronologically their personal experiences, covering from their birth date to the day when they succeed in achieving freedom. They depict their life experience as a journey in quest of freedom and self-fulfillment in the society which treats blacks unequally. The plots of the autobiographies are arranged chronologically. However, Hurston did not comply with the traditional structures of black autobiography when she wrote *Dust Tracks on a Road*. When readers take a glance at the table of contents of the autobiography, they will be impressed by its peculiar arrangement of contents. As Francoise Lionnet observes, Hurston's autobiography "presents itself as a set of interactive thematic topoi superimposed on a loosely chronological framework" (382). In fact, *Dust Tracks on a Road* can be divided into two sections. The first section seems to follow the mode of other autobiographies, while the second section completely deviates from the traditional mode and abandons narrative form, because it is composed of a series of discourses which are more like essays. In these essays, Hurston dwells on various topics such as race, love, religion, books, power, politics, and human relationships. As Raynaud states: "Everything in *Dust Tracks* points to the subversion of the autobiographical mode, which becomes invested with competing discourses—folkloric material, tall tales, residual structure from the spiritual autobiography—and which finally dissolves into 'scattering remarks' " (131). As for the first part, on the surface, it tells of her life experiences, about her happy childhood in her hometown Eatonville, her mother's death when she was only nine years old and how she managed to finish middle school and later become a student in Barnard College. But then readers will find that even in the first section, the writer places more emphasis on the representation of the history and the folk culture in Eatonville than on her personal experiences.

In conclusion, Hurston turns away from the restrictions and limitations of black autobiography both in content and form. McKay regards it as "literary ventures which experiment with the boundaries of the genre" ("The Autobiographies of Zora Neale Hurston and Gwendolyn Brooks: Alternative Versions of the Black Female Self" 280). I wonder what her autobiography, as a kind of literary venture, attempts to reveal to the readers. If her personal experience is not important, then what is the most important point she wishes to represent? I think it is not enough to limit our consideration to the discussion whether her text is true or fictional, or whether it is a success or a failure. Instead, there is still profound meaning in the autobiography for us to explore from a new perspective. When reading the autobiography, we should always bear in mind that Hurston is not only a writer, but also an anthropologist and a folklorist. I agree with Francoise Lionnet's idea that "Hurston's own concept and interpretation of black folk culture is itself the best model of how *Dust Tracks on a Road* should be conceptualized and understood" (Andrews, "African-American Autobiography Criticism: Retrospect and Prospect" 209). To comprehend *Dust Tracks on a Road*, it is of necessity to get acquainted with Hurston's view on cultural fluidity and hybridity, which has transcended the cultural view of her contemporaries. Hurston's view on culture is the key to the mystery of her autobiography *Dust Tracks on a Road*.

2.3 The Breakthrough of Hurston's View on Black Culture

2.3.1 The Influence of Franz Boas on Hurston's View on Cultures

In Barnard College, Hurston was lucky enough to become a student of the celebrated anthropologist Franz Boas, who exerted a great influence on Hurston and became her guiding spirit. Hurston's view that black people are not inferior to any people of other races is closely related to Boas' views on cultures. After examining the thoughts of Boas, we will understand Hurston's pride in her people's culture and her devotion to the collections of black folklores.

Franz Boas (1858-1942), a German-American anthropologist and a pioneer of modern anthropology, was considered the "Father of American Anthropology" and "the Father of Modern Anthropology." His main works are *The Mind of Primitive Man* (1911), *Handbook of American Indian Languages* (1911), *Folk-Tales of Salishan and Sahaptin Tribes* (1917), *Primitive Art* (1927), *Anthology and Modern Life* (1928), *Race, Language, and Culture Anthropology* (1940).

Franz Boas's important ideas are his opposition to cultural evolutionary theory and his advocating culture relativism. Franz Boas supported Darwinian theory, but he did not think that the theory could be automatically applied to cultural and historical phenomena. In fact, he was strongly opposed to cultural evolutionary theory prevalent in Europe in the 19th century developed by Lewis H. Morgan and Edward Burnett Tylor, etc. As Sidney M. Greenfield notes, in the United States, the racial variants of evolutionary theory were accepted and used to justify bondage (Greenfield 41). Boas questioned and attacked the idea that "'our' culture is special, exalted, better than others" (Lewis 453). While doing so, he tried to reformulate anthropology and brought to anthropology "an oppositional perspective" (hooks, *Yearning*: *Race, Gender, and Culture Politics* 135). Boas advocated the concept of cultural relativism. In the new framework,

Western Europeans and their former North American colonials no longer would represent the pinnacle and standard by which others were to be judged. Each culture instead was to be seen as the product of its own unique history that resulted in a set of beliefs, values and behaviors that were to be accepted on par, but different from, those of Western Europe and

North America and each other. (Greenfield 43)

Boas assumed that "human behavior was learned rather than the inevitable consequences of biology, climate or any other factors" (Greenfield 43). Historian George Stocking commented on the main contributions Boas made to the general reorientation about human beings:

> The whole thrust of his thought was in fact to distinguish the concepts of race and culture, to separate biological and cultural heredity, to focus attention on cultural progress, to free the concept of culture from its heritage of evolutionary and racial assumption, so that it could subsequently become the cornerstone of social scientific disciplines completely independent of biological determinism. (Stocking, *Race, Culture, and Evolution: Essays in the History of Anthropology* 264)

In *The Mind of Primitive Man*, Boas illustrated his understanding of the difference between primitive and civilized men, arguing that

> there is no fundamental difference in the ways of thinking of primitive and civilized man. A close connection between race and personality has never been established. The concept of racial type as commonly used even in scientific literature is misleading and requires a logical as well as a biological redefinition. (qtd. in Lewis 453)

Sidney M. Greenfield argues that "Boas' Anthropology was as much a social and political agenda as it was a scientific theory" to counter the discriminatory policy proposals (Greenfield 35). Boas' concerns about social and economic problems were shown in his proposal to the Bureau of American Ethnology and the Carnegie Foundation in 1905. In this proposal, he called for a study of the problems of the American Indians and Negro population, aiming to ameliorate poverty, discrimination and sociopolitical marginalization (Lewis 454).

Boas devoted himself to the struggle against anti-black racism and to the bettering of black people's condition. According to the cultural evolutionary theory, black people "were at the bottom of the evolutionary scale" and "were placed even below the indigenous people" (Greenfield 41). Boas fiercely attacked this idea and told black people that "if…it is claimed that your race is doomed to economic inferiority, you may confidently look to the home of your ancestors and say, that you have set out to recover for the colored people the strength that was theirs before they set foot on this continent" (Stocking 313). He not only attacked the idea that the blacks were inferior to other races theoretically, but also participated in many activities to support the African Americans. He corresponded actively with the African American leaders and important intellectuals such as W. E. B. Du Bois, Booker T. Washington, Alain L. Locke, Zora Neale Hurston, helping them to obtain jobs and foundation support, encouraging them to study the history and life of the African Americans (Lewis 455). As Vernon Williams states, Boas "displayed an astonishing degree of real empathy with the plight of African American intellectuals and the black masses" (37).

With the encouragement from Boas, W. E. B. Du Bois began to study Africa and became a leading proponent of Pan-Africanism (Lewis 455). However, there is no doubt that Hurston is the African American intellectual who was most positively influenced by Boas. According to Francoise Lionnet, Boas's anthropological ideas "could not fail to influence Zora Nearle Hurston's own attitudes about the race problem in America, to reinforce her personal tendency toward individualism, and to strengthen her belief that human beings are infinitely variable and not classifiable into distinctive national or racial categories" (412). It was Boas who helped her hold the firm belief that the black people are not inferior to any other people and that black culture has its unique values. Just as Boas stated in the commencement address in Atlanta University, "'the Negro race had contributed its liberal share' to the development of human culture" (Lewis 455). It was Boas who offered Hurston the opportunity and funds to collect black folklores in the South two weeks before she graduated from Barnard College.

Franz Boas attached much importance to the study of folklore and made great efforts to found the American Folklore Society. In fact, he was an immensely influential figure throughout the development of folklore as a discipline. He took the lead in "promoting the importance of ethnographic studies—that would lead to the systematic collection of data on the lives and cultures of peoples heretofore unstudied directly by scholars" (Greenfield 43).

Boas's idea about folklore helped to foster Hurston's interest in southern Negro culture. When confronting difficulties while collecting black folklores, Hurston sought support and help from Boas. As a firm believer in the plasticity of human beings, Boas exerted a great impact on Hurston. Boas's work paved the way for Hurston's dynamic approach to culture, making her realize the unique value of black culture. Influenced and encouraged by such a passionate and insightful mentor, Hurston was deeply immersed in collecting black folklores and this became her lifelong career and cause.

2.3.2 Hurston's View on the Fluidity and Hybridity of Black Culture

2.3.2.1 Hurston's Refutation of Black Culture to Be Inferior to Other Cultures

Funded by her mentor Frantz Boas in 1927, then sponsored by the white patron Mrs. Rufus Osgood Mason, and later awarded a Guggenheim Fellowship, Hurston was offered the opportunities to go to various places to collect black folklores three times from 1927 to 1939. Based on the materials she collected from the rural South of America, New Orleans, Louisiana, Miami and then Haiti and Jamaica, she published two collections of black folk culture, *Mules and Men* (1935) and *Tell My Horse* (1938), and some important essays such as "Characteristics of Negro Expression," "Dance Songs and Tales of the Bahamas" and "Hoodoo in America." In her works, she introduced the black folk tales, arts, spirituals, blues, dances, customs, superstitions, lies, jokes, celebrations, games of Afro-American folklore and black religious practices such as voodoo. Hurston's views on culture are fully embodied in her folklore collections, essays and novels. Her views on cultures are mainly reflected in her autobiography *Dust Tracks on a Road*, her folklore collection *Mules and Men* and her essay "Characteristics of Negro Expression."

When collecting black folklores, Hurston proved that black culture is not at all inferior to white culture, and has its own characteristics and unique values. While working in the field, Hurston always bore in mind Frantz Boas's idea of cultural relativism and his idea of liberating the concept of culture from its biological heritage. Boas contends that "achievements of races do not warrant us to assume that one race is more highly gifted than another" (Stocking 227). Echoing Boas' ideas, Hurston states in *Dust Tracks on a Road* that "Negroes are just like anybody else" (*DT* 329) and that

> light came to me when I realized that I did not have to consider any racial group as a whole. God made them duck by duck and that was the only way I could see them. I learned that skins were no measure of what was inside people. So none of the Race clichés meant anything any more. I began to laugh at both white and black who claimed special blessings on the basis of race. (*DT* 235)

Boas believed that "the Negro race had contributed its liberal share" to the development of human culture and that "the history and ethnography of Africa gave ample evidence of the skill, creativity, and ambition of their ancestors and kin" (Lewis 455). Similarly, Zora Hurston, "daughter of Eatonville, with the 'map of Florida on her tongue' and a common experience with rural southern black people" (Hemenway, *Zora Neale Hurston—A Literary Biography* 90), found a treasure of black folk culture and was fascinated by the richness of black culture. These experiences strengthen her belief that black culture is as valuable as any other cultures in the world, including the dominant white culture.

2.3.2.2 Hurston's Finding of Black Culture as a Thriving Culture

Hurston's experiences of collecting folklores enabled her to find out a truth, much to her surprise and delight. When offered the opportunity to collect black folklores, "the task was to record the songs, customs, tales, superstitions, lies, jokes, dances, and games of Afro-American folklore" (Hemenway, *Zora Neale Hurston—A Literary Biography* 84). However, the more important goal of her work was to salvage black culture, the classic goal of anthropology. Bell hooks claims that "the idea that cultures to be studied were necessarily vanishing, dying out, were… perspectives informed by white cultural imperialism" (hooks, *Yearning*: *Race, Gender and Cultural Politics* 136). Lori Jirousek also mentions racism shaping the discipline of anthropology: "Salvage anthropology assumes that simple or 'primitive,' typically non-Western cultures are disappearing so that scientists quickly must record them" (Jirousek 420). Having been strictly trained for working in the field of anthropology, Hurston did not question its goal. She was said to be "weighed down by this thought, that practically nothing had been done in Negro folklore when the greatest cultural wealth of the continent was disappearing without the world ever realizing that it had ever been" (qtd. in hooks, *Yearning*: *Race, Gender and Cultural Politics* 136). Therefore, Hurston began her anthropological work with the mission to salvage black folk culture. While committing herself to her work as a participant-observer, and collecting more and more materials about black culture, Hurston gradually discovered that "the culture she observes is thriving, not declining" (Jirousek 420). Jirousek continues her argument, "she also uncovers much that is borrowed, revamped, reordered. Hurston finds a dynamic, changing, lively 'hybrid' culture that survives not in spite of, but while including interaction with other cultures" (420). In fact, the characteristics of hybridity and adaptability are the very reason why black culture is not vanishing, but thriving.

2.3.2.3 Hurston's View on Cultural Fluidity and Hybridity

Hurston's view on black culture is illustrated in "Characteristics of Negro Expression." In this essay, she introduces various aspects of African-American culture including black folklore, dancing, music, religious practice, and so on. By describing the black cultural phenomena, she illustrates the main characteristics of black culture: originality, imitation, adaptation and hybridity.

According to Melville Herskovits, Frantz Boas' major contribution is his "concept of culture as a dynamic, changing force, to be understood only if it is recognized as a manifestation of the 'mental life' of man" (qtd. in Jirousek 418). Hurston expresses cultural fluidity in her ethnographic texts and argues that black culture is not a static, insular culture. When writing about folklore, she asserts, "Negro folklore is not a thing of the past. It is still in the making" (Hurston, "Characteristics of Negro Expression" 27).

Based on the fluidity of Afro-American culture, Hurston formed her idea of cultural hybridity. Her concepts of cultural fluidity and hybridity are of importance to the understanding of Afro-American culture. Hurston's view of hybridity is closely related to her root of culture—the philosophical ideas of ancient Africa. The Africans believe in "connectedness rather than separation" and maintain that the opposites coexist harmoniously (Collins 212). Patricia Hill Collins asserts that "in contrast to Western, either/or dichotomous thought, the traditional African worldview is holistic and seeks harmony" (Collins 212). In Chukwanyere Amalu's opinion, "Africans do not emphasize deductive logic but have inherent in their systems of thought another form of reasoning which might be termed dialectical reasoning, which is based on the idea of a concert of opposite concepts" (Njuguna). To illustrate the African philosophy further, Nana Adu-Pipim Boaduo FRC and Daphne Gumbi assert that

> Africa has distilled and encoded its experiences in science, philosophy, arts and heritage of its understanding of the world in countless ways. In brief, Africa's experiences are found encoded in its symbols, rituals, designs, artefacts, music, dances, proverbs, riddles, poetry, drum texts, architecture, technology, science and more importantly oral traditions (Tedla,

1991). The view of this list is that many of listed items appear simple on the surface; it is not until one attempts to unravel the encoded philosophies or messages within them that one is struck by their profundity. (FRC and Gumbi 46)

Deeply influenced by her childhood experiences in her Southern rural hometown Eatonville, Hurston knows well the meaning of "concert of opposites". As people firmly believe in connectedness and coexistence of various opposites, African American culture represents its vitality, dynamic force and adaptability. Although living in the white dominant culture, African Americans have taken advantage of the flexibility of their culture, and occupied what Bhabha defines as "interstitial" space, absorbing and revising some elements of the other cultures (including white culture) and changed them according to their own needs. In fact, that is Hurston's concept of cultural hybridity, which has been embodied in all aspects of African American culture.

In "Characteristics of Negro Expression," Hurston illustrates the fluidity, adaptability, hybridity and originality of black culture, covering its various aspects such as drama, language, folklore, dance, jazz, cultural heroes, religious practice (e.g. shouting). The aesthetic ideas of the black people are described in the article.

Black culture has its own distinctiveness. Black folks are imaginative and creative people who love beauty and arts. The first notable characteristic of Negro expression is their passion for drama, which permeates their entire life. In Hurston's point of view, "every phase of Negro life is highly dramatized… Everything is acted out...there is an impromptu ceremony always ready for every hour of life. No little moment passes unadorned" ("Characteristics of Negro Expression" 24). The second characteristic is their will to adorn, which shows their passionate pursuit of beauty. Bell hooks asserts that "the basis of African-American aesthetics" is their belief that "beauty, especially that created in a collective context, should be an integrated aspect of everyday life, enhancing the survival and development of community" (*Yearning: Race, Gender, and Cultural Politics* 105). In this respect, their desire for beauty is reflected in their decoration of their homes, such as their gaudy calendars, wall pockets and advertising lithographs. It is also embodied in their revision of the English language ("Characteristics of Negro Expression" 24). She argues that "perhaps his [Negro's] idea of ornament does not attempt to meet conventional standards, but it satisfies the soul of its creator" (24). The third striking features of the Negro expression are angularity and asymmetry. The former can be seen everywhere in the Negro's life, such as African sculpture, dancing, and doctrine of any sort. The latter can be found in African sculpture and carvings, and in the literature forms of prose and verse. Hurston considers Negro dancing as "dynamic suggestion," arguing that "since no art ever can express all the variations conceivable, the Negro must be considered the greater artist, his dancing is realistic suggestion, and that is about all a great artist can do" (27). Hurston's argument refutes fiercely the white supremacist ideology insistence that "black people, being more animal than human, lacked the capacity to feel and therefore could not engage the finer sensibilities that were the breeding ground for art" (hooks, *Yearning: Race, Gender, and Cultural Politics* 105).

As for the understanding of originality and imitation, the two important aesthetic concepts of Negro expression, Hurston has her own unique perspective. She first defines the meaning of originality, "it is obvious that to get back to original sources is much too difficult for any group to claim very much as a certainty. What we really mean by originality is the modification of ideas…It is his treatment of the borrowed material" ("Characteristics of Negro Expression" 28). From this perspective, "the Negro is a very original being" (28), thus denouncing the racist assumption that "the Negro is lacking in originality" (27). All the Negroes are famous mimics, but it doesn't mean that they are not original since mimicry is in itself an art. Negroes stick to their own cultural distinctiveness, on the one hand; on the other hand, they borrow and mimick the new materials from other cultures and revise them to meet their own needs. Just as Hurston says,

> While he lives and moves in the midst of a white civilization, everything that he touches is re-interpreted for his own use. He has modified the language, mode of food preparation, practice of medicine, and most certainly the religion of his new country, just as he adapted to suit himself the Sheik hair-cut made famous by Rudolph Valentino. (28)

In this way, hybridity becomes an important feature of African American culture. Just as Jirousek states, "African Americans distill cultural elements already circulating, remaking them as needed" (422). The hybridity of African American culture is reflected in the variety of folklore and music. Negroes borrow elements from other origins and combine them with their own stories, adapting them to meet their own demands. Hurston considers the variety of black folklore to be an embodiment of "the adaptability of the black man: nothing is too old or too new, domestic or foreign, high or low, for his use" (27).

In her article "'That Commonality of Feeling': Hurston, Hybridity, and Ethology," Lori Jirousek gives a detailed analysis of the hybridity of African American culture. I will use some examples from this article to dwell on hybridity. Hurston's ethnographical work *Mules and Men* collected stories including those of African origin, but also stories of European origin, highlighting black people's connection to the experiences of other people. For example, there is a story told by a young informant Julius Henry. The story originating from Europe tells how a peasant outwitted a lord. But in African American folklore, the story evolves into one of the struggles between John and his master. John defeated his master by drowning him in the end. Jirousek points out that

> the hybridity of the story itself reflects the hybridity of informants, who culturally and even biologically incorporate African, European, and perhaps other "origins." In addition, the tale speaks to the hybridity of readers whose background combine races, ethnicities, and economic classes, ancestors of whom could stand in for various figures in the tale. (421)

Jirousek also expounds the reflection of hybridity in Hurston's description of the religious practice of "shouting" and her recording of "Mother Catherine," which embody the eclectic nature of African American religion (Jirousek, 423-24).

2.3.2.4 The Contribution of Black Culture to American Culture

In Hurston's point of view, during the process of interaction with the other cultures, African American culture has made great contributions to American culture because it has not only absorbed the elements of other cultures and enriched its own culture, but it has also been absorbed by other cultures and has enriched and become part of American culture. It contributes to the richness of American culture in the fields of language and arts. Concerning language, for instance, "the Negro has done wonders to the English language" ("Characteristics of Negro Expression" 24), revising the pronunciation and enriching its vocabulary to his liking. What is more important, his revision has been adopted by others, even by the ruling class (28). Black people's most important contribution to the English language is "(1) the use of metaphor and simile; (2) the use of the double descriptive; (3) and verbal nouns" (25).

As for music, "the Jook is the most important place in America. For in its smelly, shoddy confines has been born the secular music known as blues, and on blues has been founded jazz" (29). Jazz has become an important and popular form of music, and in fact, it originated from "the Negro's modification of the white's musical instruments" (28), and "his interpretation has been adopted by the white man himself and then re-interpreted" (28). Hurston deems it to be "the exchange and re-exchange of ideas between groups" (28), by which the human civilization gains more vitality and richness. She continues to assert that "thus has arisen a new art in the civilised world, and thus has our so-called civilization come" (28). African Americans have made great contributions to American culture not only in language and music, but also in religion, folklore and other aspects.

In conclusion, Hurston contends that African culture is not inferior to any other cultures, separating biologically based concepts of race from the dynamic and changing realities of culture, drawing the conclusion that African American culture is not a vanishing, but a thriving culture. By sticking to its originality and distinctiveness and flexibly absorbing the foreign elements and interacting with other cultures in America, African-American culture has contributed to the richness of American culture as a whole.

2.3.2.5 Hurston's View on Culture Before Her Time

In fact, Hurston's view on culture, especially her concepts of cultural fluidity and diversity, has transcended the cultural view of her contemporaries. Her ideas bear some similarities to the cultural concepts of Homi Bhabha. Bhabah proposes the idea of "interstitial passage" in his *The Location of Culture*. He states that "this interstitial passage between fixed identifications opens up the possibility of a cultural hybridity that entertains difference without an assumed or imposed hierarchy" (*The Location of Culture* 4). I agree with Jirousek's idea that "prefiguring Bhabha's theory, Hurston showed African Americans and indeed all Americans to occupy 'interstitial' space, a culture constantly in flux rather than in fixed and mutually exclusive positions that form one nation" (426).

In addition, Hurston's view on race and history bears some similarities to the ideas of Frantz Fanon. Although Hurston is not contemporary with Frantz Fanon, some of her cultural ideas are echoed by Fanon in his prominent works *The Wretched of the Earth* and *Black Skin, White Masks*. Both of them try to "subvert the cultural commonplaces they both abhor" such as the concept of race (Lionnet 412), and both of them call on blacks to free themselves from bitterness and resentment caused by their disastrous history of slavery, which will enable them to acquire more freedom and introduce creativity and inventions into existence.

As has been stated above, after the publication of *Dust Tracks on a Road*, Hurston was negatively criticized by the intellectuals of the Harlem Renaissance and by the proponents of the Negritude Movement mainly because of her ambiguous attitude towards race and the blacks' history of slavery. For them, fighting against white racism and prejudice was their permanent responsibility, while Hurston seemed to "be aspiring toward some kind of 'raceless ideal' " (Loinnet 388).

In the chapter "Seeing the World as It Is," Hurston expresses her attitude towards the concept of race. "After all, the word 'race' is a loose classification of physical characteristics. It tells nothing about the insides of people" (*DT* 325). The phrases "Race Problem," "Race Pride," "Race Solidarity," and "Race Consciousness" are so important to those proponents of the Negritude Movement, but they are meaningless to her. She refuses to regard "Race Pride" as "a virtue," but "a sapping vice," which "has caused more suffering in the world than religions" (*DT* 325). "Racial Solidarity" is regarded as a "fiction" (*DT* 329). The intellectuals of the Harlem Renaissance were infuriated at her bold statement that "so Race Pride and Race Consciousness seem to me to be not only fallacious, but a thing to be abhorred. It is the root of misunderstanding and hence misery and injustice" (*DT* 326). She emphasizes that what the world needs is "less race consciousness" (*DT* 326).

Similarly, Fanon expresses his idea about color prejudice, his plea against racialist attitudes among the blacks. In his point of view, "white civilization and European culture have forced an existential deviation on the Negro" and "what is often called the black soul is a white man's artifact" (*Black Skin, White Masks* 6). Fanon stresses that color prejudice is nothing more than

> the unreasoning hatred of one race for another, the contempt of the stronger and richer peoples for those whom they consider inferior to themselves, and the bitter resentment of those who are kept in subjection and are so frequently insulted. As color is the most obvious outward manifestation of race, it has been made the criterion by which men are judged, irrespective of their social or educational attainments. (Fanon 89)

Fanon knows well that race is not only a biological trait, but also a "historically constructed phenomenon and culturally mediated artifact" (Kane 356). However, to prevent the blacks from turning themselves into racists, Fanon advocates that the blacks should not enslave themselves by becoming the slaves of Slavery. To illustrate his idea, he claims "I am not a prisoner of history. I should not seek there for the meaning of my destiny" (179). "I do not have the right to allow myself to be mired in what the past had determined" (179). "I am not the slave of the Slavery that dehumanized my ancestors" (179). Similarly, Hurston also calls for liberation from the imprisonment of history and devotion to the present and the pursuit of a better future. She turns her back upon the past, because she "see[s] no reason to keep my eyes fixed on the dark years of slavery and the Reconstruction" (*DT* 331), and because she has been "three generations removed from it, and therefore have no experience of the thing" (*DT* 332), because she has "no personal memory of those times, and no responsibility for them" (282). She is keenly aware of the negative consequence if they turn themselves into the prisoners of the past. "To me, bitterness is the under-arm odor of wishful weakness. It is the graceless acknowledgement of defeat" (280). As a result, "I see nothing but futility in looking back over my shoulder in rebuke at the grave of some white man who has been dead too long to talk about" (282). Therefore, focusing on the present and expecting the future will be of greater importance, "I will turn all my thoughts and energies on the present. I will settle for from now on" (284).

In Fanon's point of view, the Negroes can only be disalienated by refusing to "let themselves be sealed away in the materialized Tower of the Past" (Fanon 176) and refusing to "accept the present as definitive" (Fanon 176). He calls for freeing from the past, and placing more emphasis on the present and future, so that the Negroes will be able to take a real leap which "consists in introducing invention into existence" and in the endless creation (Fanon 179). The goal can be achieved "by going beyond the historical, instrumental hypothesis" (180). He emphasizes the viewpoint that "the ideal condition of existence for a human world" can be created "through the effort to recapture the self and to scrutinize the self" and "through the lasting tension of their freedom" (181).

Similarly, refusing the boundaries of class or race prejudice, Hurston prefers to embrace "the richer gift of individualism" (*DT* 323) and the freedom to explore the individual potentials. While exploring her individual self and "recapturing the self," she points out her wish: "I do not wish to close the frontiers of life upon my own self. I do not wish to deny myself the expansion of seeking into individual capabilities and depths by living in a space whose boundaries are race and nation." (*DT* 331) Hurston analyzes the reason why people "make a boast of racial, class, or national prejudice" (*DT* 331). They do so "out of a sense of incapability to which they refuse to give a voice" (331). Unlike these people, Hurston prefers to transcend the boundaries of race and nation, and manages to touch "the four corners of the horizon" (*DT* 348).

In *Dust Tracks on a Road*, Hurston ostensibly expresses her raceless ideal and shows her skepticism about a web of beliefs and ideas of black cultures. In effect, in my opinion, it is just Hurston's strategy to resist the white cultural imperialism. As she states in *Dust Tracks on a Road*, "the words do not count… The tune is the unity of the thing" (*DT* 198). Hurston's controversial statement about race does not necessarily mean that she ignores the collective responsibility as a member of the Negroes, but she just chooses to break away from the traditional strategy to express her resistance. Rather, she adopted a completely different method to hide her real intention behind what Gates refers to as "a coded system of signs, arbitrary in reference" (McKay, *Race, Gender, and Cultural Context* 181). As McKay notes, "in attempting to cope with the powerlessness and vulnerability of the racial self, blacks have employed language strategies, particularly artifice and concealment, in their relation with white America" (181). Like Fanon, Hurston knows well about the real meaning of those cultural commonplaces related to race problems, race pride or race solidarity, which are in essence no more than the creation of European colonialism, the white cultural impositions, just as Fanon views the black soul to be a white's artifact. However, owing to Hurston's subtle relationship to her dual readerships, Hurston does not illustrate it directly. In effect, in the chapter "Seeing the World as It Is," which was eliminated because of its radical political statements in the autobiography's first edition, Hurston criticizes Western imperialism fiercely. When writing about democracy, she claims, "Looking at all these things, I am driven to the conclusion that democracy is a wonderful thing, but too powerful to be trusted in any but purely Occidental hands" (*DT* 342).

It is true that Hurston shows her skepticism about the cultural commonplaces but she does not put forward any positive solutions since she is not a politician. Fanon also likes to ask questions. "O my body, make of me always a man who questions!" (*Black Skin, White Masks* 181). In this sense, "Fanon takes up the same relay" (Lionnet 412). But the questions Hurston raised are explored by

Fanon and answered in his influential works *Black Skin and White Masks* and *The Wretched of the Earth*. Fanon criticizes his fellow colonized for adopting racialist thinking and reproducing the values of the colonizer, believing firmly that "only the poetry of the future can move and inspire human beings to action and to revolution" (Lionnet 393). Although Hurston does not develop a revolutionary perspective, she suggests, just like Fanon, that "we urgently need to retrieve those past traditions that can become the source of reconciliation and wholeness, for it is more important to learn from those traditions than to dwell on pain and injustice" (Lionnet 393). Hurston will "retrieve those past tradition[s]" from the rich realm of black folk culture in her hometown Eatonville and other rural southern black communities.

In conclusion, because Hurston held such a cultural view that serves race from culture, her notion of race could not be understood by her contemporaries and was even negatively criticized by the black intellectuals, who considered her to be racially accommodationist. In fact, Zora Hurston, as the "daughter of Eatonville," (Hemenway, *Zora Neale Hurston—A Literary Biography* 90) loves her black folk and black folk culture. She just devotes herself to the presentation and celebration of black folk culture in her unique way. Her autobiography *Dust Tracks on a Road* is also one of her works which show her passion for the representation and celebration of African-American culture, although it has subverted the genre of autobiography both in form and content and has become the most controversial autobiography in African-American culture.

2.4 Representing and Celebrating Black Folk Culture as Its Interpreter

2.4.1 Representation of the Richness of Black Culture

Elizabeth Fox-Genovese argues that "the common denominator" of autobiographies of black women "derives not from the general categories of race or sex, but from the historical experience of being black and female in specific society at a specific moment and over succeeding generations" ("To Write My Self—The Autobiographies of Afro-American Women" 161). In this respect, Hurston follows the tradition of black women's autobiographies. Like Fanon who opposes the overuse of the general concept "African culture" because he regards it as a creation of European colonialism (Lionnet 389), Hurston does not represent black folk culture in the general and abstract sense, either. She knows well the difference and diversity of black culture, thinking that "nothing that God ever made is the same thing to more than one person. That is natural. There is no single face in nature, because every eye that looks upon it, sees it from its own angle. So every man's spice-box seasons his own food" (*DT* 61). Similarly, black culture is not an abstract concept. Rather, it is full of diversity and difference in different black communities. Therefore, Hurston observes and records the richly varied black folk culture based on the specific black communities of Eatonville, Polk County, New Orleans, Nassau, Jamaica and Haiti during and after the period of Reconstruction. She represents the richness and the unique traits of black cultures of the various black communities because she firmly believes that "the universal can only be known through the specific and that knowledge grounded in first-hand experience can yield more insights into the human condition and into the processes of acculturation, differentiation, and historicization to which human beings are subjected" (Lionnet 389).

In *Black Skin, White Masks*, Fanon argues that "Good-Evil, Beauty-Ugliness, White-Black: such are the characteristic pairings of the phenomenon that…we shall call 'manicheism delirium' " (141). "Whiteness" and "blackness" in culture are also the creation of European colonialism. Fanon does not think white culture and black culture are oppositions. To resist the white stereotype that the blacks do not have culture, the blacks do not have to prove to the whites that their culture is superior to white culture, because such behavior is in fact reproducing the values of white culture imperialism. He gave an example to elaborate his argument in *Black Skin, White Masks*, which tells of the white's contempt for black music, viewing jazz music as "an irruption of cannibalism into the modern world" (Fanon 176). His response to it was not to "take up a position on behalf of Negro music against white music, but rather to help my brother to rid himself of an attitude in which there was nothing healthful" (Fanon 176), because opposition to white music for jazz is to reproduce the white's values. Similarly, in *Dust Tracks on a Road*, Hurston's aim of representing black folk culture is not to prove the superiority of black culture over white culture, but to share the richness and diversity of black culture with others. Like Fanon, by resisting the imposed concepts of white culture colonialism and representing passionately the dynamic and richly varied black folk culture, Hurston adopted her unique way to resist the stereotyped idea that "Negroes are savages, brutes, illiterates" (Fanon 88). Culture is the "product of its own unique history that resulted in a set of beliefs, values, and behaviors that were to be accepted on par" (Greenfield 43). Influenced by her great mentor Boas, Hurston believes that "human behavior was learned rather than the inevitable consequences of biology, climate or any other factors" (Greenfield 43). Therefore, Hurston has a firm belief in the values of black folk culture.

2.4.2 The Community of Eatonville as the Representative of Black Culture

Just as Fanon based his analysis in *Black Skin, White Masks* on his hometown in the Caribbean island of Martinique, the French colony, emphasizing "local historically and geographically specific contingencies," (Lionnet 389) Hurston based her representation of black culture on her hometown Eatonville, Florida.

At the beginning of the autobiography, Hurston points out that "like the dead-seeming, cold rocks, I have memories within that came out of the material that went to make me. Time and place have had their say" (*DT* 3). By emphasizing the importance of "the material" and "time and place," Hurston is telling her readers the important role that the black community Eatonville played in her life. The culture there had an everlasting and positive impact on Hurston's personality and her attitude towards life. In all her life, Eatonville is the source of her spirit.

Eatonville is the first all-black town, a "pure Negro town—charter, mayor, council, town marshal and all", "the first [Negro community] to be incorporated, the first attempt at organized self-government on the part of Negroes in America" (*DT* 3). Eatonville came into being after the Civil War. After gaining the victory in the Civil War, three white young men tried their fortunes in central South Florida and settled there. Many people were attracted to move there and gradually a prosperous white community named Maitland came into being. At the same time, a number of black people moved there to seek better opportunities and a better future, because in this new area, there was "no more back-bending over rows of cotton; no more fear of the fury of the Reconstruction" (*DT* 8). Instead, there was "good pay, sympathetic white folks and cheap land, soft to the touch of a plow" (*DT* 8). That was why "relatives and friends were sent for" (*DT* 8). Therefore, "while the white estates flourished on the three-mile length of Lake Maitland, the Negroes set up their hastily built shacks around St. John's Hole" (*DT* 8). Fortunately, "on August 18, 1886, the Negro town, called Eatonville, after Captain

Eaton, received its charter of incorporation from the state capital, Tallahassee, and made history by becoming the first of its kind in America, and perhaps in the world" (*DT* 10). Therefore, in "a raw, bustling frontier, the experiment of self-government for Negroes was tried" and "White Maitland and Negro Eatonville have lived side by side for fifty-six years without a single instance of enmity" (*DT* 10-11).

Zora Neale Hurston moved to Eatonville with her family when she was three. Her father John Hurston, a mulatto "over the creek," left Alabama, married her mother Lucy Ann Potts, and moved to Eatonville in his late twenties. He had learned to read and write, which enabled him to develop his personal potentials and later become mayor of the town for three terms, serving as a preacher, helping to write the local law. The prosperous family lived a happy and quiet life there. The Hurstons owned a house of eight rooms, a five-acre garden, a yard with plenty of fruits and chickens. As a result, they had more than adequate housing and food for themselves and their eight children. Hurston's mother Lucy Anne Potts is a woman with strong will and full of independence. Unlike John Hurston, she encouraged her children to develop their creativity and potentials. Because Hurston's personality was different from the other children, Lucy paid more attention to her and developed a warm and intimate mother-daughter relationship, which became Hurston's source of spirit when she confronted setbacks and difficulties in life. As Hurston notes, "Mama exhorted her children at every opportunity to 'jump at de sun.' We might not land on the sun, but at least we would get off the ground" (*DT* 21). Lucy was always standing between her husband and her daughter. Hurston's disposition was just like her own, and she didn't want to squinch her daughter's spirit.

Growing up in such an autonomous black community as Eatonville and in such a family full of warmth and love, Hurston enjoyed a carefree childhood. She was absorbed in the culture in the black community. Her imagination and creativity were fully developed. As Hemenway points out,

> this fact of birth makes Hurston unique among black writers, and it was the major shaping forces in her life. Growing up in Eatonville meant that Zora Hurston could reach the age of ten before she would realize that she had been labeled as a 'Negro' and restricted from certain social possibilites by chance of race. (Hemenway, "Zora Neale Hurston and the Eatonville Anthropology" 192-93)

Living in the all-black community of Eatonville, Hurston "escaped the terror and victimization of segregation and racism in the southern ex-slave states and the northern industrial centers which Richard Wright and others describe in their autobiographies" (McKay, "The Autobiographies of Zora Neale Hurston and Gwendolyn Brooks" 269). Rather, in *Dust Tracks on a Road*, Hurston devoted herself to the description of the local culture of Eatonville by exposing to her readers "a total Black reality where Black people do not represent issues: they represent their own, particular selves in a Family/Community setting that permits relaxation from the hunted/warrior posture…" (qtd. in Raynaud 134).

Following the tradition of black female autobiographies, Hurston identified her individual self with the collective self of the black community. She found her individual self as part of the black community. But unlike the other black female autobiographers, Hurston did not focus on her specific personal experiences, but on the rich cultures of her community. Instead of narrating her own stories, she would rather act as the cultural interpreter for the black community. As McKay puts it, "Hurston reinforced her identity within the black community not as autobiographer but as self-appointed cultural interpreter for the community from which she came" ("The Autobiographies of Zora Neale Hurston and Gwendolyn Brooks" 182). Since early childhood, Hurston had realized that "the heart and spring of the town" was Mayor Joe Clark's store, where men gathered together and sat on boxes and benches, "pass[ing] this world and the next one through their mouths. The right and the wrong, the who, when and why was passed on, and nobody doubted the conclusion" (*DT* 61). The men made jokes with each other, gossiped about others' adultery because "there were no discreet nuances of life on Joe Clarke's porch" (*DT* 62). In Eatonville, people expressed their emotions directly, without having to hide their feelings. "There was open kindnesses, anger, hate, love, envy and its kinfolks, but all emotions were naked, and nakedly arrived at. It was a case of 'make it and take it.' You got what your strengths would bring you" (*DT* 62). The men's attitudes toward the nuances of life was also the embodiment of "the spirit of that whole new part of the state at the time, as it always is where men settle new lands" (*DT* 62).

For Hurston, the store porch was the most interesting place she could ever think of. She seized every opportunity "to allow whatever was being said to hang in [her] ear," and to hear "adult double talk" (*DT* 62). But what she really loved to hear was "the menfolks holding a 'lying' session," when the men "strain[ed] against each other in telling folk tales. God, Devil, Brer Rabbit, Brer Fox, Sis

Cat, Brer Bear, Lion, Tiger, Buzzard, and all the wood folk walked and talked like natural men" (*DT* 63-64). Being an anthropologist and folklorist, unlike the other writers and artists in the Harlem Renaissance, Hurston knew well that "the qualities of black culture which the artists in that movement were striving to capture resided in folklore… [and] that the folk represented not an aesthetic or a spiritual force to be merely intellectualized in art but rather a people struggling for life in all its positive and negative aspects" (McKay, "The Autobiographies of Zora Neale Hurston and Gwendolyn Brooks" 182). As Frantz Fanon argues, "when a story flourishes in the heart of a folklore, it is because in one way or another it expresses an aspect of 'the spirit of that group' " (Fanon 45-46). Hurston was keenly interested in the folk tales told by such story-tellers as "Lige," who told the tale about "how and why Sis Snail quit her husband, for instance" (*DT* 64). A woman story-teller named Gold told the story about the origin of the black race, which "pleased [her] more than what [she] learned about race derivations later on in Ethnology" (*DT* 66). In this tale, the concept of race was deconstructed. Black people were viewed as only a heap of multitudes who overslept and missed the hour to get their right color from God. This tale is in fact also a challenge and resistance to the colonial imposition on black people. As Fanon states, "it [color prejudice] is nothing more than the unreasoning hatred of one race for another… The light-skinned races have come to despise all those of a darker color, and the dark-skinned peoples will no longer accept without protest the inferior position to which they have been relegated" (89).

In effect, Hurston had heard dozen of those tales in "the lying session." As a successful preacher, Hurston's father John Hurston and his preacher associates often held big story-telling sessions on the front porch and very funny stories would be told (*DT* 69). As Hurston noted in her essay "Characteristics of Negro Expression," the great variety of Negro folklore "shows the adaptation of the black man: nothing is too old or too new, domestic or foreign, high or low, for his use. God and the Devil are paired" (27). Most people in the village were familiar with those tales of God, the Devil, animals and natural elements. The telling of tales had become an indispensable part of their life, which enriched their life immensely.

Always exposed to such pleasing environment, encouraged by her mother's spirit of independence and pursuit of freedom, Hurston had immersed herself in the culture of the black community and put her imagination and creativity into full play. The folk tales and the relaxing atmosphere stirred up her own fancies.

As Hemenway points out, "the Saturday night music and the Sunday morning praying, the singing, working, loving, and fighting of black rural life would become the fecund source for her adult imagination" ("Zora Nearle Hurston and the Eatonville Anthropology" 195). Hurston "picked up the reflections of life around [her] with [her] own instruments, and absorbed what [she] gathered according to [her] inside juices" (*DT* 61). She "picked up glints and gleams out of what [she] heard and stored it away to turn it to [her] own uses" (*DT* 69). Hurston began to make full use of her own imagination to make up her own stories. The animals, the wind, the trees, everything in nature seemed to be able to communicate with her. They kept talking to her and telling her things. Knowing the background of Eatonville and her family, I think there is no wonder why a black girl would long for "a fine black riding horse with white leather saddle and bridles" (38). Though her request for such a horse was rejected by her father, she made up one for herself and in her imaginative world, she often rode the prancing horse and saw things in far places. She was eager to know more about the outside world, so she invited her friend Carrie to "walk out to the horizon and see what the end of the world was like" (*DT* 36). She made friends with nature, naming a tree as "the loving pine." Influenced by the early childhood experiences, Hurston dreamed of touching "the four corners of the horizon" (*DT* 348). Hurston was deeply fascinated by the richness of the black folk culture. As a young girl, she grew up happily as a member of the Eatonville community.

Unfortunately, Hurston's mother died when she was still young. Her father remarried immediately after her mother's death. Hurston and her siblings were forced to leave their hometown and her happy childhood came to an abrupt end. She had to face the adversities in the outside world on her own. However, thanks to the strength and power she acquired in Eatonville, she was able to face up to the difficulties in life without changing and distorting her disposition. As McKay puts it, "throughout her life the South remained her source of spiritual strength, the locus of her genius, and always her place to which she returned" ("Autobiographies of Hurston and Brooks" 272). Several years later, after graduating from Barnard College, sponsored by her celebrated mentor Frantz Boas, she obtained the opportunity to go back to her hometown Eatonville to collect black folklores, which enabled her to write her first folklore collection *Mules and Men*. Bell hooks argues that

her return "home" to do field work was on one level a gesture of self-recovery; Hurston was returning to that self she had been forced to leave behind in order to survive in the public world of a huge Northern city...Back in Eatonville she could experience herself both as autonomous individual and as someone connected in a deeply emotional and spiritual way to the life of the community. The return home had such an impact on Hurston's psyche that she could not simply transcribe the material uncovered there as though it were only scientific data. It was vividly connected in her mind to habits of being and a way of life. (*Yearning: Race, Gender, and Culture Politics* 141)

Armed with the anthropological knowledge and a unique cultural view, Hurston examined the black folk culture in Eatonville, New Orleans, Haiti and Jamaica with a new perspective. While doing the field work, she first approached the work with the "objectivity" required in the professional academic work, but she didn't gain a lot. Then she changed her method and played the role both as a member of the community and as a participant-observer, exploring the characteristics of black folk cultures, understanding the diversity and hybridity of black culture more deeply.

In the chapter entitled "Research," Hurston described her experiences to collect black folk culture in such places as Polk County, New Orleans, Bahama. Acting both as an anthropologist and a participant-observer, Hurston represented the richness, flexibility, diversity and hybridity of black folk culture. Just as the folks in her hometown Eatonville held "lying sessions," Hurston also organized "lying sessions" frequently when she did her field work, which helped her collect many folklores and songs in an effective and reliable way. Knowing well the importance to build up intimate relationships with the informants, she created a relaxing and exciting atmosphere so that the informants would take part in the story-telling sessions more actively. As she put it,

I enjoyed collecting the folk-tales and I believe the people from whom I collected them enjoyed the telling of them, just as much as I did the hearing. Once they got started, the "lies" just rolled and story-tellers fought for a chance to talk. The one thing to be guarded against, in the interest of truth, was over-enthusiasm. (*DT* 197)

Hurston described the cultures in Polk County, Florida, where the black people enjoyed and celebrated life in their own way. "Black men scrambling up ladders into orange trees. Singing, laughing, cursing, boasting of last night's love, and looking forward to the darkness again" (*DT* 181). At night, they expressed their passion for life in the jooks, singing and dancing. They sang songs which "are born out of feelings with an old beat-up piano, or a guitar for a mid-wife" and danced the square dance, "dancing the scronch. Dancing the belly-rub. Knocking the right hat off the wrong head, and backing it up with a switch-blade" (*DT* 182).

As is known to us, the jook (i.e. a small roadside establishment in the southeastern United States where you can eat and drink and dance to music provided by a jukebox) is one of the most valuable contributions the black people have made to American culture. It was in the jook that the popular music blues and jazz were born. As Hurston put it,

> musically speaking, the jook is the most important place in America…The singing and playing in the true Negro style is called "jooking"… the songs grow by incremental repetition as they travel from mouth to mouth and from jook to jook for years before they reach outside ears. Hence the great variety of subject-matter in each song. ("Characteristics of Negro Expression" 29)

In Polk County, the black people enjoyed themselves heartily in the jooks singing, dancing and gambling. As Hurston noted, "and the night, the pay night rocks on with music and gambling and laughter and dancing and fights" (*DT* 184). Hurston viewed this as "the primeval flavor of the place" (*DT* 185).

Hurston left Polk County for New Orleans, Louisiana, and South Florida again, then Miami, and then she decided to go to Bahamas. She soon made a valuable discovery— "This music of the Bahaman Negroes was more original, dynamic and African, than African Negro songs" (*DT* 192). In order to know more about it, she left for Bahamas' capital Nassau, where she "ran to every Jumping Dance that [she] heard of, learned to 'jump,' collected more than a hundred tunes and resolved to make them known to the world" (*DT* 194). After returning to New York in 1932, Hurston managed to introduce Bahaman songs and dances to the audience at the John Golden Theater, aiming to "show what beauty and appeal there was in genuine Negro material, as against the Broadway concept" (*DT* 194). Fortunately, her purpose was achieved since the concert aroused a tremendous interest in "genuine Negro material" and "primitive Negro dancing" (*DT* 194). She was proud of her achievement in "show[ing] the wealth and beauty of the material to those who were in the field" (*DT* 194).

Hurston realized that the Bahamans were extremely prolific song-makers.

As she put it, "the humble Negroes of America are great song-makers, but the Bahaman is greater. He is more prolific and his tunes are better" (*DT* 197). The Bahaman Negroes showed their originality and adaptability while making songs. For them, "nothing is too big, or little, to be 'put in sing' " (*DT* 197).

For the black people, culture is not a fixed and static concept. Rather, it is a dynamic and changing force. While studying folkloric forms, Hurston discovered the plasticity of "subject matter" and the hybridity of black folk culture. Hurston presents black culture as "in process, always current, active, and flexible, gathering materials from everywhere" (Jirousek 421-22). Lionnet argues that the content of Negroes' folktales and "lying" sessions "is not rigid and unchanging but varies according to the tale-telling situation. It is the contextual frame of reference, the situation of the telling, that determines how a tale is reinforced by each new teller" (385). Hurston depicts the adaptability of the process of singing songs as follows:

> For instance, if a song was going good, and the material ran out, the singer was apt to interpolate pieces of other songs into it. The only way you can know when that happens, is to know your material so well that you can sense the violation. Even if you do not know the song that is being used for padding, you can tell the change in rhythm and tempo. The words do not count. The subject matter in Negro folk-songs can be anything and go from love to work, to travel, to food, to weather, to fight, to demanding the return of a wig by a woman who has turned unfaithful. The tune is the unity of the thing. And you have to know what you are doing when you begin to pass on that, because Negroes can fit in more words and leave out more and still keep the tune better than anyone I can think of. (*DT* 197-98)

The performance of songs are not fixed, but improvisational. If necessary, more materials can be added to it. The subject matter can be anything. This is a typical example to show the adaptability and hybridity of black culture. But it is also crucial to note that while adapting their songs to the specific situation, the singers should know "what they [are] doing," and "keep the tune," because "the tune is the unity of the thing" (*DT* 198). That means adaptability, hybridity and creativity are the main traits of black folk culture, but the black people would never give up their unique features.

In conclusion, in her autobiography *Dust Tracks on a Road*, Hurston placed more emphasis on the representation and interpretation of black folk culture. Through the "spy-glass" of anthropology and as a cultural interpreter, Hurston passionately presented the diversity and vitality of black cultures in the Southern areas. She created what Houston Baker calls "the black hole," "a subcultural (underground, marginal, or liminal) region in which a dominant, white culture's representations are squeezed to zero volume, producing a new expressive order" (Baker 152).

Chapter Three

Inheriting and Surpassing Tradition in Angelou's *I Know Why the Caged Bird Sings*

3.1 The Influence of the Tradition on Angelou's *I Know Why the Caged Bird Sings*

Unlike Hurston who "stepped outside the boundaries of conventional patterns in black autobiography" (McKay, "The Autobiographies of Zora Neale Hurston and Gwendolyn Brooks" 264) and subverted the traditions of black autobiography both in form and content in order to represent her strong passion for black folk culture, Maya Angelou followed the traditions of both black male and female autobiographies and used the autobiographical writing to represent both the personal experiences as a black young woman and the collective experiences of black people as a whole race. Unlike Hurston who subverted the concept of race, Angelou inherited "the political consciousness" and regarded the "race problem" as an important issue in her autobiography. James Olney claims the importance of Angelou's autobiography: "If black autobiography is a paradigm, the history of Maya Angelou's *I Know Why the Caged Bird Sings* is a paradigm of a paradigm" ("Autobiography and the Cultural Moment: A Thematic, Historical, and Bibliographical Introduction" 15). Angelou adopted "the fully developed black female autobiographical form that began to mature in the 1940s and 1950s" (Braxton, *Black Women Writing Autobiography—A Tradition Within a Tradition* 184).

Angelou has written six serial autobiographies: *I Know Why the Caged Bird Sings* (1969), *Gather Together in My Name* (1974), *Singin' and Swingin' and Gettin' Merry Like Christmas* (1976), *The Heart of a Woman* (1981), *All God's*

Children Need Traveling Shoes (1986) and *A Song Flung Up to Heaven* (2002). Among these six autobiographies, the third and fifth volumes are written in the form of travel narratives, the second, the fourth and the last volumes are written in the form of novels, only the first volume, which is a collection of proses, is written in the traditional way of autobiographical writing. Joanne M. Braxton emphasizes its important literary value by asserting that "speaking in terms of its literary merits, it is perhaps the most aesthetically satisfying autobiography written by a black woman in this period [in the post-civil rights era]" (Braxton 185). In fact, *I Know Why the Caged Bird Sings* is widely recognized as one of the greatest American black autobiographies by critics such as Dolly A. McPherson, George K. Kent and Sidonie Anne. Therefore, I will base my discussion of Angelou's autobiographies mainly on the first volume *I Know Why the Caged Bird Sings*.

In *I Know Why the Caged Bird Sings*, Angelou explored the traditional themes in black autobiography such as seeking for freedom from the social, economic and other forms of enslavement, the fight against oppression from the white dominant culture, the strength of the black community and the way of resistance against the oppression, the important role of female elders in the black community. In the following part, I will elaborate the impact of these traditional elements of black autobiography on Angelou's autobiographies, mainly on *I Know Why the Caged Bird Sing*. According to George E. Kent, "*I Know Why* [*the Caged Bird Sings*] creates a unique place within black autobiographical tradition, not by being 'better' than the formidable autobiographical landmarks described, but by its special stance toward the self, the community, and the universe, and by a form exploiting the full measure of imagination necessary to acknowledge both beauty and absurdity" (75).

3.1.1 The Journey from Enslavement to Freedom

As has been stated in Chapter One, the slave narrative has exerted an everlasting impact on the later development of black autobiography, since it has established some prototypal thematic and structural patterns for black autobiography, which keep recurring in later black autobiography. The thematic matrix in the slave narrative is to fight against "the fetters of mankind and the yearning of all living things for freedom" (qtd. in Schultz 82). Sidonie Anne Smith writes about the pattern established in the slave narrative: "In black American autobiography the opening almost invariably recreates the environment of enslavement from which the black self seeks escape. Such an environment was literal in the earliest form of black autobiography, the slave narrative, which traced the flight of the slave northward from slavery into full humanity" ("The Song of a Caged Bird: Maya Angelou's Quest After Self-Acceptance" 367). In some sense, the slave narrative is the story about a journey, a journey from the South to the North, a journey from the imprisonment of slavery to freedom, a journey from an enslaving community that has denied the rights and dignity of black people to a community where the narrator can find a niche for himself and fulfill his own social role. Later black autobiographies inherited the thematic pattern of seeking freedom, because even after slavery had been abolished, black people still suffered serious racial discrimination and social injustice. As Megna-Wallace observes,

> although legally free after 1865, the legacy of slavery remained with blacks, most of whom were still economically, socially, and psychologically dependent on whites. Poor educational opportunities, severely limited employment options, and segregation, as well as white violence and intimidation, all worked to keep blacks in an inferior social position and to persuade many that they were indeed inferior. (19)

Unable to enjoy the real freedom and rights claimed in the Constitution, black people were still on the way to seeking for freedom, equality and justice in their real sense and continued fighting against the hostility from the dominant white culture, which remained the main themes of black autobiographies. Therefore, the black autobiography is, to some degree, still a story about a journey from imprisonment to freedom. However, in post-bellum autobiographies, "the literal enslavement is replaced by more subtle forms of economic, historical, psychological, and spiritual imprisonment from which the black self still seeks an escape route to a 'North' " (Smith, "The Song of a Caged Bird: Maya Angelou's Quest After Self-Acceptance" 367). As Dolly A. McPherson asserts, "the journey to a distant goal, the return home, and the quest which involves the voyage out, achievement, and return are typical patterns in black autobiography" (*Order out of Chaos*: *The Autobiographical Works of Maya Angelou* 120). George E. Kent asserts that "black autobiographies take us on a journey through chaos, a pattern established by the narratives of escaped slaves" (73).

In *I Know Why the Caged Bird Sings*, Angelou also inherited the pattern of writing about her journey from social and spiritual imprisonment to freedom and liberation, telling about her childhood, about how she was just like a bird struggling to free itself from the cage and celebrate its victory.

The opening of the autobiography is full of symbolic meanings. It was an Easter congregation in Stamps, Arkansas in the 1930s. A young, awkward black girl named Marguerite, standing before the Colored Methodist Episcopal Church, failed to memorize the lines of a poem. Not knowing what to do next, she just repeated the first two lines again and again. "What you looking at me for?/I didn't come to stay…" People laughed at her because of her well-known forgetfulness. Little Marguerite felt so ashamed of herself for her own awkwardness and her "ugly appearance" that she fled from the church, running back home, running, peeing and crying. In fact, Little Marguerite failed to memorize the following lines of the poem not because she really forgot the poem, but because she was too sensitive to her "ugly appearance," because she was trapped in the bodily and spiritual imprisonment, which seemed to have exerted an important influence on her. As a little black girl, she was also influenced by the white standards of physical beauty. Since she was young, she had a sense of inferiority because she was regarded as an ugly girl, and she felt ashamed of her "skinny legs" (*CB* 2), her "shit color" (17) and her "small and squinty" eyes (2). She felt that she was living in a "black ugly dream." But to her joy, several days before the Easter congregation, she found that Momma was revising a beautiful dress for her although it was donated by a white. She had been expecting to wear the lavender dress so that she would look like a movie star. "I was going to look like one of the sweet little white girls who were everybody's dream of what was right with the world" (1). She felt excited at the wonderful idea and was expecting the arrival of the occasion when she could surprise all the people, showing them that she was in fact a white girl with blond hair. She imagined that people around her would give her respect and plead for her forgiveness and they would understand why she "never picked up a southern accent or spoke the common slang" (2). She wanted to let people know the fact that she was "really white" and it was "a cruel fairy stepmother, who was understandably jealous of [her] beauty" who has turned her into "a too-big Negro girl, with nappy black hair, broad feet and a space between her teeth that would hold a number-two pencil" (2).

Marguerite's severe self-hatred deriving from her skin and appearance is typical of the state of mind of African-American women. "As a consequence of lacking power, of being victims of racism, and of the failure of developing a positive sense of self, African-American women, however, often suffer psychologically and spiritually from self-hatred" (Blackburn 143). Because "black women are always judged by white standards, with blond, blue-eyed, white-skinned women of regular features [as] the ideal," they often have low self-esteem and negative self-images (Blackburn 144).

In fact, Marguerite's self-hatred and dreaming of becoming a white girl are the evidence to show the accomplishment of white cultural imposition on the black community. According to Frantz Fanon, in the collective unconscious in Europe, the Negro symbolizes "evil, sin, wretchedness, death, war, famine" (Fanon 147) and "blackness, darkness, shadow, shades, night, the labyrinths of the earth, abysmal depths" (Fanon 146), while on the other hand, white symbolizes "the bright look of innocence, the white dove of peace, magical, heavenly light" (Fanon 146). White children are regarded as lovely angels while black children are viewed as evil and ugly. "A magnificent blond child—how much peace there is in that phrase, how much joy, and above all how much hope! There is no comparison with a magnificent black child: literally, such a thing is unwonted" (Fanon 146). What is worse was that even "in the collective unconscious [of black people themselves], black=ugliness, sin, darkness, immorality. In other words, he is Negro who is immoral" (Fanon 149). Fanon argues that "the Negro selects himself as an object capable of carrying the burden of original sin. The white man chooses the black man for this function, and the black man who is white also chooses the black man. The black…is the slave of this cultural imposition. After having been the slave of the white man, he enslaves himself. The Negro is in every sense of the word a victim of white civilization" (Fanon 148). "The Negro makes himself inferior. But the truth is that he is made inferior" (Fanon 115).

Influenced by the white cultural imposition, young Maya was trapped in self-loathing and self-shame. She was eager to wake from her black ugly dream, hoping that a beautiful dress would change her fate. However, to her disappointment, the beautiful dress turned out to be only "a plain ugly cut-down from a white woman's once-was-purple throwaway" (*CB* 2). Unable to accept the truth that her dream of becoming a white girl could not be realized, she couldn't focus any attention on the poem and forgot the lines. Unable to face such a heavy blow, she ran away from the church, and she couldn't help urinating. Her severe bitterness and pressure needed an outlet to relieve herself.

> So I ran down into the yard and let it go. I ran, peeing and crying, not toward the toilet out back but to our house…I laughed anyway, partially for the sweet release. Still, the greater

joy came not only from being liberated from the silly church but from the knowledge that I
wouldn't die from a busted head. (*CB* 3)

Her "peeing" is not only the physical reaction of the extreme pressure, but also
symbolizes that the girl was struggling to find ways to liberate herself from her
spiritual enslavement and cage of self-hatred. Her "laughing" also predicts her
strategy to use her full imagination to reveal the absurdity in society. The opening
part of the autobiography prefigures the thematic content of the book: how the
black girl facing both the enslavement imposed on her by the white dominant
society and the imprisonment created by herself makes her way to fight against
the low self-image so as to find a way for full self-acceptance and self-fulfillment.
Though it is a long way to go and a way full of setbacks and hostility, she was
eventually able to free herself from the gloomy reality and sang her songs of
transcendence.

3.1.2 The Power of Words as a Way to Freedom

Emphasizing the power of words is one of the central themes of black
autobiography established in the slave narratives such as *The Narrative of the
Life of Frederick Douglass, an American Slave* (1845), which was inherited
by later autobiographies such as Richard Wright's *Black Boy*, Maya Angelou's
I Know Why the Caged Bird Sings. In fact, African-American culture attaches
much importance to "the force, responsibility and commitment of the word," and
African Americans believe that "the word alone alters the world" (qtd. in Cudjoe
281). According to Cudjoe, "in both the metaphorical and literal sense, speech
and language became instruments of liberation in Afro-American life, and the
magical incantation of the word and its transformative power gave sustenance
and hope to Afro-Americans even in their darkest hours" (282). Fully aware of
the magical power of words, Afro-Americans use the word as "a powerful and
sensitive weapon for the survival of the Afro-American," "a shield from the cruel
reality of American life" and "an extended arena" to struggle for freedom of Afro-
Americans (Cudjoe 282).

In *I Know Why the Caged Bird Sings*, Angelou gained her awareness of
the full power of words by going through some aching experiences, which later
enabled her to use language as a weapon against white oppression and as an
instrument for her self-assertion and self-fulfillment.

When still very young, Marguerite was attracted instinctively by the magical power of words. She cultivated keen interest in reading novels written both by white and black writers. As a voracious reader, she enjoyed the world created by the giant writers. She writes:

> During these years in Stamps, I met and fell in love with William Shakespeare. He was my first white love. Although I enjoyed and respected Kipling, Poe, Butler, Thackeray and Henley, I saved my young and loyal passion for Paul Lawrence Dunbar, Langston Hughes, James Weldon Johnson and W. E. B. Du Bois' "Litany at Atlanta." But it was Shakespeare who said, "When in disgrace with fortune and men's eyes." It was a stage with which I felt myself most familiar. (*CB* 11)

Angelou's passion for books enabled her to develop her imagination fully. In the sterile and gloomy life in Stamps, she created an imaginative world where she could communicate with those greatest writers, which laid a solid foundation for her later literary career.

However, Angelou realized the frighteningly negative power of words after she was raped by her mother's boyfriend Mr. Freeman. Knowing that Mr. Freeman was murdered, Angelou felt extremely guilty because she thought his death was partly caused by her lie at his trial. She was frightened by the potentially fatal power of words, "I could feel the evilness flowing through my body and waiting, pent up, to rush off my tongue if I tried to open my mouth. I clamped my teeth shut, I'd hold it in. If it escaped, wouldn't it flood the world and all the innocent people?" (*CB* 72) She deliberately refused to talk to anyone except her brother Bailey. As a result, Angelou enslaved herself in the world of muteness for a whole year until Mrs. Bertha Flowers, "the aristocrat of Black Stamps" (*CB* 77), "threw [her] the first life line" (*CB* 77), who helped her and confirmed to her the positive power of words. With the help of Mrs. Flowers, Angelou acknowledged that "the imagination can harness the power of words to great ends" (Pierre Walker 176).

Mrs. Flowers told Marguerite about the importance of words, "but bear in mind, language is man's way of communicating with his fellow man and it is language alone which separates him from the lower animals" (*CB* 82). She emphasized the beauty of spoken words, "words mean more than what is set down on paper. It takes the human voice to infuse them with the shades of deeper meaning" (*CB* 82). To Marguerite, the idea of "the human voice infusing words" seemed so "valid and poetic" (*CB* 82). When Mrs. Flowers read to her the first page of *A Tale of Two Cities* by Dickens, Marguerite appreciated the poetic beauty of her words, "I heard poetry for the first time in my life…Her voice slid in and curved down through and over the words. She was nearly singing" (*CB* 84). Marguerite admired the graceful and knowledgeable black woman so much that she "[had] remained throughout [her] life the measure of what a human being can be" (*CB* 78). For Marguerite, staying with Mrs. Flowers was the first of her "lessons in living" (*CB* 83), a precious gift and a kind of "enchantment" (*CB* 84) to her, which enabled her to be fully aware of the positive power of words and the beauty of spoken words. This unforgettable experience "leads her to appreciate the African-American poetic tradition as she never had before" (Pierre Walker 176).

In the chapter of graduation, after hearing the insulting speech of a white lecturer, all the black students as well as their parents became indignant and were inspired to sing songs. Marguerite was deeply moved by the magical power of the beauty of the poem by James Weldon Johnson and the Negro national anthem composed by J. Rosamond Johnson. "While echoes of the song shivered in the air…The tears that slipped down many faces were not wiped away in shame." (*CB* 156) At this moment, Marguerite "was a proud member of the wonderful, beautiful Negro race" (*CB* 156). Inspired by the singing of the Negro national anthem, the black people survived, "the depths had been icy and dark, but now bright sun spoke to our souls" (*CB* 156).

Knowing the powerful strength of words, Maya Angelou did not fear the negative power of words again. Instead, just like Richard Wright, she used her imagination to "harness the power of words to [her] own artistic and political ends" (Pierre Walker 176). As the "extension of the word" (Cudjoe 282), Angelou's autobiographical statement has become the instrument as well as the weapon to achieve liberation and assertion of her individual and collective identity.

3.2 The Voice of the American Black Community

3.2.1 The Racial Oppression of the American Black Community

Owing to their unique disastrous experience of slavery, American black autobiographers consider themselves as an inseparable part of the whole group and should take on the responsibility of voicing for the whole group so that other people will know more about what the whites have done to them. Cudjoe asserts that "the Afro-American autobiography must be seen as constructed, constituted, and formed by the specific practices and discourses of a specific people and their response to their time and place. It is not so much a unique statement of a particular individual but part of the signifying practices of an entire people" (Cudjoe 277). As a result, in black autobiography, the personal voice intermingles with the collective voice. As Butterfield points out, "the self belongs to the people, and the people find a voice in the self" (3). In effect, the aim of autobiographical writing is not to represent the individual exploits, but to give testimony to the social oppression of their race. According to Butterfield, the responsibility of the self in the black autobiography is to draw "sustenance from the past experience of the group, giving back the iron of its endurance fashioned into armor and weapons for the use of the next generation of fighters. The autobiographical form is one of the ways that black Americans have asserted their right to live and grow" (Butterfield 3).

For Angelou, the writing of autobiography is "a conscious assertion of identity, as well as the presentation of an alternate version of reality seen from the point of view of the black female experience" (Braxton 201). In *I Know Why the Caged Bird Sings*, Angelou narrated her experience with more emphasis on denouncing the oppression that the southern segregated black community suffered. Angelou expressed her attitude towards her goal of writing—"the effort to convey a sense of collective experience" (Megna-Wallace 5): "I'm using the first-person singular, and trying to make that first-person plural, so that anybody can read the work and say, 'Hmm, that's the truth, yes, uh-huh,' and live in the work." (qtd. in Megna-Wallace 5) In an interview with Claudia Tate, when answering whether she considered her works to be autobiographical novels or autobiographies, Angelou also emphasized the importance of shouldering the responsibility of speaking for the whole race:

> They are autobiographies. When I wrote *I Know Why the Caged Bird Sings*, I wasn't thinking so much about my own life or identity. I was thinking about a particular time in which I lived and the influences of that time on a number of people. I kept thinking, what about that time? What were the people around young Maya doing? I used the central figure—myself—as a focus to show how one person can make it through those times. (Tate 6)

In her autobiography, Angelou portrayed her childhood spent in Stamps, Arkansas in the 1930s, when "segregation was a deeply ingrained part of southern culture and governed all aspects of social interaction" (Megna-Wallace 15). According to Megna-Wallace, after emancipation, the whites regarded the African Americans as a threat to them, so they devised the following methods to suppress the blacks: "Jim Crow legislation, disenfranchisement, judicial discrimination, debt peonage, and violent intimidation were included in the repertory of social control techniques." (26) As a result, strikingly different from Hurston who spent a happy childhood in the community of Eatonville, where the black people enjoyed their freedom and autonomy, Maya experienced a childhood full of harshness, brutality and violence in the community of Stamps caused by the Jim Crow laws. Angelou observes that

> in Stamps the segregation was so complete that most Black children didn't really, absolutely know what whites looked like. Other than that they were different, to be dreaded, and in that dread was included the hostility of the powerless against the powerful, the poor against the rich, the worker against the worked for and the ragged against the well dressed. I remember never believing that whites were really real. (CB 20)

The gap between the black and the white caused by the racial discrimination was so wide that when Maya and her brother Bailey occasionally crossed the black area of Stamps and reached the white part of town, they felt that "the pleasure fled…After we left Mr. Willie Williams' Do Drop Inn, the last stop before whitefolkville, we had to cross the pond and adventure the railroad tracks. We were explorers walking without weapons into man-eating animal's territory" (CB 20). Bell hooks also described her similar experiences when walking "away from the segregated blackness of [their] community into a poor white neighborhood," she remembered the sense of fear, "because we would have to pass that terrifying whiteness—those white faces on the porches staring us down with hate. Even when empty or vacant, those porches seemed to say 'danger,' 'you do not belong here,' 'you are not safe' " (hooks, *Yearning: Race, Gender and Cultural Politics* 41).

At that time, it was common for black children to be in fear of everything related to the whites, because for the sake of safety, black children were taught during their earliest developmental years that "all whites had the right to abuse and exploit blacks without fear of serious censure or consequences. Blackness was associated with inadequacy and subservience" (Megna-Wallace 22). Growing up in such an environment, Angelou became more aware of the racial subordination and impotence of black people.

In the segregated Stamps, just like in all the other southern rural areas, the Negroes remained economically and socially powerless, having poor educational and job opportunities. "Many jobs were not open to the African Americans, and they typically held the lowest paid jobs" (Megna-Wallace 15). Angelou recalled the harsh living conditions of the cotton pickers: "In the Store the men's faces were the most painful to watch" (*CB* 100). Although working long hours, they lived a difficult life. "No matter how much they had picked, it wasn't enough" (*CB* 7). After working like horses and oxen, they "tried to smile to carry off their tiredness as if it was nothing, the body did nothing to help the mind's attempt at disguise" (*CB* 100-01), with their "backs and shoulders and arms and legs resisting any further demands" (*CB* 7). Struggling hard for survival, they tried "to earn enough for the whole year with heavy knowledge that they were going to end the season as they started it. Without the money or credit necessary to sustain a family for three months. In cotton-picking time the late afternoons revealed the harshness of Black Southern life" (*CB* 7). Witnessing the harsh life of the southern cotton pickers, Angelou would fly into inordinate rage when confronting "the stereotyped picture of gay song-singing cotton pickers" (*CB* 7). In fact, even after slavery was abolished, the blacks "remained economically, socially and psychologically dependent on whites who remained in almost complete economic and social control" (qtd. in Megna-Wallace 23). What's more, "because many [blacks] had been trained to accept white control, their lack of education and skills, the level of antagonism toward blacks, and their dependency tie to whites with power, many blacks—although woefully oppressed—were unable to struggle against the unjust exercise of power they experienced" (qtd. in Megna-Wallace 23).

The Southerners not only had to work extremely hard for survival, they also had to confront the white violence and intimidation. Maya keenly felt the atmosphere of deprivation and violence prevailing in Stamps. For the blacks, it was not unusual to confront the commonplace dangers in their daily life. For example, the threat and terror of lynching remained a consistent theme in the autobiography, which Angelou described in Chapters 3, 6 and 25. As Angelou puts it: "High spots in Stamps were usually negative: draughts, floods, lynchings and deaths" (*CB* 76). Megna-Wallace considers lynching "as a method of social control" after the Emancipation, "as slavery had successfully controlled African

Americans prior to the Civil War" (Megna-Wallace 25).

In Chapter 3 of the book, Angelou described the painful memory about an attempted lynching, of which wretched Uncle Willie was likely to become a target. One day, a former sheriff informed her grandmother nonchalantly of the news, "Annie, tell Willie he better lay low tonight. A crazy nigger messed with a white lady today. Some of the boys'll be coming over here later" (*CB* 14). The incident had an everlastingly negative effect on Maya's psychological development. "Even after the slow drag of years, I remember the sense of fear which filled my mouth with hot, dry air, and made body light" (*CB* 14). Those white boys, the members of the Ku Klux Klan, who would practice lynching, harbored unreasonable hatred towards black people, "The 'boys'? Those cement faces and eyes of hate that burned the clothes off you if they happened to see you lounging on the main street downtown on Saturday" (*CB* 14). The blacks were "hated, despised, detested… by the entire race" (Fanon 89). Angelou was not only horrified by the frightening atmosphere caused by the incident, but also felt indignant at the unfair treatment black people had to endure. "His [the former sheriff's] confidence that my uncle and every other black man who heard of the Klan's coming ride would scurry under their houses to hide in chicken dropping was too humiliating to hear" (*CB* 14). In spite of her indignation, Uncle Willie was forced to hide in an empty bin covered with layers of potatoes and onions, and Maya's grandmother Mrs. Henderson knelt praying for Willie's safety. Fortunately, the Klansmen didn't come that night, otherwise, "they would have surely found Uncle Willie and just as surely lynched him. He moaned the whole night through as if he had, in fact, been guilty of some heinous crime" (*CB* 15).

According to Megna-Wallace, "lynching was a widespread phenomenon after Reconstruction and during the first third of the 20th century, particularly in the South, and that the African Americans were by far the most frequent victims of lynching" (25). The fear for lynching was part of the life of the community of Stamps. One evening, Bailey came back home late because he missed his mother so much that he watched a movie starred by a woman who looked like his mother over and over again. Before Bailey came back home safely, his grandmother felt extremely worried about him, fearing that he had become a victim of lynching. At the thought of the possible result, her grandmother couldn't hide her anxiety and fear. "Her apprehension was evident on the hurried movements around the kitchen and in her lonely fearing eyes. The black woman in the South who raises sons, grandsons, and nephews had her heart-strings tied to a hanging noose. Any break from routine may herald for them unbearable news" (*CB* 95). The deepest fear in black women derived from the sense of insecurity, from "the constant threat of physical violence and intimidation by whites against blacks" (Megna-Wallace 17).

In Chapter 6, Maya and Bailey heard people talking about a man killed and thrown into a pond. It was said that "the man's things had been cut off and put in his pocket and he had been shot in the head, all because the whitefolks said he did 'it' to a white woman" (*CB* 190). What was worse, however, Bailey later witnessed the rotten corpse of another black victim of lynching, but he found that a white man even grinned at the death of the black man. Thoroughly shocked and horrified at the frightening experience, Bailey couldn't help asking: "Why do they [white men] hate us [black men] so much?" (*CB* 167). By asking such a question, Bailey "was away in a mystery, locked in the enigma that young southern black boys start to unravel… from seven years old to death. The humorless puzzle of inequality and hate. His experience raised the question of worth and values, of aggressive inferiority and aggressive arrogance" (*CB* 168). As a small black boy, Bailey could not understand that mob violence is "an instrument of social control over a 'threatening' southern black population" (qtd. in Megna-Wallace 26).

In the segregated South, racism pervaded every aspect of social life. "The two races went to different hospitals, were usually limited to treatment by doctors and dentists of their own race, attended separate schools and churches, used separate public restroom facilities and drinking fountains…" (Megna-Wallace 15) Mrs. Annie Henderson knew well about the differences legitimated by Jim Crow laws, but she decided to take her granddaughter to see the white dentist Lincoln when Maya suffered a severe toothache. She was confident that Dentist Lincoln would do her a favor because she once did him a big favor, lending him money so that he would not lose his building. However, Lincoln's reaction was totally beyond her expectation, "Annie, you know I don't treat nigra, colored people..." (*CB* 159). His policy was "I'd rather stick my hand in a dog's mouth than in a nigger's" (*CB* 160). Feeling indignant over Lincoln's reaction, Mrs. Henderson demanded that Lincoln should give her back ten dollars as the interest she didn't ask for. Maya, the little girl who faced the cruel racism, felt greatly humiliated, "it seemed terribly unfair to have a toothache and a headache and have to bear at the same time the heavy burden of Blackness" (*CB* 159). Maya made up another version of Henderson's resistance to Lincoln's racism, which was direct and fierce resistance to the unfair treatment the blacks had to suffer at that time. In her imagination, her courageous and dignified grandmother gave her order to the ignominious dentist: "I order you, now and herewith. Leave Stamps by sundown." "Now, that brings me to my second order. You will never again practice dentistry. Never!" (*CB* 162-63).

Angelou described the complicated feelings of ups and downs she experienced on the graduation day, when she first experienced excitement and expectation as a top student of the graduating class of 1940, then the humiliation and despair when she heard the racist speech made by a white man named Edward Donleavy and eventually a strong pride in the wonderful, beautiful Negro race inspired by the community's collective singing of the Negro national anthem. At first, all the members of the graduating students and their parents were anticipating the graduation day, "the hush-hush magic time of frills and gifts and congratulations and diplomas" (*CB* 152). However, their enthusiasm was totally spoiled by Donleavy's speech which was full of severe racial discrimination. His speech humiliated Angelou so greatly that it nearly destroyed her confidence in her race and hope for the future. This speech made her realize the destructive impact of racism on the black people. Donleavy was a representative of the dominant whites, implying that "the white kids were going to have a chance to become Galileos and Madame Curies and Edisons and Gauguins, and our boys (the girls weren't even in on it) would try to be Jesse Owenses and Joe Louises" (*CB* 151). Jesse Owenses and Joe Louises are their heroes, but they are not the only heroes of black people. In the minds of the dominant whites, "we were maids and farmers, handymen and washerwomen, and anything higher that we aspired to was farcical and presumptuous" (*CB* 152). "We were lower types of human beings. Only a little higher than the apes…we were stupid and ugly and lazy and dirty and, unlucky and worst of all, that God Himself hated us and ordained us to be hewers of wood and drawers of water, forever and ever, world without end" (*CB* 113). Angelou felt the impotence and powerlessness of black people:

> It was awful to be Negro and have no control over my life. It was brutal to be young and already trained to sit quietly and listen to charges brought against my color with no chance of defense. We should all be dead, one on top of the other…As a species, we were an abomination. All of us. (*CB* 153)

Faced with the humiliation and bitterness as a member of the Black race, Angelou again felt the suffocating burden of race imposed on them: "I thought about colors I hated: ecru, puce, lavender, beige and black" (*CB* 154). According to an investigation done by Frantz Fanon, white people associated Negroes with "biology, penis, strong, athletic, potent, boxer, Joe Louis, Jesse Owens, Senegalese troops, savage, animal, devil, sin" (128). Because of the cultural imposition, "the black man naturally feels that he is in closer touch with 'the lower animals' than with the white man, who is so far superior to him in every respect" (qtd. in Fanon 134). The Negroes were regarded as an illiterate race that had no culture. Not surprisingly, Angelou described her indignation at being considered to be the people of only having biological toughness with no brains or minds. "There was no 'nobler in the mind' for Negroes because the world didn't think we had minds, and they let us know it" (*CB* 154). As Cudjoe puts it, "the major crime of the dominant white society resides in its attempt to reduce all Negroes to a sense of impotence and nothingness. This is the internal 'rust' that threatens the development of the personal identity of all black people in America" (288). Young Maya was almost defeated by the cultural colonization of the white. Fortunately, it was the speech of the graduating black student Henry Reed and the community's singing of the Negro national anthem that instilled in her the pride of the Black race.

3.2.2 The Strength of the American Black Community

In *I Know Why the Caged Bird Sings*, Angelou not only reveals the difficult life of the black people against a predatory white world, but also represents the strength and richness of the black community just as Hurston represents the diversity and richness of black folk culture in her hometown Eatonville. In some sense, the community of Stamps is Angelou's source of strength, in the same way that Eatonville is Hurston's source of power. The difference between those two communities lies in the fact that the people in Eatonville were more fortunate and were likely to enjoy their own autonomy, which enabled Hurston to be freed from the sense of racial oppression, while Angelou keenly felt the brutal oppression of the white supremacist society. As McPherson puts it, "Maya Angelou, like many other black autobiographers, describes the southern black community as one that nurtures its members and helps them to survive in such an antagonistic environment" ("Initiation and Self-Discovery" 30). In spite of the hostile social environment, the community was still the place where the oppressed black could find their strength and warmth in life thanks to the close bonding of the community, the mutual help from the members, "the resilience of black Americans and their ability to cope with the inequities of American racism" (McPherson, "Initiation and Self-Discovery" 32). The descriptions of the richness and warmth of the life in Stamps testify to "the sense of relationships in the black community—the cooperative alliances that enable blacks to survive, with grace and exuberance, the most difficult circumstances" (McPherson, "Initiation and Self-Discovery" 32). For Angelou, "the black community is the essential community" (Schultz 88). When people in the community were in difficulties, others were ready to help. When they were humiliated by the white supremacist society, they sought support and strength from the community. The close bonding of the community provides them the "possibilities for love and laughter that often persist in the face of poverty and oppression" (McPherson, "Initiation and Self-Discovery" 32). The positive role that the community played in enhancing the cohesion among the members of the community were embodied in their various community activities, such as "church gatherings, storytelling sessions in the family-owned store, and cooperative work projects (such as annual hog slaughterings, preserving and canning activities, and work in the cotton fields)" (Estes-Hicks 68). Poverty in life did not defeat them in seeking happiness in life. All the members of the community took active part in various mutual community activities, which gave them a genuine sense of belonging and security.

For instance, people helped each other during the killing season. "In Stamps the custom was to can everything that could possibly be preserved. During the killing season, after the first frost, all neighbors helped each other to slaughter hogs and even the quiet, big-eyed cows if they had stopped giving milk" (*CB* 19). Both men and women were actively involved in the activities which were held in the cheerful and harmonious atmosphere. "The missionary ladies of the Christian Methodist Episcopal Church helped Momma prepare the pork for sausage," children "brought wood for the slick black stove" and "the men chopped off the larger pieces of meat" (*CB* 19).

Angelou described "the episodes of beauty" which "relieved the monotony of life in Stamps" (Cudjoe 289). In Chapter 20, Angelou had a poetic description of the happy time when the community held the biggest outdoor event of the year—summer picnic fish fry in the clearing by the pond. "All churches were represented, as well as the social groups (Elks, Eastern Star, Masons, Knights of Columbus, Daughters of Pythias), professional people (Negro teachers from Lafayette County) and all the excited children" (*CB* 115). This was a feast for all the people. Musicians, busy ladies and excited children enjoyed themselves. Musicians brought them "cigar-box guitars, harmonies, juice harps," ladies showing off "their baking hands," proven fishermen and weekend amateurs sitting "on the trucks of trees at the pond," a gospel group rehearsing "on one corner of the clearing" and children singing and playing balls (*CB* 115-16). "Their harmony, packed as tight as sardines, floated over the music of the county singers and melted into the songs of the small children's ring games" (*CB* 116). In the big festival, people enjoyed the leisure time, delicious food, music, which showed the richness of their entertainment. At this moment, people temporarily forgot the harshness and oppression of life and obtained a strong sense of belonging to a community full of optimism, humor and creativity, showing their passion and love for life.

The African-American church played a key role in uniting the rural community and enhancing the cohesion of the community so that southern blacks were able to survive the brutal reality. As "the institution that has had the greatest impact on the African-American community," the church was "a source of comfort and inspiration to them as they endured the horrifying conditions of slavery," provided "solace to African Americans in the face of racism, violence, and poverty," and functioned as "a unifying force in the community" (Megna-Wallace 87). Harry V. Richardson asserts that "it [the church] has held in common unity more Negroes than any other organization, and it has had more influence in molding the thought and life of the Negro people than any other single agency" (qtd. in Megna-Wallace 88-89).

For Maya Angelou, when she stayed with her grandmother Mrs. Henderson, the church was an inseparable part of her life. In the third volume of her autobiography series, *Singin' and Swingin' and Gettin' Merry Like Christmas*, Angelou wrote about the dominant role of the church in her family life:

> I had grown up in a Christian Methodist Episcopal Church where my uncle was superintendent of Sunday School, and my grandmother was Mother of the Church. Until I was 13 and left Arkansas for California, each Sunday I spent a minimum of six hours in church. On monday evenings Momma took me to Usher Board Meeting; Tuesday, the Mothers of the Church met; Wednesday was for prayer meeting; Thursday, the Deacons congregated; Fridays and Saturdays were spent in preparation for Sunday. (13) (qtd. in Megna-Wallace 88)

Mrs. Henderson, the most capable woman in the community, acted as Mother of the Church. She was fiercely religious and her firm belief in God was the origin of her strength and the sustaining force in her life. Deriving "spiritual sustenance and fortitude from the 'Bread of Heaven'" (Braxton 190), Mrs. Henderson used her religious conviction to direct her children and grandchildren, requiring Maya and Bailey to obey the religious rules and participate in all the religious activities. Growing up in such a religious environment, Maya Angelou acknowledged the positive role of religious activities although she also realized the absurdity and negative aspects of activities in the church.

In *I Know Why the Caged Bird Sings*, Angelou described church-related activities, which not only brought spiritual inspiration to the black people, but also laid a solid foundation for the community's solidarity. A case in point is the black people's devotion to the annual revival meeting. Even after working hard at daytime, they were expecting to take part in the revival meeting. For them, this was a solemn and sacred occasion to embrace God, when they would not "indulge in human concerns or personal questions" (*CB* 102). People were full of eager anticipation, "people…streamed toward the temporary church. The adults relayed the serious intent of their mission…. Their minds were concentrated on the coming meeting, soul to soul, with God" (*CB* 102). They sang songs and spirituals, expressing their emotions through groans, shouts and shrieks, which gave them great comfort and helped them to gain confidence. "Their faces shone with the delight of their souls. The mean whitefolks was going to get their comeuppance" (*CB* 107). They strongly believed in the conviction of "faith, hope and charity" and "the greatest of these is charity" (*CB* 108). They derived great satisfaction and confidence in the future from the congregation, forsaking their distress for a little while, believing that "even if they were society's pariahs, they were going to be angels in a marble white heaven" (*CB* 108).

In *I Know Why the Caged Bird Sings*, Angelou described the church activities in some other chapters, for example, the opening chapter about what happened on the Easter Day and the chapter about the funny behavior of Sister Monroe. The religious ideas had penetrated through every aspect of their life. Although many scholars argue that "like violence and segregation, the message of the church has been used to ensure white dominance over blacks" (Megna-Wallace 90), to some degree, the black people have subverted the church's function of manipulating them expected by the whites, and have transformed the church as an organization to strengthen the bonding of the community and a place to express their resistance.

As McPherson notes, in the South, "religion, sports, and education functioned in a way that encouraged the discriminated class to accept the status quo. But Angelou demonstrates how the blacks in Stamps subverted those institutions and used them to withstand the cruelty of the American experiences" ("Initiation and Self-Discovery" 38).

Although Angelou also criticized the absurdity of the church, she knew well the constructive and positive influence of church activities on the black community. As Joanne M. Braxton argues, "unlike Wright, she [Angelou] evokes this ridicule [of the church] and paints this portrait without condescension—still recognizing the solvency of the basic spiritual trust" (Braxton 191). In fact, "among rural Negroes the church is still the only institution which provides an effective organization of the group, an approved and tolerated place for social activities, a forum for expression on many issues, an outlet for emotional repressions, and a plan for social living. It is a complex institution meeting a wide variety of needs" (qtd. in Megna-Wallace 91).

Owing to the communal activities in their daily life and in the church, members of the community shared their joys and sorrows. Nobody was isolated from the rest of the community. When they were in difficulty, others would be ready to help them. Generous donating was common although "whatever was given by Black people to other Blacks was most probably needed as desperately by the donor as the receiver" and the generosity "was indulged on pain of sacrifice" (*CB* 40). When a black man was in danger of becoming the would-be victim of lynching for assaulting white womanhood, Mrs. Henderson helped him to escape in spite of the danger of involving herself in it. When a man was in grief because of the death of his wife, Mrs. Henderson and Uncle Willie showed great concerns for him, consoling him and encouraging him to live on. When Maya was locked in the cage of muteness caused by the rape, Mrs. Flowers threw the "first life line" to her (*CB* 77) and gave her the "lessons in living" (*CB* 83). When Bailey did not come back home on time in the evening, his grandmother was worried and the neighbors also showed deep concerns for him. In an interview with Randall Tsututa, Angelou pointed out: "But the people around us also helped raise us. They watched us when we were out of the house. They knew that Mamma was getting up in age and Uncle Willie could not get around easily, so they watched us and reported our actions to Mamma and Uncle Willie" (qtd. in Megna-Wallace 117). According to McPherson, in the southern black community, "one member's concern becomes the community's concern because members, in their practice of the rituals of extended family relationships, are related not only through the community but through the church as well" (McPherson, "Initiation and Self-Discovery" 31).

I agree with Estes-Hicks that "Maya's grandmother's store, 'the lay center of activities in town,' gave the writer a Hurston-like post from which to observe the rich life of the small-town Arkansas in the thirties during her ten-year stay in the South" (Estes-Hicks 68). In the store, which was built in the heart of the Negro area, Maya observed the harshness of the cotton pickers and the difficult life of the people during the Great Depression. It was also in the store, however, that she witnessed the vitality and strength of the community. "In those tender mornings the Store was full of laughing, joking, boasting and bragging. One man was going to pick two hundred pounds of cotton, and another three hundred" (*CB* 6).

People would gather in the store when important things related to the black people happened. Those special occasions provided them the chance to promote their racial solidarity and pride in their race. For example, the black people would gather here to listen to the radio broadcasting about the boxing match between their hero Joe Louise and his white opponent Carnera. For them, the boxing match became "a tableau in which black America came face to face with white America" (Cudjoe 286). In this way, "sports, as it were, became just another arena where the struggle for justice and liberation was carried on" (Cudjoe 288).

Joe Louise inspired pride in African Americans and he was "the idol of every Negro home in the United States" (Megna-Wallace 124). All the people came here, including men, women and children:

> The LAST INCH of space was filled, yet people continued to wedge themselves along the walls of the Store. Uncle Willie had turned the radio up to its last notch so that youngsters on the porch wouldn't miss a word. Women sat on kitchen chairs, dining-room chairs, stools and upturned wooden boxes. Small children and babies perched on every lap available and men leaned on the shelves or on each other. (*CB* 111)

Joe Louise's victory in boxing was significant to them, because it was a way to demonstrate their dignity and worth to white people. Not surprisingly, all of them felt nervous at first. When Louise was going down, people became extremely worried. For them, whether Joe Louise would defeat the opponent or not meant a lot to them. If he was defeated, it meant that his race was under the harsh oppression by white people. Joe Louise, the Brown Bomber, the national hero for the blacks, fought not only for himself, but more for the dignity and value of his people. When news came that Joe Louise defended heavyweight championship, the black people were proud of the hero. Joe Louise had proved to the world that they were the strongest people in the world. The people in Stamps who gathered in Mrs. Henderson's store were so proud of the remarkable achievement of their whole race that they celebrated the precious moment just as it was a festival.

3.2.3 The Strategies of Racial Protest

3.2.3.1 The Black Family as a Site of Resistance

Living in the severe hostile environment, the black community was forced to find their way out for survival. Fortunately, the strong communion, the sense of belonging and togetherness, the strength and power they found in the community enabled them to manage to survive. Bell hooks argues that "the experience of rural living, poverty, racial segregation, and resistance struggle" offered "ways of knowing, habits of being, that can sustain us as a people" (hooks, *Yearning*: *Race, Gender, and Cultural Politics* 38). In the antagonistic environment, they found their unique ways of resistance against the white supremacist society. As far as "resistance" is concerned, the Vietnamese Buddhist monk Thich Nhat Hahn gives the following definition:

> Resistance means opposition to being invaded, occupied, assaulted and destroyed by the system. The purpose of resistance, here, is to seek the healing of yourself in order to be able to see clearly...I think that communities of resistance should be places where people can return to themselves more easily, where the conditions are such that they can heal themselves and recover their wholeness. (qtd. in hooks, *Yearning*: *Race, Gender, and Culture Politics* 43)

For the southern black communities, the black family was the most important place for resistance. Bell hooks argues that

> despite the brutal reality of racial apartheid, of domination, one's homeplace was the one site where one could freely confront the issue of humanization, where one could resist. Black women resisted by making homes where all black people could strive to be subjects, not objects, where we could be affirmed in our minds and hearts despite poverty, hardship,

and deprivation, where we could restore to ourselves the dignity denied us on the outside in the public world. (*Yearning: Race, Gender, and Culture Politics* 42)

Bell hooks continues to illustrate the importance of homeplace as an instrument for struggling against the white oppression:

Throughout our history, African Americans have recognized the subversive value of homeplace, of having access to private space where we do not directly encounter white racist aggression. Whatever the shape and direction of black liberation struggle…domestic space has been a crucial site for organizing, for forming political solidarity. Homeplace has been a site of resistance. Its structure was defined…by our struggle to uplift ourselves as a people, our struggle to resist racist domination and oppression. (*Yearning: Race, Gender, and Culture Politics* 47)

In *I Know Why the Caged Bird Sings*, Angelou described the blacks' various ways to protest against oppression. When interviewed by Tate and answering Tate's question, "How do you integrate protest in your work?" Angelou said: "Protest is an inherent part of my work. You can't just not write about protest themes or not sing about them. It's a part of life. If I don't agree with a part of life, then my work has to address it" (Tate 7-8). Realizing the significance of revealing the ways of resistance, Angelou first described the importance of homeplace as the place for cultivating children's good manners and life habits, for retaining their grace and dignity. For example, in Angelou's family, Mrs. Henderson always indoctrinated her grandchildren with the two commandments that "THOU SHALL NOT be dirty" and "THOU shall not be impudent" (*CB* 21), convincing us that "not only was cleanliness next to Godliness, dirtiness was the inventor of misery" (*CB* 22). All the members of the community believed that

the impudent child was detested by God and a shame to its parents and could bring destruction to its house and line. All adults had to be addressed as Mister, Missus, Miss, Auntie, Cousin, Unk, Uncle, Buhbah, Sister, Brother, and a thousand other appellations indicating familial relationship and the lowliness of the addressor. Everyone I knew respected these customary laws, except for the powhitetrash children. (22)

The family's positive instruction helped their children build up their grace and dignity. Compared with the powhitetrash childen, black children were clean and polite, which meant that they were people with self-esteem and self-respect. In the black homeplace, the family elders, especially elderly females, would teach their children and grandchildren to utilize the daily activities as a way to fight against oppression, and endowed "everyday activities such as washing, raking a yard, or minding one's manners with symbolic value as a way of resisting bigotry" (Pierre Walker 174). Walker argues that "making every minute of the day a symbolic means of fighting segregation in turn means that segregation is not a helpless and hopeless situation" (174).

3.2.3.2 Mrs. Henderson's Subtle Resistance

Living in the brutal reality of white oppression, Mrs. Henderson developed her own way of resistance—what Stephen Butterfield called the weapon of "the most dignified course, silent endurance" and what Pierre A. Walker referred to as "subtle resistance," which was the typical way of resistance adopted by most of the members of the community. Pierre A. Walker argues that the tactic of subtle resistance was "the more effective strategy for reacting to racism and segregation than rage and indignation" and its powers lay in the fact that black people could use the weapon to "preserve [their] human dignity" "without risking harm to life, liberty, or property" (173-74).

Mrs. Henderson told her grandchildren that when confronting whites, "the less you say to whitefolks (or even powhitetrash), the better" (*CB* 22). She tried to use the useful resistance experiences to protect her grandchildren:

> Momma intended to teach Bailey and me to use the paths of life that she and her generation and all the Negroes gone before had found, and found to be safe ones. She didn't cotton to the idea that whitefolks could be talked to at all without risking one's life. And certainly they couldn't be spoken to insolently. In fact, even in their absence they could not be spoken of too harshly unless we used the sobriquet "They." If she had been asked and had chosen to answer the question of whether she was cowardly or not, she would have said that she was a realist. Didn't she stand up to "them" year after year? (*CB* 39).

Angelou attributed her Momma's cautious attitude towards the whites to the influence of slavery and her Momma's "African-bush secretiveness and suspiciousness," which were confirmed by "centuries of promises made and promises broken" (*CB* 164). The following saying could best illustrate her Momma's subtle resistance: "'If you ask a Negro where he's been, he'll tell you where he's going.' To understand this important information, it is necessary to know who uses this tactic and on whom it works" (*CB* 164).

In Chapter 5 about Mrs. Henderson's confrontation with the powhitetrash girls, Angelou described "one of the most usually subtle, ambiguous, understated confrontation scenes in the history of the form" (Butterfield 210). Angelou views it as the "most painful and confusing experience I had ever had with my grandmother" (*CB* 23) and she thinks that "my lifelong paranoia was born in those cold, molasses-slow minutes" (*CB* 24). This was a typical case in which Mrs. Henderson adopted her strategy of subtle resistance to defeat the powhitetrash girls' humiliation and maintain her human dignity. The racial oppression could be fully embodied in the plot. McPherson regards it as "a vivid recapturing of black/white tensions in the South of the 1930s" ("Initiation and Self-Discovery" 29).

Three dirty impudent white girls, who had nothing but their superiority of their white skin given by the white domination, tried every means of agitation to humiliate Mrs. Henderson, the most respectable elderly lady in the black community, making fun of her in various means, calling Mrs. Henderson impudently by her first name, aping and mocking her, making puppet dance like clowns and even showing their pubic hair. The white girls attempted "to use their race as an overbearing instrument of power" and practiced "the rituals of white power with the full sanction of the white community" and tried to "reduce the black woman to their level" (McPherson, "Initiation and Self-Discovery" 29). Young Maya, hiding behind the door, burst into a rage, wishing to use "the rifle behind the door" (*CB* 24) to fight against them directly: "I wanted to throw a handful of black pepper in their faces, to throw lye on them, to scream that they were dirty, scummy peckerwoods…" (*CB* 25). However, facing the humiliation imposed on her by the mean white girls, Mrs. Henderson used her subtle resistance to defeat the girls. She did not express her anger on her face. Instead, she showed calmness, humming spirituals, calling the white girls Miz. When seeing the girls coming, Mrs. Henderson stood with an erect posture, seeming to "be pulling for the top of the oak tree across the road," (*CB* 24) which showed her calmness and courage to face the challenge. When confronting the white girls' provocation, Mrs. Henderson kept humming spirituals, as if nothing had happened, "she sang on. No louder than before, but no softer either. No slower or faster" (*CB* 25). It meant that Mrs. Henderson was patient enough to face the white girls' humiliation. Eventually, the white girls felt they were bringing contempt upon themselves and left dejectedly. It was Mrs. Henderson who won the victory eventually, "her face was a brown moon that shone on me. She was beautiful. Something had happened out there, which I couldn't completely understand, but I could see that she was happy" (*CB* 27). Young Maya realized that "whatever the contest had been out front, I knew Momma had won" (*CB* 27). Not being a coward, Mrs. Henderson was forced to use the realistic strategy of resistance because of "the sanctions of the caste system which supports the children's behavior," but she refused to "recognize in them anything but white children" and refused to "register their offensiveness, or humanity, by deviating from the normal formulas of respect toward whiteness…Her triumph must be silent, unnoticed by those whom she has vanquished" (Butterfield 211-12). As McPherson puts it, "seeking to preserve her own integrity and to transcend the ugliness of their actions, Mrs. Henderson wins a psychological victory by using this weapon to transcend the limitations of her social world" ("Initiation and Self-Discovery" 29). In fact, the weapon of subtle resistance later served "as a basis from which Maya can later move to protesting and combating racism actively" (Pierre Walker 174).

Similarly, in the chapter of the dentist, Mrs. Henderson also used her realistic strategy of subtle resistance to fight against the racist dentist Lincoln who would rather "stick [his] hand in a dog's mouth than in a nigger's" (*CB* 160). Unlike the imaginary version created by Maya, Mrs. Henderson didn't behave like a hero and order the white dentist to leave Stamps and stop practicing dentistry. Rather, she asked Lincoln to pay ten dollars to her for the loan she once gave to him. Unable to understand her Momma's reaction, young Maya had to create an imaginary Mrs. Henderson who had the superhuman powers to manipulate the white dentist.

In fact, Mrs. Henderson's strategy of resistance was used by most people in the black community. For them, survival was of the greatest importance. So in Angelou's third autobiography *Gather Together in My Name*, she recalled the most violent and the final conflict between the grandmother and the granddaughter. When coming back to Stamps and visiting the General Merchandise Store, Angelou again confronted the contempt and humiliation of the white saleswomen: "In that moment I became rootless, nameless, pastless" (*Gather Together in My Name* 76). Unlike her grandmother, Angelou directly used the weapon of language to fight back. But to her surprise, her Momma did not approve of her radical way of resistance. Instead, her Momma responded to her dangerous behavior by slapping her in the face, because for Momma who regarded subtle resistance as the most secure way to fight against white people, she harbored a deeply-rooted anxiety that Angelou would invite danger to herself because of her direct and open protest against the white's dominance. Knowing well that her grandmother did so just for the sake of protecting her, Angelou bade farewell to her grandmother and left Stamps immediately. And she never expected that was the last time she saw her beloved Momma.

3.2.3.3 Singing Songs as a Way of Resistance

Apart from the subtle resistance which was most frequently adopted by the black community, they also used songs to express their resistance against the white supremacist society. Singing songs has been a tradition to fight against the oppression in the black community (Nero 239). Elizabeth Fox-Genovese argues:

> Unbreakable bars closed black communities in upon themselves…Within those cages, black communities developed their own vibrant life…Singing in the face of danger, singing to thwart the stings of insolence, singing to celebrate their Lord, singing to testify to a better future, singing with the life blood of their people, black women defied their imprisonment. The cages constrained, but did not stifle them. The songs of confinement grounded the vitality of their tradition, launched the occasional fledgling to freedom. ("Myth and History: Discourse of Origins in Zora Neale Hurston and Maya Angelou" 29-30)

In *I Know Why the Caged Bird Sings*, for example, when facing the humiliation of the white girls, Mrs. Henderson "uses the vehicle of song as a mechanism to triumph over her restrictions and limitations" (Nero 239). She hummed a hymn and sang on until the powhitetrash girls left. Then, she turned back to the store and sang: "Glory, glory, halluelujah, when I lay my burden down" (*CB* 27). Mrs. Henderson's religious conviction and the singing of songs were the origin of her strength. By using the power, she was calm and courageous enough to face up to the denigration and humiliation from the white dominant society.

The remarkable power of singing songs as a force to fight against the racism of the white was fully displayed in the chapter of the graduation scene. On the day of graduation in 1940, the speech delivered by the guest speaker Donleavy "was laden with half-hearted inspirations representative of a larger, mainstream society's low expectations of black people" (Barnwell 228). The spirit-killing speech conjured up the displacement and self-hatred among the black people. However, it was the speech given by Henry Reed, the valedictorian, and the singing of the Negro national anthem "Lift Ev'ry Voice and Sing" that lifted the morale of black people. After delivering the inspiring valedictory address of "To Be or Not to Be," Henry Reed turned his back to the audience and sang, nearly speaking: "Lift ev'ry voice and sing/ Till earth and heaven ring/ Ring with the harmonies of Liberty…" (*CB* 154-55). All the people joined in the singing, including the students, the parents and the children. They sang: "We have come over a way that with tears/ has been watered,/ We have come, treading our path through/ the blood of the slaughtered" (*CB* 156). For the first time, Angelou understood the overwhelming power and remarkable beauty of songs and poetry. With all the members in the black community joining in the singing, they enhanced their racial pride and solidarity. "We were on top again. As always, again. We survived. The depths had been icy and dark, but now a bright sun spoke to our souls. I was no longer simply a member of the proud graduating class of 1940; I was a proud member of the wonderful, beautiful Negro race" (*CB* 156).

It was on this occasion that Angelou came to realize the power of poetry and songs, and the vital role that the poets played on their way to freedom. "Oh, Black known and unknown poet, how often have your auctioned pains sustained us? Who will compute the lonely nights made less lonely by your songs, or by the empty pots made less tragic by your tales?" (*CB* 156). Angelou realized the important guiding roles of poets: "We might raise monuments and sacrifice to the memories of our poets…We survive in exact relationship to the dedication of our poets (include preacher, musicians and blues singers)" (*CB* 156).

Fully aware of the sacred mission of poets in the cause of the liberation of the whole race, Angelou became such a poet herself, writing numerous poems to boost the morale and pride of the black race, making her contribution to the cause of liberation of the blacks. In her poem "Still I Rise," she writes:

> You my write my down in history/ With your bitter, twisted lies,/ You may trod me in the very dirt/ But still, like dust I'll rise… you may shoot me with your words,/ You may cut me with your eyes,/ You may kill me with your hatefulness, But still, like air, I'll rise./ …. Leaving behind nights of terror and fear/ I rise/ Into a daybreak that's wondrously clear/ I rise/ Bringing the gifts that my ancestors gave,/ I am the dream and the hope of the slave./ I rise/ I rise/ I rise. (Angelou, *Poems* 154-55)

Angelou's beautiful poems motivated the spirit of the blacks and gave them inspiration and encouragement to fight for freedom and for a brighter future.

3.3 The Song of a Black Female Self

3.3.1 Maya's Journey to Self-Discovery

In *I Know Why the Caged Bird Sings*, Angelou followed the black autobiography tradition: undertaking the responsibility of giving the voice of the collective group. A black autobiographical statement is regarded as "a public rather than a private gesture," with "me-ism giving way to our-ism" (Cudjoe 280). As a member of the black community of Stamps, Arkansas, Angelou described the voice of the black community, revealing the severe racial oppression, the impotence and subordination of the black people as well as the strength they derived from the close bonding of the black community, their use of resistance strategies such as the subtle racial resistance and their communal actions such as singing songs to fight against the white domination and racial prejudice. As an outstanding poet, a great artist, a brave fighter, Angelou has never forgotten her mission as "a proud member of the wonderful, beautiful Negro race" (*CB* 156) and her autobiography bore witness to "the collective experience—to black powers of survival and creativity as well as to white oppression" (Fox-Genovese, "My Statue, My Self: Autobiographical Writing of Afro-American Women" 184).

Like other Afro-American writers who "have written themselves as persons and as women under special conditions of colonization," (Fox-Genovese, "My Statue, My Self: Autobiographical Writing of Afro-American Women"184) Angelou described her personal growth as a black girl in the South in the 1930s and 1940s. *I Know Why the Caged Bird Sings* is not only "a personal testimony to oppression" (Fox-Genovese, "My Statue, My Self: Autobiographical Writing of Afro-American Women" 178) or a story about the strength as well as the sufferings of black people, it is also a coming-of-age story about a black girl's survival, about how a black girl with extreme self-hatred and self-doubt grows into an independent girl full of self-assurance and self-determination. This is a story about how a caged bird undergoes painful experiences and makes its way to fly into the blue sky. This is a story about how a caged bird seeks its freedom and finally achieves its liberty. This is a song celebrating how a black girl breaks her imprisonment and finds out the way to express her self-worth. In contrast with the young girl in the opening chapter, who dreams of becoming a white girl, Maya, when the story ends, has become "a proud member of the wonderful, beautiful Negro race" (*CB* 156) and a confident mother, who was courageous enough to confront the challenges of life. According to Butterfield, "*I Know Why the Caged Bird Sings* is not really the struggle of the bird; it is the exploration of the cage, the gradual discovery of its boundaries, the loosening of certain bars that she can slip through when the keepers' backs are turned" (Butterfield 207-08).

The story narrates the childhood life of the black girl Marguerite Johnson from 3 to 16 years old when she became a mother, covering the years when she stayed with her grandmother in the southern community of Stamps, Arkansas, and later with her mother in Los Angeles and San Francisco. Angelou revealed how difficult life was for a black girl in the segregated southern communities: "If growing up is painful for the southern black girl, being aware of her displacement is the rust on the razor that threatens the throat. It is an unnecessary insult." (*CB* 3) Maya struggled hard for survival under "the interlocking structures of gender, class and race" (Fox-Genovese, "My Statue, My Self: Autobiographical Writing of Afro-American Women" 178). As Angelou puts it, "the black female is assaulted in her tender years by all those common forces of nature at the same time that she is caught in the tripartite crossfire of masculine prejudice, white illogical hate and Black lack of power" (*CB* 231). The process of growth to Maya was a process from "being ignorant of being ignorant to being aware of being aware" (*CB* 230).

In her autobiography, Angelou "conveys the diminished sense of herself that pervaded much of her childhood" (qtd. in Hagen 152). When Maya was only three, her parents ended their disastrous marriage and sent her and her four-year-old brother Bailey from California to Stamps, Arkansas under the care of her grandmother Mrs. Annie Henderson. She still remembered the tags attached to their wrists "which instructed—'To Whom it May Concern' " (*CB* 3-4). The sense of being abandoned by their parents loomed large in the minds of young Maya and Bailey and remained a painful experience all their lives. Feeling deserted by their parents, Maya and Bailey had imagined that both of her parents had died until one Christmas when they received presents from their mother. "I couldn't believe that our mother would laugh and eat oranges in the sunshine without her children" (*CB* 42). Maya and Bailey could not understand the reason why their mother and father abandoned them: "Why did they send us away? And what did we do so wrong? So Wrong? Why, at the age of three and four, did we have tags put on our arms to be sent by train alone from Long Beach, California, to Stamps, Arkansas, with only the porter to look after us?" (*CB* 43) When Maya was faced with the unexpected gift, she felt grieved, "a wretched feeling of being torn engulfed me" (*CB* 44). The sense of abandonment by her parents was so destructive that she thought nobody loved her. As Sidonie Ann Smith argues, a child internalizes such rejection by parents and translates it as a rejection of self, "ultimately the loss of home occasions the loss of self-worth" ("The Song of a Caged Bird: Maya Angelou's Quest After Self-Acceptance" 369). In the community of Stamps, Maya felt the displacement. The reaction of the town to the two children was to "[close] in around us, as real mother embraces a stranger's child. Warmly, but not too familiarly" (*CB* 4). Before Maya became familiar with the Store, she felt that "we were locked up in a Fun House of Things where the attendant had gone home for life" (*CB* 5).

Besides, her appearance was often criticized by others. Unlike graceful Bailey, Maya was regarded as "big, elbowy and grating," and was described by her playmates as "being shit color" (*CB* 17). Even the elders sometimes said "unkind things about [her] features" (*CB* 17). Seeing her handsome father, she couldn't believe she was his daughter, "maybe he wasn't my real father. Bailey was his son, true enough, but I was an orphan that they picked up to provide Bailey with company" (*CB* 45). Therefore, there was no wonder that in the opening scene, young Maya asked: "What you looking at me for?/ I didn't come to stay…" (*CB* 1). Faced with the audience, the wretched girl felt completely out of place. She was so sensitive to her negative body image that she could not focus on the reciting of the poem. When realizing that her dream of becoming a pretty white girl could not be realized, she was so frustrated that she forgot the lines of the poem. Feeling embarrassed and ashamed, she had no choice but to run away, crying, screaming, laughing and urinating. As a girl who was enveloped in the cage of her negative body image and the sense of being abandoned by parents, Maya was like a caged bird that was trying to seek ways to escape.

Those years when they stayed in Stamps, Maya lived in such a sense of displacement and insecurity. What's worse, "the aura of personal displacement is counterpointed by the ambience of displacement within the larger black community," because "the black community of Stamps is itself caged in the social reality of racial subordination and impotence" (Smith, "The Song of a Caged Bird: Maya Angelou's Quest After Self-Acceptance" 369). As analyzed in the previous part of the chapter, the people in the black community lived in the shadow of what Smith refers to as "the white apparition." White oppression pervaded in every corner of their life. They lived in extreme poverty and just managed to get by on small incomes no matter how hard they worked; they were also suffering from the psychological panic for fear of becoming victims of lynching that would be likely to happen anywhere anytime; they had to endure other various forms of white oppression that had penetrated into every aspect of life. As Cudjoe argues, "the inherent suicidal tendency of an oppressive and racist society" had pushed the black people "to the brink of spiritual waste and physical destruction" (288). For Maya, such an antagonistic social environment "becomes the point of departure from which she struggles to salvage a sense of dignity and personhood, the necessary prerequisite to expressing any sense of womanhood" (Cudjoe 288).

When she was about eight, Angelou's father came back to Stamps and sent them to their mother's home in St. Louis. She felt out of place in the new place: "St. Louis was [a] new kind of hot and a new kind of dirty…For all I knew, we were being driven to Hell and our father was the delivering devil" (*CB* 49). She regarded St. Louis as "a foreign country" and she would never get used to the life there. For Maya, moving to St. Louis was another experience of geographical displacement. She never expected that a catastrophe that would leave her lifelong trauma was around the corner. In the new home, her mother's boyfriend Mr. Freeman lived with them. Sometimes, she was allowed to sleep with her mother and Mr. Freeman in a large bed. As a little girl who was so eager for love from parents, she even thought of Freeman as her real father. However, one day when her mother was not at home, Freeman raped the little girl. It was such a disastrous experience for her. "The act of rape on an eight-year-old body is a matter of the needle giving because the camel can't. The child gives, because the body can, and the mind of the violator cannot" (*CB* 65). After Bailey gave the information to Grandmother Baxton, Vivian's mother, Mr. Freeman was arrested and put to court. Although he was given a sentence of one year and one day, he was released that very day. But then news came that he was killed, maybe by her maternal uncles. Maya felt guilty for Freeman because she thought her lie in court was partly responsible for his death. Frightened by the fatally negative power of words, she refused to talk to anybody except her beloved brother Bailey because she feared that "if I talked to anyone else, that person might die too. Just my breath, carrying words out, might poison people and they'd curl up and die like the black fat slugs that only pretended" (*CB* 73). In addition to the cage of the negative body image and the impotence of the black community, she was also trapped in the cage of muteness. In order to isolate herself from the rest of the world and to achieve "perfect personal silence" (*CB* 73), Maya refused to speak and preferred to act only as a listener. Irritated by her silence, her relatives in St. Louis chose to send her back to Stamps.

The book was once severely criticized because of the true depiction of rape. However, despite the controversy, Angelou considered it meaningful to write the truth: "You write so that perhaps people who hadn't raped anybody yet might be discouraged, people who had might be informed, people who have not been raped might understand something, and people who have been raped might forgive themselves" (Braxton, "Symbolic Geography and Psychic Landscapes" 12). In fact, Angelou wrote about it because she tried to "tell the truth and preserved it in all artistic forms" (Tate 11). According to Mary Vermillion, "in order to challenge racist stereotypes that associate black women with illicit sexuality, both writers [Jocob and Angelou] obscure their corporeality…by transforming the suffering connected with rape into a metaphor for the suffering of their race" (137). Angelou used "her rapist's violation of her body and will to explore the oppression of her black community" (Vermillion 137). Although for most people, "rape can destroy a woman's autonomy and self-image," Angelou "transform[ed] this potentially destructive event into an opportunity to celebrate [her] resistance to somatophobia and negative stereotypes about the black female body" (Vermillion 144). Selwyn R. Cudjoe argues, "the rape of this eight-year-old by an almost-impotent male who, it would seem, is unable to enjoy a relatively mature and respectful relationship with an adult black woman, can only be seen as symbolic of one aspect of this internal dimension of black life" (Cudjoe 289). Cudjoe considers that "the villain is a society that reduces men to impotence and women to lives of whoredom, and makes children the victims of their father's lust and impotence" (289).

Maya's trauma caused by the rape would be healed in Stamps, Arkansas—the community of her source of strength. "Her psychological and emotional devastation finds a mirror in Stamps' social devastation. Stamps gives her back the familiarity and security of a well-known cage. She climbs back happily, losing herself in her silent world, surrendering herself to her own worthlessness" (Smith, "The Song of a Caged Bird: Maya Angelou's Quest After Self-Acceptance" 371). She crept into "the cocoon" of "the barrenness of Stamps" and "the resignation of its inhabitants" (*CB* 74). She was trapped in the cage for a whole year until

Mrs. Flowers threw her "the first life line" (*CB* 77) and gave her the "lessons in life" (*CB* 83). Mrs. Flowers not only taught her the power of words, especially the power of spoken words, but also told her about the importance of mother wit:

> She said that I must always be intolerant of ignorance, but understanding of illiteracy. That some people, unable to go to school, were more educated and even more intelligent than college professors. She encouraged me to listen carefully to what county people called mother wit. That in those homely sayings was crouched the collective wisdom of generations. (*CB* 83)

Her meeting with Mrs. Flowers was of great significance for Angelou's awareness of self-worth and her identification of her racial identity. In the past, the little black girl lived in the world full of total solitude and displacement, in total self-hatred and self-condemnation. However, for the first time in her life, she realized she was a girl with her own individual worth: "I was liked, and what a difference it made. I was respected not as Mrs. Henderson's grandchild or Bailey's sister but for just being Marguerite Johnson" (*CB* 85). The feeling of being liked by "the aristocrat of Black Stamps" she admired most was as a precious gift to her, the aura of which lingered on all her life. Besides, the beautiful appearance of Mrs. Flowers inspired her pride in her race: "It would be safe to say that she made me proud to be Negro, just by being herself" (*CB* 79). The communication with Mrs. Flowers enabled her to "experience the incipient power of her own self-worth" (Smith, "The Song of a Caged Bird: Maya Angelou's Quest After Self-Acceptance" 371).

When Maya worked as a maid for the white woman Mrs. Cullinan at the age of ten, she confronted directly the insult from the old white woman, which turned out to be a critical turning point that stimulated her awareness of her individual identity. Just for the sake of convenience, Mrs. Cullinan changed her name into "Mary" instead of "Margaret." Mrs. Cullinan's renaming Maya "echoes the larger tradition of American racism that attempts to prescribe the nature and limitations of [a] black person's identity" (McPherson, "Initiation and Self-Discovery" 37). For white people, black people were just objects and white people had the right to give them whatever names they liked. In this sense, they denied the humanity of black people. However, the blacks could not stand being renamed: "Every person I knew had a hellish horror of being 'called out of his name.' It was a dangerous practice to call a Negro anything that could be loosely construed as insulting because of the centuries of their having been called nigger, jigs, dinges, blackbirds, crows, boots and spooks" (*CB* 91). Unwilling to use her grandmother's subtle resistance, Maya, with the encouragement from her brother Bailey, fought against Cullinan's insulting behavior by deliberately breaking Mrs. Cullinan's favorite casserole and two of the green glass cups. Totally shocked by Maya's rebellious reaction, the white woman eventually shouted out: "Her name's Margaret, goddamn it, her name's Margaret" (*CB* 93). By doing so, Angelou assumed "the consciousness of rebellion as the stance necessary for preserving her individuality and affirm[ed] her self-worth" (Smith, "The Song of a Caged Bird: Maya Angelou's Quest After Self-Acceptance" 372). Dolly A. McPherson regards Maya's encounter with the white woman as a "decisive step toward self-definition" to free herself from the cage: "Only after Maya determines to risk Mrs. Cullinan's outrage and to defy the expectations of others is she able to begin to loose herself, psychologically, from the dehumanizing atmosphere of her environment" ("Initiation and Self-Discovery" 38).

One of the important aspects of young Maya's self-discovery was her gradual acceptance of her racial self. Young Maya had grown from a little girl who hated her "shit" black skin into a girl proud of being a member of the black race. Confronting the severe white oppression and the blacks' harsh living condition, she felt ashamed of their people's obedience and impotence. "I thought them all hateful to have allowed themselves to be worked like oxen, and even more shameful to try to pretend that things were not as bad as they were" (*CB* 101). She couldn't understand why the blacks would like to go to church despite a day's hard work and their weariness. The idea came to her that "my people may be a race of masochists and that not only was it our fate to live the poorest, roughest life but that we liked it like that" (*CB* 102). "It was awful to be Negro and have no control over my life…We should all be dead…" (*CB* 153). It was when she met Mrs. Flowers that she recognized the beauty of the black race for the first time. Owing to the close bonding of the community of Stamps and the collective activities such as church activities, gathering together to listen to the broadcasting about Joe Louis' boxing match, the singing of songs on the gradation day, she came to realize the strength of the race and cultivated a sense of pride in the black race and became "a proud member of the wonderful, beautiful Negro race" (*CB* 156). When she later moved to San Francisco and was transferred to George Washington High School, her sense of identification with her black race was further enhanced. "For the first semester, I was one of the three black students in the school, and in that rarefied atmosphere I came to love my people more. Mornings as the streetcar traversed my ghetto I experienced a mixture of dread and trauma" (*CB* 182). "In the evenings on the way home the sensation were joy, anticipation and relief …. I recognized that I was again in my country" (*CB* 182). Maya was no more the girl dreaming of becoming a white girl, instead, she identified herself as a member of her race and found her sense of belonging as part of the collective community.

Despite her identification of her racial identity, Maya was still on the way to her self-discovery. At the age of 13, Mrs. Henderson sent Maya and Bailey to San Francisco to live with their mother. Several years ago when they were sent to St. Louis, Maya felt totally out of place. In contrast, "In San Francisco, for the first time, I perceived myself as part of something," because "the air of collective displacement, the impermanence of the life in wartime and the gauche personalities of the more recent arrivals tended to dissipate my own sense of not belonging" (*CB* 179). According to Sidonie Smith, "the fluidity of the new environment matched the fluidity of her emotional, physical, and psychological life. She could feel in place in an environment where everyone and everything seemed out-of-place" ("The Song of a Caged Bird: Maya Angelou's Quest After Self-Acceptance" 372). The city of San Francisco, "friendly but never gushing, cool but not frigid or distant, distinguished without the awful stiffness" (*CB* 180), enhanced her sense of belonging. She writes: "To me, a thirteen-year-old black girl, stalled by the South and southern black life style, the city was a state of beauty and a state of freedom" (*CB* 180).

Another significant experience was the trip to a small Mexican town with her father, who later got heavily drunk, leaving her alone to deal with the problem on her own. At first, she was at a loss about what to do and complained about the cruel fate: "How pitiless were the Fates and how helpless was this poor black girl" (*CB* 200). But then, she decided to drive the car herself to go back to Los Angeles, although she never learned how to drive. She was determined to control her own fate all by herself: "The challenge was exhilarating. It was me, Marguerite, against the elemental opposition. As I twisted the steering wheel and forced the accelerator to the floor I was controlling Mexico, and might and aloneness and inexperienced youth and Bailey Johnson, Sr., and death and insecurity, and even gravity" (*CB* 202-03). This experience helped Maya to build up her confidence in her ability to take control of her fate by herself no matter what difficult condition she would face.

Back to California, Maya had a big fight with her father's lover Dolores and was wounded. As a result, she left her father without saying goodbye to him. She would not return to her mother's home, either, because she was in fear of her mother's revenge on Dolores. So she just wandered in San Diego and then joined a junkyard of commune composed of homeless children of different races. The one-month life spent with the homeless children changed her view of life. As she states,

after a month my thinking processes had so changed that I was hardly recognizable to myself. The unquestioning acceptance by my peers had dislodged the familiar insecurity. Odd that the homeless children, the silt of war frenzy, could initiate me into the brotherhood of man… The lack of criticism evidenced by our ad hoc community influenced me, and set a tone of tolerance for my life. (*CB* 216)

The experience enabled Angelou to imagine a world where people of all races are equal to each other and live harmoniously with each other. "The commune experience also confirms Angelou's determination to exercise further control over her being and helps her to establish a valuable new direction for her personal growth" (McPherson, "Initiation and Self-Discovery" 43).

Maya decided to go to work and wanted to work as a streetcar driver. Though it was difficult for her to get the job, she triumphed owing to her strong determination and countless struggles. Eventually, she "was hired as the first Negro on the San Francisco streetcars" (*CB* 229). Maya became "so much wiser and older, so much more independent, with a bank account and clothes that [she] had bought for [herself]" and she "had learned and earned the magic formula which would make [her] a part of the gay life [her] contemporaries led" (*CB* 230). Obtaining the job as the first black streetcar driver in San Francisco, Maya became more independent and confident, believing that she could achieve any goals she would set for herself. After having experienced the difficulty of seeking employment, she understood more deeply about what black women suffered in the white patriarchal society. She advocated that black women should deserve more respect and acceptance. She asserted that "the formidable character" of American Negro females was "an inevitable outcome of the struggle won by survivors and deserve[d] respect if not enthusiastic acceptance" (*CB* 231).

Maya assured herself of her racial self and social identity, and she was proud of becoming a member of her race and was confident of her own intelligence and ability, but she was still not sure about her sexual identity. Since childhood, she had no confidence in her appearance. Although becoming a white girl was no more her dream, she still felt upset about her appearance because she was not as beautiful as the other girls. She noticed that her voice was heavy, with her hands and feet being far from being feminine and dainty, her breasts sadly underdeveloped: "My voice is too deep and my feet are big, and I have no hips or breasts or anything. And my legs are so skinny" (*CB* 236). After reading the novel *The Well of Loneliness*, a book about lesbians, she was worried about her own sexual identity. It occurred to her that maybe she was also a latent lesbian. In order to prove to herself she was a normal girl, she needed a boyfriend to "clarify [her] position to the world and, even more important, to [herself]. A boyfriend's acceptance of [her] would guide [her] into that strange and exotic land of thrills and femininity" (*CB* 238). So Maya took the initiative to deal with her problem by choosing a boy of casual acquaintance as her target, asking him directly: "Would you like to have a sexual intercourse with me?" (*CB* 240). The boy asked: "You mean, you're going to give me some trim" (*CB* 240). "He thought I was giving him something, and the fact of the matter was that it was my intention to take something from him" (*CB* 240). Still suspicious about her sexual identity, she then found herself pregnant. Although pregnancy was not what she had expected, at least it proved to herself that she was not a lesbian. Encouraged by her mother, she gave birth to her son. "My son was born. Just as gratefulness was confused in my mind with love, so possession became mixed up with motherhood. I had a baby. He was beautiful and mine. Totally mine" (*CB* 245). With the encouragement of her mother, Maya was courageous enough to shoulder the responsibility of raising her son. McPherson points out that "the birth of Maya's son is a celebration of a new life, of Maya's own rebirth as a young mother, and of Maya's discovery of her creative self" ("Initiation and Self-Discovery" 44). Stephen Butterfield argues that "the experience of the baby connects the woman to the ages of human birth, death, hope and wonder beyond the artificial conventions of race" (213). As Sidonie Smith notes, "the birth of the baby brings Maya something totally her own, but, more important, brings her to a recognition of and acceptance of her full, instinctual womanhood" ("The Song of a Caged Bird: Maya Angelou's Quest After Self-Acceptance" 374). In this way, the girl "has succeeded in freeing herself from the natural and social bars imprisoning her in the cage of her own diminished self-image by assuming control of her life and fully accepting her black womanhood" (Smith, "The Song of a Caged Bird: Maya Angelou's Quest

After Self-Acceptance" 374). After a sixteen-year journey, Maya grew from a sensitive little girl into an independent woman with confidence, hope and love. After painful experiences of exploration and reflection, she accomplished the journey to self-discovery.

3.3.2 Celebrating Female Bonding and Motherhood

Living in the South where life is full of harshness and brutality, where growing up black and female is a painful experience, Maya managed to survive and became a girl with self-assurance and self-determination. There are some crucial elements that helped her in the process of self-discovery and self-fulfillment: the strength from the close bonding of the community, the discovery of the power of language and poetry, love from the community and her family, and most importantly, the close and warm female bonding. The fact that Maya was lucky enough to be loved and protected by the people around her proved to be the source of the power and her sense of security, and it equipped her with more courage and power to confront the oppression from outside the black community. In some sense, this autobiography is a celebration of the female role models in the black community, such as her grandmother Mrs. Henderson, Mrs. Flowers, her mother Vivian Baxter. In *I Know Why the Caged Bird Sings*, Angelou not only admired her Momma, her mother and Mrs. Flowers, but also revered "the tradition in which they participated and the way in which they prepared her, as best they could, to cope with the realities of being black and female" (Braxton 198). According to George E. Kent, "Grandmother Henderson of Stamps, Arkansas, represents the religious tradition; Mother Vivian Baxter, more of the blues-street tradition" (Kent 75). Grandmother's "spirit of religion combined with simple, traditional maxims shapes the course of existence and the rituals of facing up to something called decency" (Kent 75), while her mother's blues-street tradition made Maya know the importance of independence, self-reliance and flexibility, and enabled her to be better equipped to survive in an unstable white society. Mrs. Flowers taught her the power of words and books, and the importance of the oral culture of the black community.

In *Singin' and Swingin' and Gettin' Merry Like Christmas*, she credited her independence to the positive influence of her grandmother and her mother.

My pride had been starched by a family who assumed unlimited authority in its own affairs.

> A grandmother, who raised me, my brother and her own two sons, owned a general
>
> merchandise store… My beautiful mother, who ran business and men with autocratic power,
>
> taught me to row my own boat, and paddle my own canoe, hoist my own sail. She warned,
>
> in fact, "If you want something done, do it yourself." (qtd. in Megna-Wallace 120)

According to Joanne M. Braxton, *I Know Why the Caged Bird Sings* treats traditional themes of black female autobiography, including the "importance of the family and the nurturing and rearing of one's children, as well as the quest for self-sufficiency, self-reliance, personal dignity, and self-definition" (*Black Women Writing Autobiography—A Tradition Within a Tradition* 184). Singing black motherhood and celebrating the role model of nurturer-protector remain a theme of Angelou's series of autobiographies. According to Mary Jane Lupton, "the theme of motherhood remains a unifying element, with Momma Henderson being Angelou's link with the black folk tradition" ("Singing the Black Mother— Maya Angelou and Autobiographical Continuity" 131). In *I Know Why the Caged Bird Sings*, Angelou explored the relationship between her and her grandmother, between her and her mother, while in her subsequent autobiographies, she continued to examine the contact between her and her grandmother, between her and her mother, with more focus on the relationship between her as a mother and her son Guy. As Stephen Butterfield puts it, "continuity is achieved by the contact of mother and child, the sense of life begetting life that happens automatically in spite of all confusion—perhaps also because of it" (213).

In *I Know Why the Caged Bird Sings*, Momma Henderson exerted the most important influence on young Maya. In some sense, she was considered as her mother's substitute. Braxton asserts that Momma "fulfils the archetypal role of the outraged mother" (189). In the African-American family, grandmothers played a vital role both in slavery and after emancipation. "During slavery, the Negro grandmother occupied in many instances an important place in the plantation economy and was highly esteemed by both the slaves and the masters…When emancipation came, it was often the old grandmother who kept the generations together." (qtd. in Megna-Wallace 118). Mildred A. Hill-Lubin also argues for the importance of grandmother as "a significant force in the stability and the continuity of the black family and the community" (qtd. in Lupton 132). Mrs. Henderson was a typical representative of such southern grandmothers. She was selected by Hill-Lubin as an example "of the strong grandmother in African-American literature—the traditional preserver of the family, the source of folk

wisdom, and the instiller of values within the black community" (Lupton 132).
George E. Kent argues that Grandmother Henderson enabled Maya to understand
the "folk religious tradition" (76). It was from the religious tradition that
Grandmother Henderson obtained her strength and wisdom to "give much order to
the children's lives, to set the family in initial order in California, and to provide
them with the minimum resources to struggle for a world more attractive" (Kent
76).

For young Maya, it was Momma's unconditional love for her that gave her
a sense of security and helped chip away her dreadful sense of displacement
and isolation. It was Momma who set a good example and gave directions of
life for her and Bailey, instilling into their minds the power of religion and the
courage to face white oppression. It was Momma who taught her the importance
of maintaining dignity and independence. Mrs. Henderson not only gave them a
home and love, but also showed deep concerns about their psychological health.
When she found that Bailey was in a psychological crisis after witnessing the
dead body of a lynched victim, she sent them to their mother's home decisively.
When Maya was enslaved in the cage of isolation and silence, Momma, extremely
worried about her, was wise enough to turn to Mrs. Flowers for help. Her action
was of great significance for Maya to free herself from the cage of muteness.

In an interview with Joanne M. Braxton, when asked about how she was able
to heal herself in terrible experiences, Angelou expressed the importance of love
from her family members, especially Momma's immense love for her. "I can't
remember a time when I wasn't loved by somebody…My grandmother loved
me and Uncle Willie loved me UNCONDITIONALLY…even when I became
so weird that they couldn't understand me—they loved me. They loved me even
then…" (qtd. in Braxton, "Symbolic Geography and Psychic Landscapes" 12).
Angelou regarded love from her grandmother as "a healing lard, an ointment,
a lotion" and "true therapy" (12). No matter what the society talked about her,
Angelou knew that her grandmother always said she was somebody (12).

In Angelou's memory, her Momma never kissed or indulged her, but she
knew that Momma loved her deeply in her heart. "Her world was bordered on all
sides with work, duty, religion and 'her place.' I don't think she ever knew that a
deep-brooding love hung over everything she touched. In later years I asked her if
she loved me and she brushed me off with: 'God is love. Just worry about whether
you're being a good girl, then He will love you'" (*CB* 47).

In Angelou's second autobiography *Gather Together in My Name*, she recalled the conflict between her and her Momma. When Momma knew that Angelou conflicted with two white saleswomen, Momma's extreme concern for Maya's safety led her to hit Maya in the face and immediately sent her away to the safe place. Angelou knew that Momma did so just for the sake of her security. For Momma, survival was of the greatest importance. Angelou didn't realize that she would never see her grandmother again. In her third volume *Singin' and Swingin' and Gettin' Merry Like Christmas*, when Angelou was in hospital to have an operation, her grandmother died. When she got the news, she was in deep grief:

> Ah, Momma, I had never looked at death before, peered into its yawning chasm for the face of the beloved. For days my mind stagger out of balance…I would never find Momma. If I were as good as God's angels and as pure as the Mother of Christ, I could never have Momma's rough slow hands pat my cheek or braid my hair. (41)

In the elegiac passage on Momma's death, Angelou wrote a funeral song based on the black gospel tradition. To achieve the effect of solemnness, she used the words like *chasm, precipice, angels* and *beloved*, which she used to achieve humorous effects in the description of Sister Monroe in *I Know Why the Caged Bird Sings* (Lupton 135). According to Lupton, the gospel motif in the elegiac passage on Momma's death shows that Angelou rediscovered the power and beauty of black spirituals: "The spirituals and gospel songs were sweeter than sugar. I wanted to keep my mouth full of them and the sounds of my people singing felt like sweet oil in my ears" (qtd. in Lupton 135). In memory of Momma's death in this way, Angelou expressed the profound influence of Momma's folk religious tradition on her. As she grew up and became mature, she could understand the strength and beauty of the black people's religion better, and thus had a deeper understanding of her grandmother. The sense of love, warmth and security and the strength her grandmother gave her unconditionally was a treasure throughout her life.

When Momma talked to Mrs. Flowers described in *I Know Why the Caged Bird Sings*, young Maya "hated her for showing her ignorance to Mrs. Flowers" (*CB* 78). However, many years later she realized that "they [Momma and Mrs. Flowers] were as alike as sisters, separated only by formal education" (*CB* 78). Mrs. Flowers once told her: "Some people, unable to go to school, were more educated and even more intelligent than college professors" (*CB* 83). Years later, Angelou came to realize that her Momma was one of such people.

Another woman who had a profound and positive influence on Angelou is her mother Vivian Baxter, who instilled in her the impact of what George E. Kent refers to as "the blues-street tradition" (Kent 75). According to Kent, "in this fast life area of black tradition, the children receive great kindness and considerable impact from built-in instabilities…She [Vivian] herself is the embodiment of bold aggressiveness and self-reliance" (77). Vivian Baxter was a typical representative of the carrier of the blues tradition in that she was optimistic, independent and self-reliant. Angelou's feelings toward her mother was, to some degree, ambivalent. On the one hand, the parting from her mother in her childhood was a painful experience. Not knowing why her mother abandoned her and her brother, she imagined that she had died; on the other hand, she admired her mother for her beauty, for her intelligence and self-reliance. When meeting her mother at the age of eight, she described her mother's remarkable beauty and she thought her mother "was too beautiful to have children" (*CB* 50). After she moved to California to live with her mother, her admiration for her mother seemed to be growing. She appreciated her mother's way of thinking and her way of dealing with problems. When her children stayed with her, Vivian would create a cheerful atmosphere. When she knew that Maya wished to become a streetcar driver, she encouraged her to do her best. She taught Maya that "there was nothing a person can't do, and there should be nothing a human being didn't care about" (*CB* 225). Vivian had a store of aphorisms to give her guidance. "Life is going to give you just what you put in it. Put your whole heart in everything you do, and pray, then you can wait" or "God helps those who help themselves" (*CB* 228). Her philosophy for life was that she "hoped for the best, was prepared for the worst, so anything in between didn't come as a surprise" (*CB* 234). When she knew that Maya was pregnant, "there was no overt or subtle condemnation. She was Vivian Baxter Jackson" (*CB* 244).

In the subsequent autobiographies *Gather Together in My Name* and *Singin' and Swingin' and Gettin' Merry Like Christmas*, Angelou continued to explore the mother-child relationship. Since she herself was a mother, she also explored the relationship between her and her son Guy. In *Gather Together in My Name*, Angelou described how difficult it was for a black young single-mother to raise her son and she was aware of the fact that mother and child are separate individuals (Lupton 139). In *Singin' and Swingin' and Gettin' Merry Like Christmas*, she narrated the conflict between her career and mothering, and was torn between a "good" mother and a "bad' mother (Lupton 141). In *The Heart of a Woman*, Maya Angelou became "a strong and aggressive black mother rather than a mother torn by self-doubt" (Lupton 142). "Powerful, protective of her son, Angelou has become… a reincarnation of Momma Henderson" (Lupton 142). In her fifth autobiography *All God's Children Need Traveling Shoes*, Angelou reaffirmed the meaning of motherhood through her identification with Africa (Lupton 145). Her son Guy became a college student in Ghana and stayed there to complete his degree. "Guy has become, through his interaction with the Ghanaians, a 'young lord' of Africa, given back to the Mother Continent freely" (Lupton 145).

In Angelou's series of autobiographies, singing the positive roles of female bonding and celebrating the grandmother-child and mother-child relationships remain a recurring theme. For the African Americans, women played the role models and became a vital strength in preserving and inheriting their traditions.

3.4 Surpassing American Black Autobiographical Tradition

Maya Angelou used the autographical genre to write a series of six volumes of autobiographies, starting with *I Know Why the Caged Bird Sings* (1969) and ending with *A Song Flung Up to Heaven* (2002). For Maya Angelou, the genre of autobiography is "a special form, consciously chosen as her most effective genre" (Lupton, *Maya Angelou: A Critical Companion* 30). In an interview with Jackie Kay, Angelou said that "I think I am the only serious writer who has chosen the autobiographical form as the main form to carry my work, my expression" (qtd. in Lupton, *Maya Angelou: A Critical Companion* 30). In her works, Angelou followed the tradition of African-American male and female autobiographies. For Angelou, "the writing of autobiography is a conscious assertion of identity, as well as the presentation of an alternate version of reality seen from the point of the black female experience" (Braxton, *Black Women Writing Autobiography—A Tradition Within a Tradition* 201).

While Maya Angelou's autobiographies are regarded as a kind of representative works which follow the convention of black autobiography, they have also surpassed the traditions of black autobiographies in several aspects. Maya Angelou has made some remarkable innovations both in form and themes of her autobiographical writings.

Firstly, Angelou employs the special form of serial autobiographies. "A serial autobiography is a set of two or more related texts that reflect on, predict, and echo each other, so that they are seen as parts of a whole" (Lupton, *Maya Angelou: A Critical Companion* 32). The serial autobiography writing is part of the American literary tradition. For example, Frederick Douglass wrote two autobiographies which are closely related to each other: *Narrative of the Life of Frederick Douglass* (1945) and his second one *My Bondage and My Freedom* (1855). Richard Wright also wrote his serial autobiographies *American Hunger* (1944) and *Black Boy* (1945). However, Angelou made full use of the genre of serial autobiographies as a vehicle for self-expression. When Angelou wrote her first autobiography *I Know Why the Caged Bird Sings*, she didn't expect that serial autobiographical writing would become the most ideal instrument for her reflection on life. Lupton thinks that Angelou's writing of her third volume *Singin' and Swingin' and Gettin' Merry Like Christmas* (1976) "marks a historical moment in the history of African-American autobiography. At this time, no other well-known black female autobiographer had taken her story into a third volume" (98). No one could expect that Angelou would create six serial autobiographies, in which she narrates her life stories and personal growth as a black woman, an affectionate mother, a passionate artist, and a fighter for the black people. Serial autobiography writing offers her a flexible space to reflect on the first four decades of her life. As Lupton put it, "the continuous fluctuation of the serial form allows the writer a freedom not available in the fixed, single autobiography" (32).

Secondly, Angelou interprets the autobiographical form creatively by deviating from traditional autobiographical patterns. In Maria Lauret's opinion, Angelou tried to challenge the usual structure of the autobiography by critiquing, changing, and expanding the genre (98).The most striking feature of her serial autobiographies lies in the fact that she blends different genres in her autobiographies, which would help her avoid repetition and monotony. Among the six autobiographies, there is a collection of proses *I Know Why the Caged Bird Sings* (1969); two travel narratives *Singin' and Swingin' and Gettin' Merry Like Christmas* (1976) and *All God's Children Need Traveling Shoes* (1986), and three novels *Gather Together in My Name* (1974), *The Heart of a Woman* (1981) and *A Song Flung Up to Heaven* (2002). Angelou's introduction of hybrid genres to her serial autobiographical writing is an important innovation in American autobiographical writing. The first volume *I Know Why the Caged Bird Sings* (1969) consisting of a series of proses is regarded as a paradigm of autobiographical writing. The third and the fifth volumes are interlaced with travel narratives: the stories are arranged according to the motif of movement or travel, covering many places from Europe, Africa to America. The movement from journey to journey is the narrative line of these two volumes. For example, *Singin' and Swingin' and Gettin' Merry Like Christmas* (1976) shifts its focus from America to a European location, and *All God's Children Need Traveling Shoes* (1986) tells stories about Angelou's African journey from 1962 to 1965. The second, the third and the last volumes are more like novels, with elaborately-designed plots and full descriptions of characters. In those three volumes, Angelou adopts fiction-writing techniques.

Besides, Angelou tried to write "autobiography as literature," which was regarded by her publisher Robert Loomis as "the most difficult thing anyone could do" (Tate 6). Angelou accepted the challenge and has made great achievements. In her serial autobiographical writing, Angelou uses various fiction-writing techniques such as metaphor, irony, the development of plot and the choice of settings. For example, irony is a device frequently employed by Angelou. A case in point is the comic description about Sister Monroe's funny behavior in the church, an ironic narration about the renaming episode of Mrs. Cullina in *I Know Why the Caged Bird Sings*. Owing to the employment of fiction-writing techniques, Angelou's autobiographies are viewed as autobiographical fiction by some critics including Mary Jane Lupton, Eugenia Collier, and so on. For example, according to Lupton, "Angelou amplifies the autobiographical tone by using dialogue—by having another character or characters speak to the narrator" (*Maya Angelou: A Critical Companion* 29). However, in an interview with Claudia Tate, Angelou emphasized that her works were autobiographies rather than autobiographical novels, underlining the fact that when she was writing, she was thinking more about "a particular time in which I lived and the influences of that time on a number of [black] people" (Tate 6).

But the fact that Angelou considered her works as autobiographies rather than autobiographical novels didn't deny the fictional aspects of her works. Lupton argues that to achieve the artistic effect, Angelou "diverge[d] from the conventional notion of autobiography as truth" (Lupton 34). As Richard Coe points out, in autobiography the "border-line between fact and poetry is impossible to determine" (qtd. in Hagen, *Heart of a Woman, Mind of a Writer, and Soul of a Poet: A Critical Analysis of the Writings of Maya Angelou* 17). For Angelou, when she wrote her works, she didn't just record the life literally. Instead, she would carefully select the materials for the development of plots. In the process of writing, "some events stood out in my mind more than the others. Some, though, were never recorded because they either were so bad or so painful, that there was no way to write about them honestly and artistically without making them melodramatic" (Tate 7). Therefore, she would use some strategies such as humor, comic irony and self-parody to make her writing more impressive. McPherson points out that "Angelou's effective use of self-parody is something new in black autobiography and, thus, creates a unique place in black autobiographical tradition" (124). Angelou employs those strategies skillfully in many circumstances.

In Angelou's six autobiographies, there is the combination of realism and modernism, the blending of fact and fiction, and the lyrical descriptions of the surroundings and her feelings, etc. Each of the autobiographies is elaborately structured: most of them are based on the narrative line of the movement from journey to journey. Eugenia Collier thinks that in her autobiographies, there are "vividly conceived characters and careful development of theme, setting, plot, and language" (Lupton 30).

In each of the autobiographies, Angelou created important heroes and heroines, for example, her grandmother Mrs. Henderson, her mother Vivian, her brother Bailey, Mrs. Flowers, etc. in *I Know Why the Caged Bird Sings*; her girlfriend Louise Kendricks, those manipulative and unfaithful men who took advantage of her such as Curly, L.D. Tolbrook, Troubador Martin in the second volume *Gather Together in My Name*. In her third volume *Singin' and Swingin' and Gettin' Merry Like Christmas* (1976), the main characters are her husband Tosh Angelos, her son Guy, her mother Vivian, and the grandmother Annie Henderson, etc. In each of the autobiographies, there are deliberate arrangements of dramatic plots, for example, in *Singin' and Swingin' and Gettin' Merry Like Christmas* (1976), the main plots are her marriage and the intense conflict between her and her husband, her relationships with her son and her mother, the death of her grandmother and the fate of her brother Bailey. In this volume, Angelou made an effective placement of opposing incidents, narrating a sequence of conflicts and oppositions, which makes the book more dramatic.

Angelou's autobiographies have surpassed the black autobiography tradition not only in form, but also in themes. Angelou wrote the series of autobiographies to dwell on themes that were common in black female autobiographies, such as race oppression, white dominance, the celebration of female bonding in the black community, the difficulty for black females to survive, the calling for black women's independence and self-realization. Selwyn R. Cudjoe argues for the importance of Angelou's autobiographies in Afro-American literature:

> As a statement, Angelou presents a powerful, authentic and profound signification of Afro-American life and the changing concerns of the Afro-American life and the changing concerns of the Afro-American woman in her quest of personal autonomy, understanding, and love. Such a statement, because of the simple, forthright, and honest manner in which it is presented, is depicted against the larger struggle of Afro-American and African peoples for their liberation and triumphs. It is a celebration of the struggle, survival, and existence of Afro-American people. (Cudjoe, *Maya Angelou: The Autobiographical Statement Updated* 285).

But her works should not be viewed only as a black autobiography or only as a woman's autobiography. Harold Bloom points out that Angelou's appeal lies in "her remarkable literary voice, [which] speaks to something in the universal American 'little me within the big me' " (qtd. in Barnwell 220). In fact, her autobiographies described not only the life conditions of black men and women, but also the universal experiences of the whole mankind, and explored the universal themes—"death and rebirth, movement from innocence to experience, idealism versus cynicism, the search for selfhood, and the importance of determining one's own self-definitions" (McPherson, *Order out of Chaos* 129). Each of the serial autobiographies puts emphasis on different themes, but some of the themes remain Angelou's main concerns. For example, in *I Know Why the Caged Bird Sings*, imprisonment and self-discovery are the main themes. *Gather Together in My Name* (1974) mainly explores motherhood, constant change of work, the meaning of race and the eagerness for a stable life. Her relationship with her son and struggling for self-fulfillment continue to be the main concerns of the third autobiography *Singin' and Swingin' and Gettin' Merry Like Christmas* (1976) and the fourth one *The Heart of a Woman* (1981). In *All God's Children Need Traveling Shoes* (1986), the themes are motherhood, race, the search for an African identity and the search for a genuine sense of belonging as a human being. As McPherson notes, "Catholic in her sympathies, Angelou understands and regrets the suffering and misery not just of the black people but of humankind. Her coherent orchestration of these themes and her humorous, sometimes bitterly satiric portrayal of her creative life have established her as a significant voice" (McPherson, *Order out of Chaos* 129).

Angelou had such universal ideas because she considered herself not only as a black woman, but first as a human being, just like anybody else in the world, "I am a human being. I refuse to indulge any man-made differences between myself and another human being" (Tate 7). For example, in her second volume *Gather Together in My Name* (1974), Angelou narrates the difficult life of a young black mother who was fighting against drugs, prostitution and failure in life. In order to survive and rear her son, Angelou struggled hard for life, changing jobs frequently, working as a cook, a dancer, a dish-washer, a barmaid, even as a prostitute, facing the setbacks again and again, and having fragmented relationships with her relatives and other people. In this autobiography, which is more like a novel, by delineating an alienated individual, Angelou reflects the solitude, isolation and despair of the people in the fragmented society—the typical state of mind of human beings in the modern times. Here is not only a story of a black mother, but also one of a person in the spiritual wasteland in the modern times. Fortunately, undergoing the sufferings, the strong-willed woman still survived, with great hopes for the future.

As McPherson puts it, "how an understanding of the self leads to a feeling of kinship with humankind is excellently demonstrated in Angelou's autobiographical prose" (*Order out of Chaos* 125). Just as Angelou puts it herself, "'I speak to the black experience, but I am always talking about the human condition—about what we can endure, dream, fail at, and still survive.' In this spirit, she faithfully depicts her home ground as a version of the universal human experience" (qtd. in Braxton, *Black Women Writing Autobiography—A Tradition Within a Tradition* 182).

For example, one of the most touching and universal themes in Angelou's serial autobiographies is her continuous exploration of the family relationships. Priority is given to the depiction of the complicated and precious feelings between the members of the family, her close relationship with her brother Bailey, her deep attachment to her grandmother Mrs. Henderson, her ambiguous feelings for her mother, her devoted love for her son Guy. Family becomes the source of warmth and spiritual power for her. Among the members of her family, her relationship with her Momma is one of the warmest parts of the serial autobiographies, and perhaps one of most touching depictions in American literature. Her grandmother will not show her love by telling her directly, or by hugging her. But Mrs. Henderson's devoted love for Angelou and her brother Bailey is the strong source of spiritual power throughout their lives. Mrs. Henderson is a capable and tough woman full of wisdom, love, self-respect and strength, helping her grandchildren to become strong-willed and dignified people in her own way. She devoted her immense love to her grandchildren even after they left their hometown. For example, in *Gather Together in My Name*, there was an intense conflict between Mrs. Henderson and Angelou because of Angelou's rebellious confrontation with two white saleswomen. Momma's instinctive intention to protect her from being hurt by the white people caused her to hit Angelou in the face. As a result, Angelou was ordered by Momma to leave Stamps as soon as possible. Angelou never expected that that was the last time she stayed with her grandmother. Unfortunately, when Momma died, Angelou was in hospital for an operation. To relieve herself of the immense grief, Angelou tried to seek strength from religion, just as her grandmother did all her life.

Besides, the motif of motherhood remains a dominant theme throughout the whole series. Readers are deeply impressed by Angelou's devoted depiction of the complicated relationship between mother and child, for example, her relationship with her mother, and her relationship with her son. As a woman struggling for survival and for the development of her career, it was difficult to strike a balance between self-fulfillment and nurturing her son. When separating from her son, she would be overwhelmed by an intense sense of guilt and pain. When an automobile accident happened to her son, she was extremely worried and then she decided to stay in Accra, Ghana until her son recovered. Angelou is a woman with great achievements in many aspects, but for her, the most important thing in life is to become a responsible mother. Motherhood is a dominant theme which will move her readers deeply.

In conclusion, Angelou has surpassed the traditions of black autobiographies both in form and themes. By employing her unique various writing skills such as the special form of serial autobiography, the blending of various genres in her serial autobiography, the fictional techniques such as comic irony, self-parody and imagination, by creating vivid images that are not stereotyped, Angelou explored the universal themes: how human beings endure sufferings and setbacks, how they struggle for survival and hope, thus instilling in her works a sense of universality. Not only the blacks but also the people of all races would be moved by her deep understanding of human strength as well as weakness, laughter and sorrows.

Chapter Four

A New Quest for Identity in Lorene Cary's *Black Ice*

4.1 The Black Students' Dilemma in Dominant White Culture

4.1.1 Cary's Psychological Trauma Caused by the Blacks' History of Slavery

Lorene Cary' autobiography *Black Ice* is so well received that it has established Cary's reputation in the literary circle. In this memoir, Lorene Cary narrated her experience of the two years from 1972 to 1974 when she stayed in the formerly all-white, all-male St. Paul preparatory school in New Hampshire in New England as one of the first black students.

Lorene Cary's parents attached much importance to their daughter's education, so when their neighbor Mrs. Evans informed them of the good news that the exclusive boarding school St. Paul's School was "interested in finding black girls" (*BI* 8), they decided to seize the opportunity, because the education in St. Paul's "was more than knowledge; it could mean credentials, self-confidence, power" (*BI* 8). Knowing the news, young Cary was very excited and felt confident enough to compete with those white rich students. She was eager to make "a precocious launch into the wide world of competition" (*BI* 8), because she believed that she had been raised for this opportunity:

> Why else had my mother personally petitioned the principal of Lea School so that I could
>
> attend the integrated showcase public grade school at the edge of the University of

Pennsylvania's reach—out of our West Philly district? Why else would she have dragged
me across the street on my knees when I balked on the morning before the big I.Q. test,
the one that could get me into the top first-grade class, the class on which...and a special
individualized reading series were bestowed? (*BI* 32)

As an intelligent and ambitious girl, Cary was full of hope for the bright future.
She thought to herself: "Wasn't it time for me to play my part in that mammoth
enterprise—the integration, the moral transformation, no less, of America? I had
been waiting for this the way a fairy princess waits for a man" (*BI* 32-33). Cary
was confident that she would be intelligent enough to compete with the white
students and achieve success.

However, when Cary studied in the school, she underwent painful
experiences and serious psychological crises. Cary found that the strength she
derived from her black community was not powerful enough for her to deal
with the problems she would confront in St. Paul's. To a degree, like other black
autobiographies, *Black Ice* not only dwells on Cary's personal coming-of-age
story, it is also an autobiography which demonstrates the blacks' struggle of
liberating themselves "from the crippling social and psychological effects of
the dominant ideology and culture" (Cudjoe 273). As Cudjoe puts it, "the Afro-
American autobiography must be seen as constructed, constituted, and formed by
the specific practices and discourses of the specific people and their response to
their time and place" (Cudjoe 277). So is the autobiography *Black Ice*, in which
Cary described the specific situation of a certain group of black people in the
specific time. It reveals the ambivalent and complicated condition of the black
students as trailblazers who studied in the formerly all white elite school right
after the Civil Rights Movement. During their stay in the dominant white schools,
they were obsessed by the complicated and mixed feelings of pain, remorse and
alienation. "Instead I found my own adolescence, in all its hormonal excess,
waiting for me at St. Paul's: old rage and fear, ambition, self-consciousness, love,
curiosity, energy, hate, envy, compulsion, fatigue" (*BI* 4). The description in *Black
Ice* is different from the narration of Hurston or Angelou. Unlike Hurston who
grew up in the autonomous black Eatonville, Lorene Cary was not as optimistic
as Hurston and did not have such a transcendent concept of the problem of race.
Unlike Angelou who witnessed the racial discrimination directly but derived
much strength from both her grandmother's religious tradition and her mother's
blues tradition, Lorene Cary did not suffer from the overt racial discrimination

such as the fear of lynching or being refused by the white dentist to treat her toothache. Instead, when Lorene Cary was admitted by St. Paul's, it was right after the Civil Rights Movement and the black people were told that "Black is Beautiful" (*BI* 5). Therefore, what Cary suffered was not the blatant oppression and discrimination from the whites, but more from the cage of psychological trauma caused by the heavy burden of the history of slavery, of segregation, of memory of racial oppression. As Regina Blackburn notes, "the issue of identity, of defining and understanding this black self" is a recurrent theme in black women's autobiographies (136). In fact, the issue of identity crisis, especially racial identity crisis, became the dominant problem that Cary had to confront and deal with. As McKay puts it, "Cary's complex interrogation of the racial self in the white world and tensions in intrafamilial relationships signals new advances in the development of black autobiography" ("The Narrative Self: Race, Politics, and Culture in Black American Women's Autobiography" 104). As a bright black girl, she was confident of her own ability, believing that she was competitive enough to turn out in the white world. In some sense, she was proud of herself and her race. She believed that "we had been bred for it just as surely as they [white students]. The point was that we were there to turn it out" (*BI* 59). In contrast to the rich whites, she even thought she possessed more advantages than the whites. However, on the other hand, she was keenly aware of her racial identity as a black. "I was more aware of being black at St. Paul's than I was of being a girl" (*BI* 200). Staying in the white dominant St. Paul's, she was overwhelmed by the stereotyped idea of the white's superiority over the blacks. So she was always torn apart between pride and self-hatred. "I remembered the self-loathing, made worse by a poised bravado, as close as my own skin, that I wore over it" (*BI* 5). As Blackburn notes, one of the themes of black female autobiography is "the assigning of some value to the black self," which "could be a source of pride and contentment, but more often the sense of blackness brought shame, self-hatred, and self-depreciation. This low or negative self-evaluation caused some women to exist in an ambivalent state, torn between pride and self-hatred" (136).

In *Black Ice*, during the two years when Lorene Cary stayed in St. Paul's, she experienced such an ambivalent state of mind, torn apart between her awareness of race pride and her self-loathing. She was obsessed by the feeling of self-hatred: "Just like a nigger. Nothin' worse than a sorry nigger. …I hate to say it, but you know these niggers ain't shit…What is wrong with us? …Can you tell me what is wrong with my people? … Niggers flies I do despise. The more I see niggers, The more I like flies" (*BI* 79).

For a fifteen-year-old black girl, who was isolated from her own community, the ambivalent feelings were so destructive that she realized "how profoundly St. Paul's had shaken me, or how damaged and fraudulent and traitorous I felt when I graduated" (*BI* 4). In St. Paul's, it was not easy for her to slip into white culture; what's worse, she felt as isolated from the blacks as she was from the whites. Nowhere could she find her sense of belonging. I agree with Gonzalez's opinion that her ambivalent confusion about her identity as a black girl and a student in the dominant white St. Paul's can well be explained by what W. E. B. Du Bois refers to as "double-consciousness." In his work *The Souls of Black Folk*, Du Bois illustrates the typical state of mind of the African Americans:

> The Negro is...born with a veil, and gifted with second-sight in this American world—a world which yields him no true self-consciousness, but only lets him see himself through the revelation of the other world. It is a peculiar sensation, this double-consciousness, this sense of always looking at one's self through the eyes of others, of measuring one's soul by the tape of a world that looks on in amused contempt and pity. One ever feels his twoness— an American, a Negro; two souls, two thoughts, two unreconciled strivings; two warring ideals in one dark body, whose dogged strength alone keeps it from being torn asunder. (Du Bois 12)

The lasting effects of the collective memory of the black's history were mainly embodied in the following aspects: firstly, Cary held the belief that no one could be trusted, let alone white people, so Cary didn't have trust in the education in St. Paul's, neither would she trust her white teacher and white classmates; secondly, Cary, together with the black students, was torn apart in the dilemma of trying hard to succeed in the white world and maintaining her racial loyalty; thirdly, as a black girl, she was forced to confront "the wrongs, and sufferings, and mortifications peculiarly their own" (qtd. in Cudjoe 273), which black women had to endure.

As Gonzalez states, "the sequels of slavery, the oppression and the segregation suffered by whole generations of African Americans lead inevitably to a feeling of mistrust that will mark the relationship with white people as well as the negotiation of the ethnic self" (Gonzalez 124). Cary remembered the story about "trusting no man" told by her Pap. The story is about how a father used his unique way to teach her daughter Izzy to protect herself by trusting no man. The father first encouraged Izzy to jump from the top of the steps to where he was, promising her that he would catch her. Trusting her father, the girl gathered up her courage and jumped toward her father's arm, but her father stepped aside, and consequently, the girl fell on the hard ground and was wounded. She cried: "Papa, why didn't you catch me, Papa? Why did you let me fall?" (*BI* 132). The father taught Izzy the lesson: "Listen to me, Izzy, and listen carefully. 'Learn this once and never forget: Trust no man' " (*BI* 132).

So when Cary was admitted to St. Paul's, she underwent ambivalent psychological experiences. As a highly intelligent girl, on the one hand, she was confident of her facility in learning and was determined to become one of the top students; on the other hand, inheriting the burden of the slavery history of her race, she had an innate sense of inferiority. So when confronting the white world in St. Paul's, she would become self-conscious and over-sensitive. Any unpleasant trivial episodes would lead to her self-doubt. It was difficult for the girl to trust anything or anybody in the school. For example, she was doubtful about the real aim of the school's admitting black students, tortured by the idea that St. Paul's admitting black students might only be a social experiment, or that black kids were imported to the school just for the sake of acting as foils to the white kids, and helping out the white kids' education. Influenced by the trauma inherited from the past history of slavery, the little black girl didn't believe that the dominant white society would offer such a good opportunity for the black children, the offspring of slaves.

Bearing such deeply-ingrained self-doubt about her black skin, Cary adopted a doubtful attitude toward everybody, including her teachers, the black peers and her white classmates. She was tortured by her attitudes toward both the white teachers and the black teachers. In her opinion, the white teachers were too harsh on black students' errors because they had prejudice against the black students. When feeling extremely frustrated because of her unsatisfactory academic performance, she tried to seek help from her teachers. But for the over-sensitive girl, her white teachers' encouragement and consolation seemed to signify some unpleasant implications: she thought that her teachers didn't expect good performance from black students. As for the black teachers, she also doubted whether they were loyal to their race or not.

Meanwhile, Cary found it hard to slip into the world of her white classmates. Even when having a party with her white girl classmates, the issue of race would become a sensitive topic which would arouse her righteous anger. Cary discovered that these girls "seemed more certain than I that they deserved our good fortune… they took it as their due" (*BI* 83). Any topic related to race would hurt and irritate her. She felt lonely and alienated from the white world in St. Paul's. She wrote of her feeling of rage and hate: "In the aftermath of Black Is Beautiful, I began to feel black and blue, big and black, black and ugly. Had they done that to me? Had somebody else? Had I let them? Could I stop the feelings? Or hide them?" (*BI* 5). This statement is the true portrayal of her psychological trauma in those days.

In fact, in some sense, her efforts and hard work were acknowledged by her teachers as well as her classmates. She was elected the first girl vice-president of her class. On the graduation day, she was granted the Rector's Medal. But feeling of mistrust still lingered in her mind throughout the years when she stayed in St. Paul's. Fortunately, when Cary returned to St. Paul's fifteen years later and became a teacher, she reexamined the experiences in her school days and interpreted them in a completely fresh perspective.

4.1.2 The Obsession with the Problem of Racial Loyalty

On the one hand, Cary had great difficulty in slipping into the white dominant culture; on the other hand, she felt the privilege she enjoyed in the elite school was a betrayal to her race. When Cary got the news that she was accepted by St. Paul's, she told her two closest girl friends, who were also as intelligent as she was. She felt like a traitor, feeling guilty that "how was it that I should have this opportunity and they should not" (*BI* 35). When coming home from St. Paul's, she visited her best friends. But to her grief, she found that there was a great gap between them. It was difficult for her to explain the condition in her new school and they "had to work hard just to keep talking" (*BI* 99). She felt even out of place at her own home. "At my own house I felt as if I were fighting for a new position in the family order, while Mama pretended not to notice and Dad maybe didn't notice for real. Everywhere I went I felt out of place…. I felt as if I no longer belonged anywhere" (*BI* 99-100).

In St. Paul's, Lorene Cary never forgot her mission as a member of her black community. "I remembered duty and obligation—to my family, to the memory of dead relatives, to my people" (*BI* 5). "My duty was to compete in St. Paul's classrooms. I had no option but to succeed and no doubt that I could will my success" (*BI* 58). All the black students understood "the desperate mandate, the uncompromising demands, and the wild, perfect, greedy hope for it" (*BI* 58). "If we could succeed here—earn high marks, respects, awards; learn these people, study them, be in their world but not of it—we could fulfill the prayers of our ancestors" (*BI* 59). Cary was worried about being assimilated by the white culture. In St. Paul's, she found some black kids who never spoke to the other blacks at all, because "they clearly wanted to assimilate. We shunned them back. They appeared not to notice" (*BI* 73). When Cary herself was elected vice president of her class, the other black students couldn't understand her and also despised her as a traitor of her race.

However, Lorene Cary's quotation from James Baldwin expressed her confusion about the issue of racial loyalty. According to Baldwin, the feeling that "I was as isolated from Negroes as I was from whites" is "what happens when a Negro begins, at bottom, to believe what white people say about him" (*BI* 78). Cary was also worried whether she would preserve her racial loyalty and whether she would also be assimilated. Her feeling of disloyalty was aggravated when the white people told them that they were special blacks: "What did these white people say in a hundred ways but that we were somehow different from the common run of the black people out there in America? What did they say but that we were special, picked out for a special destiny?" (*BI* 78). Cary was ashamed "even to consider the possibility, but it was hard not to believe sometimes" (*BI* 78). As Gonzalez puts it, Cary viewed herself "as a traitor for having trespassed into the white upper-class world, for having gone beyond the dividing racial line" (125).

Her concern about what Gates refers to as the issue of "divided loyalty" is fully embodied in her story of the woman stepping out of her skin (Gates, "Divided Loyalties in Black and White" 2). A woman slipped out of her skin at night and flew around in the darkness. When her husband found out what was happening, he was advised to rub salt on the inside of her skin. So when the woman came back and tried to slip back into her skin, she shrieked with pain: "Skin, skin, ya na know me?" (*BI* 130). According to Gonzalez, skin is a metaphor standing for "the ethnic and cultural identity of the self" (127). The fact that the woman slipped out of the skin means that she attempted to relieve herself of the burden of her ethnic community and black culture. By flying around in the darkness, she tried to cross the dividing line of cultures. But it is impossible for her to straddle between the two cultures without suffering great pain. In this way, the story warned Lorene Cary of "the dangers of crossing boundaries and flirting with the lures of assimilation" (Gonzalez 128).

Cary not only suffered a lot of turmoil caused by her ethnic self, her strong sense of self-hatred and self-doubt was also aggravated by an undesirable first sex experience with her boyfriend Ricky, who raped her when she fell asleep. Then she "felt a sharp pain…a big, blunt pain, dull and stupid like a bowel movement in the wrong place" (*BI* 107). After the miserable experience, she felt it a shame and she hated herself. What was more, she was hurt by Ricky's narration about his relationship with another girl who had given birth to a baby for him but was only regarded by Ricky as "nothing but a whore" (*BI* 111). She wondered who she was and whether she was also "Nothing-But-a-Whore" (*BI* 111). This experience added to her sense of shame and self-hatred. She writes: "When I thought of the sex debacle, I was overwhelmed with shame... my shame soaked up and protected me from the rage underneath. Only now and then did I see the results of the slick, silent anger: tiny moments of self-hatred like dead fish washed up to the beach" (*BI* 111). Both Lorene Cary and Maya Angelou experienced the rape trauma, but unlike Maya who was given much comfort and help from her relatives such as her brother, her Momma and Mrs. Flowers after she caged herself in the world of muteness, Lorene Cary didn't tell anybody about it and had to take on the burden all by herself. She was overwhelmed by the anger and shame beneath the ostensible silence. "Lorene Cary's desire to fly is repeatedly aborted on the grounds of either race or gender" (Gonzalez 127).

In *Black Ice*, Lorene Cary describes the painful experiences in the white dominant world and tells the story of "confront[ing] head-on the hurt and the pain that is the price blacks pay for claiming their racial selves in their American lives" (McKay, "The Narrative Self: Race, Politics, and Culture in Black American Women's Autobiography" 104). However, even faced with identity crises in both race and gender, Cary managed to survive and made great achievements by finding "strategies of survival that turn her momentary disillusion into the renewed energy and strength typical of female predecessors" (Gonzalez 126). In spite of her first mediocre academic performances and her psychological turmoil, she adapted herself to the new environment as soon as possible. She was successfully elected vice president of her class and later became a member of the Disciplinary Committee; when graduating, she became the first black student to receive the Rector's Award. Therefore, *Black Ice* is a story that "sings its own song of black liberation which also embraces the challenge to survive by transforming the would-be victim of race and sex into a self-empowered free self" (McKay, "The Narrative Self: Race, Politics, and Culture in Black American

Women's Autobiography" 104). In the two years in St. Paul's and the later years after gradation, Cary explored the way of crossing the dividing line between black culture and white culture. According to McKay, "it is painful and healing as it brings together the complex, inseparable strands of the American/ African-American Self" (104).

4.2 Homi Bhabha's Theory of Hybridity and the Advantages of Marginal Space

4.2.1 Bhabha's Theory of Hybridity

Lorene Cary's *Black Ice* explored the possibility of crossing the dividing line of black and white races. I will use Homi Bhabha's theory to analyze her attempt to cross the racial dividing line.

Homi Bhabha is an influential Indian-American post-colonial theorist. The concept of hybridity is one of the most important ideas proposed by Bhabha. He doesn't view colonizer and colonized as isolated concepts. Rather, he emphasizes the interrelationship and interdependence between them. To explain the hybridization of cultures, Bhabha proposes some important terms such as "liminal space," "liminal negotiation" and "third space of enunciation."

In *The Location of Culture*, Homi Bhabha holds that "it is the trope of our times to locate the question of culture in the realm of the *beyond*" (1), because "our existence today is marked by a tenebrous sense of survival, living on the borderlines of the 'present' " (1). We live "in the moment of transit where space and time cross to produce complex figures of difference and identity, past and present, inside and outside, inclusion and exclusion" (1). Therefore, we should "move away from the singularities of 'class' or 'gender' as primary conceptual and organizational categories" (1). Instead, we should "think beyond narrative of originary and initial subjectivities and focus on those moments or processes that are produced in the articulation of cultural difference" (1). He points out that "these 'in-between' spaces provide the terrain for elaborating strategies of selfhood—singular or communal—that initiate new signs of identity and innovative sites of collaboration, and contestation, in the act of defining the idea of society itself" (1-2).

Bhabha explores the possibility of "liminal negotiation": "It is in the emergence of the interstices—the overlap and displacement of domains of difference—that the intersubjective and collective experiences of *nationess*, community interest, or cultural value are negotiated" (*The Location of Culture* 2). Bhabha asserts:

> Terms of cultural engagement, whether antagonistic or affiliative, are produced performatively. The representation of difference must not be hastily read as the reflection of *pre-given* ethnic or cultural traits set in the fixed table of tradition. The social articulation of difference, from the minority perspective, is a complex, on-going negotiation that seeks to authorize cultural hybridities that emerge in moments of historical transformation. (*The Location of Culture* 2)

Bhabha quotes what the artist and writer Renee Green said in a conversation:

> I used architecture literally as a reference, using the attic, the boiler room, and the stairwell to make associations between certain binary divisions such as higher and lower and heaven and hell. The stairwell became a liminal space, a pathway between the upper and lower areas, each of which was annotated with plaques referring to blackness and whiteness. (qtd. in Bhabha, *The Location of Culture* 4)

According to Bhabha, "the stairwell as liminal space, in-between the designation of identity, becomes the process of symbolic interaction, the connective tissue that constructs the difference between upper and lower, black and white. The hither and thither of the stairwell, the temporal movement and passage that it allows, prevents identities at either end of it from settling into primordial polarities. This interstitial passage between fixed identifications opens up the possibility of a cultural hybridity that entertains difference without an assumed or imposed hierarchy" (Bhabha, *The Location of Culture* 4).

In this way, "Bhabha posits hybridity as such a form of liminal or in-between space, where the 'cutting edge of translation and negotiation' (Bhabha 1996) occurs and which he terms 'the third space' " (Meredith 2). Thus, the third space is

> a mode of articulation, a way of describing a productive, and not merely reflective, space that engenders new possibility. It is an "interruptive, interrogative, and enunciative" (Bhabha 1994) space of new forms of cultural meaning and production blurring the limitations of

existing boundaries and calling into question established categorisations of culture and identity. (Meredith 2)

Bhaba argues that by stepping into this third space, we "may open the way to conceptualizing an international culture, based not on exoticism or multi-culturalism of the diversity of cultures, but on the inscription and articulation of culture's hybridity" (Bhabha, "Cultural Diversity and Cultural Differences" 209). He believes that "it is in this space that we will find those words with which we can speak of Ourselves and Others. And by exploring his hybridity, this 'Third Space', we may elude the politics of polarity and emerge as the others of our selves" (Bhabha, "Cultural Diversity and Cultural Differences" 209).

Bhabha's theory of hybridity and the liminal negotiation will throw light on Cary's exploration of the possibility of crossing the racial divide.

4.2.2 The Advantages of Marginal Space

W. E. B. Du Bois illustrates the double consciousness typical of the African Americans:

> The Negro is a sort of seventh son, born with a veil, and gifted with second-sight in the American world—a world which yields him no true self-consciousness…One ever feels his twoness—an American, a Negro; two souls, two thoughts, two unreconciled strivings; two warring ideals in one dark body, whose dogged strength alone keeps it from being torn asunder. (Du Bois 12)

On the other hand, Du Bois also points out the advantages of the double consciousness:

> The history of the American Negro is the history of this strife—this longing to attain self-conscious manhood, to merge his double self into a better and truer self. In this merging he wishes neither of the older selves to be lost. He would not Africanize America, for America has too much to teach the world and Africa. He would not bleach his Negro soul in a flood of white Americanism, for he knows that Negro blood has a message for the world. He simply wishes to make it possible for a man to be both a Negro and an American, without being cursed and spit upon by his fellows, without having the doors of opportunity closed roughly in his face.

> This, then, is the end of his striving: to be a co-worker in the kingdom of culture, to escape both death and isolation, to husband and use his best powers and his latent genius. These powers of body and mind have in the past been strangely wasted, dispersed, or forgotten. (Du Bois 13)

Bell hooks also points out the advantages of the status of marginality:

> As such, I was not speaking of a marginality one wished to lose—to give up or surrender as part of moving into the center—but rather of a site one stays in, clings to even, because it nourishes one's capacity to resist. It offers to one the possibility of radical perspective from which to see and create, to imagine alternatives, new worlds. (*Yearning*: *Race*, *Gender*, *and Culture Politics* 149-50)

Bell hooks argues that we can take advantage of the marginal space:

> I am located in the margin...We come to this space through suffering and pain, through struggle. We know struggle to be that which pleasures, delights, and fulfills desire. We are transformed, individually, collectively, as we make radical creative space which affirms and sustains our subjectivity, which gives us a new location from which to articulate our sense of the world. (*Yearning*: *Race*, *Gender*, *and Culture Politics* 153)

In this way, we are more likely to achieve a sense of wholeness:

> The sense of wholeness, impressed upon our consciousness by the structure of our daily lives, provided us with an oppositional world-view—a mode of seeing unknown to most of our oppressors, that sustained us, aided us in our struggle to transcend poverty and despair, strengthened our sense of self and our solidarity. (*Yearning*: *Race*, *Gender*, *and Culture Politics* 149)

Lorene Cary, studying in St. Paul's, experienced a turbulent psychological crisis. The only therapy was the folklores inherited from the old generations of her race. As a self-conscious black girl, she could only understand the folk stories in a negative way: protecting herself by putting no trust in anybody. At that time, she didn't know the advantages of being the marginalized people. But when she grew up and gained more social experiences, she would be sure to agree with Du Bois and bell hooks that the special status of marginality would offer her the advantage to gain a fresh insight into the world, the race, the culture, and the wholeness of our selves.

4.3 Exploring the Possibility of Crossing the Racial Divide in *Black Ice*

When Lorene Cary studied in St. Paul's School, she was obsessed by the sense of what Du Bois referred to as "double-consciousness," and she found it hard to cross the racial dividing line. On the one hand, she knew well that the opportunity to receive education in St. Paul's meant a brighter future to her; on the other hand, she felt as if she was a "traitor for having trespassed into the white upper-class world and having gone beyond the dividing racial line" (Gonzalez 125). She lived the two years full of self-doubt and remorse, and managed to survive owing to her strong sense of responsibility for turning out in St. Paul's for her people. She had been exploring the way to strike her balance between a black girl and a student in St. Paul's.

Fortunately, fifteen years later when she came back to St. Paul's as a teacher and one of the trustees, she seemed to have figured out the way to strike the balance between her racial self and the self as a member of America. She knew it was likely that being black "did not [only] mean handicap, shame, or denial" (*BI* 229). The writing of the autobiography became "a journey into social ethnic integration" as well as "a journey into the integration of her selves towards personal wholeness" (Gonzalez 131). In the process of writing, the adolescent Cary who was "prideful, funny, ashamed, anxious, cocky, and scared" (*BI* 228) demanded "compassion, forgiveness, reunification" (*BI* 228). By writing the autobiography, the adult Cary had accepted the past and integrated with the past self into personal wholeness. Meanwhile, she gained keen insight into and new meaning of the ambivalent condition of the past. It is also a process of exploring the possibility of crossing the racial divide through the autobiographical act. She writes about the great significance of the writing of the autobiography:

I began writing about St. Paul's School when I stopped thinking of my pre-school experience. The narratives that helped me, that kept me company, along with the living, breathing people in my life, were those that talked honestly about growing up black in America. They burst into my silence, and in my head, they shouted and chattered and whispered and sang together. I am writing his book to become part of that unruly conversation, and to bring my experience back to the community of minds that made it possible. (*BI* 6)

4.3.1 The Source of Power—Black Culture and Its Storytelling Tradition

While exploring the possibility of crossing the racial divide, Cary focused on two aspects. Firstly, she identified herself with the black community, regarding herself as a member of the whole race, clinging to the root of black culture. She drew strength from her own community. Whenever she was frustrated, she had recourse to her mother's spirit of "turning out" for encouragement and power: "Turning out, I learned, was not a matter of style; cold indignation worked as well as hot fury. Turning out had to do with will. I came to regard my mother's will as a force of nature, an example of and a metaphor for black power and black duty" (*BI* 58). As a member of the race, she never forgot her duty to compete with the white students for her people. When the graduation day was drawing near, she began to blame herself for somewhat forgetting her mission: "What had I done, I kept thinking, that was worthy of their faith? How had I helped my race? How had I prepared myself for a meaningful future? What plan did I have to make lots of money and be of service?" (*BI* 212) When she was in a psychological crisis, she would rely on her great-grandfather's storytelling tradition to go through the difficult time. The folk storytelling served as a healing therapy for her: "What the stories do is tell me why—why the old people looked at us with such unforgiving eyes, why they pushed us away, but wouldn't let go. Without the stories, I'd have nothing to explain the cacophony in my head in the indigo New Hampshire night" (*BI* 236). "Nowhere else will I get the rhythm of these stories, the ghosts and their magic. …Without the stories and the songs, I am mute" (*BI* 236-37).

4.3.2 Finding One's Place by Crossing the Racial Dividing Line

With time passing by, Cary gained more experiences and insight into her own problems, realizing that her identity crisis was partly due to her own separation from both the whites and the blacks in St. Paul's, that her "black skin, that fine, fine membrane that was meant to hold in my blood, not bind up my soul" (*BI* 237). Two years later when Cary graduated from St. Paul's, she was filled with mixed feelings of "love and gratitude, hate, resentments, shame, admiration, loss" (*BI* 219). She felt remorse because "for the first time that year, I was not ready to leave St. Paul's. I had had all my time, all my chances. I could never do it again, never make it right. I had not loved enough" (*BI* 218). She came to realize that she had not made full use of the two years in St. Paul's because of the cage of isolation and alienation she had made for herself. Consequently, "these powers of body and mind have…been strangely wasted, dispersed, or forgotten" (Du Bois 13).

Cary didn't describe much about the life after she graduated from St. Paul's, but by reading the beginning and the end of her autobiography, we may safely conclude that she must have made profound reflections upon the life in St. Paul's and must have always been exploring some ways to cross the racial divide so as to "merge [her] double self into a better and truer self" (Du Bois 13). The adult Cary would be likely to agree with what bell hooks argues for the advantages of marginality. According to hooks,

> to be in the margin is to be part of the whole but outside the main body…Living as we did—on the edge—we developed a particular way of seeing reality. We looked both from the outside in and from inside out. We focused our attention on the center as well as on the margin. We understand both. This mode of seeing reminded us of the existence of a whole universe, a main body made up of both margin and center. Our survival depended on an ongoing public awareness of the separation between margin and center and on ongoing private acknowledgement that we were a necessary, vital part of that whole. (*Yearning: Race, Gender and Cultural Politics* 149)

Cary has been exploring the ways to become a "co-worker in the kingdom of culture, to escape both death and isolation, to husband and use [her] best powers and [her] talent genius" (Du Bois 13).

In addition, Cary's idea also coincides with Bhabha's concept of negotiation of the Third Space, which helpes create the hybridization of cultures. "Despite the exposure of the third space to contradictions and ambiguities, it provides a spatial politics of inclusion rather than exclusion that initiates new signs of identity, and innovative sites of collaboration and contestation" (Meredith 3). Meredith argues that "the hybrid strategy opens up a third space of/for rearticulation of negotiation and meaning" (3). Meredith points out:

The hybrid identity is positioned within this third space, as "lubricant"... in the conjunction of

cultures. The hybrid's potential is with their innate knowledge of "transculturation" (Taylor,

1991), their ability to transverse both cultures and to translate, negotiate and mediate affinity

and difference within a dynamic of exchange and inclusion. (Meredith 2)

The concept of hybridity is "celebrated and privileged as a kind of superior cultural intelligence owing to the advantage of in-betweeness, the straddling of two cultures and the consequent ability to negotiate the difference" (qtd. in Meredith 2).

Therefore, armed with such an idea of creating hybrid cultures, Cary "stopped thinking of [her] pre-school experience as an aberration from the common run of black life in America" (*BI* 6). Her unique perspective enabled her to reexamine the life in St. Paul's and view the past experiences with a fresh point of view. Cary believed that it was likely to change the condition of the blacks' isolation from the whites. She asserted that "the isolation I'd felt was an illusion, and it can take time and, as they say at St. Paul's, 'the love and labor of many,' to get free of illusions" (*BI* 6). "According to Bhabha, this hybrid third space is an ambivalent site where cultural meaning and representation have no primordial unity of fixity." (Meredith 3) "It is that Third Space, though unrepresentable in itself, which constitutes the discursive conditions of enunciation that ensure that the meaning and symbols of culture have no primordial unity or fixity, that even the same signs can be appropriated, translated, rehistoricized and read anew" (Bhabha, *The Location of Culture* 37).

Therefore, Cary had a new understanding of her experiences in St. Paul's when she examined them from the perspective of negotiating in the liminal third space. In St. Paul's, she had a mistrust in the attempt of the school's admitting black students and was always obsessed with the interrogation: "Were we black kids a social experiment?" (*BI* 5). Cary often felt that she was only "a marginal other" in the white dominant society. As a result, she was trapped in the cave of isolation, failing to find a sense of belonging in the school, overwhelmed by the sense of self-hatred brought about by her identity as a member of the black race.

In the eyes of the adult Cary, the fact that St. Paul's School admitted black students was an opportunity for the blacks to contribute to the "mammoth enterprise—the integration, the moral transformation" of America (*BI* 5). Black students should make full use of the "marginal space" to see, to imagine "alternatives, new worlds" (hooks, *Yearning: Race, Gender and Cultural Politics*

149). Cary advocated "the integration of both sides of the ethnic self, in this case the Black side and the American side into a whole being who is a composite of multiple selves, 'refusing the boundaries which assign her exclusively to one place or the other' " (Gonzalez 128-29). As Du Bois states, "the history of the American Negro is the history of this strife—this longing to attain self-conscious manhood, to merge his double self into a better and truer self" (13). The adult Cary will agree that black people should free themselves from the trauma caused by the history of slavery, because clinging to the miserable history will always put them into a painful state of mind and will deprive them of their hope for a better future. Rather, the black people should make full use of the advantages of the marginal status to have a comprehensive understanding of the value of both the white culture and their own culture, believing that they are also members of the Americans, and their culture is an indispensable part of American culture.

Nevertheless, what Cary advocated was "hybridity," but not "assimilation." She wrote: "If we could succeed here—earn high marks, respects, awards; learn these people, study them, *be in their world but not of it*—we would fulfill the prayers of our ancestors" (*BI* 59, emphasis mine). As Gonzalez points out, "Cary is not choosing assimilation into the white culture and society but rather a 'healthy' integration in it as well as the inclusion—rather than exclusion—of the different but not opposing selves of the African-American person" (129). As Du Bois points out:

> In this merging [of the double self into a better and truer self] he wishes neither of the older selves to be lost. He would not Africanize America, for America has too much to teach the world and Africa. He would not bleach his Negro soul in a flood of white Americanism, for he knows that Negro blood has a message for the world. He simply wishes to make it possible for a man to be both a Negro and an American, without being cursed and spit upon by his fellows, without having the doors of opportunity closed roughly in his face. (13)

In fact, Cary was strongly opposed to the assimilation by white culture. She thought of it as a shame that some black people who had been assimilated regarded their own child as a monkey from the zoo if she was too dark and that "little girls cry out to God in the dark for good hair" (*BI* 233-34). The hybridity that Cary advocated would not "sound like dying a cultural death" (*BI* 233). What she pursued was "an image of wholeness, inclusion; moving circles that come together, overlap, drift apart" (*BI* 233). Otherwise, "why else were we, like married women, so concerned to find the right compounds and hyphenates? Black American (big B, small b), Afro-American, Afric-American, people of color, Afro-Caribbean, Anglo-African, people of the diaspora, African-American?" (*BI* 233) Obviously, Cary "advocates the idea of wholeness and inclusion instead of the insurmountable dividing line of separation" (Gonzalez 130). Gonzalez considers *Black Ice* "a paean to hybridity" (130) and "the always problematic inbetweenness of ethnic self in the United States" (Gonzalez 130) was transformed into the "self-empowered free self" (McKay, "The Narrative Self: Race, Politics, and Culture in Black American Women's Autobiography" 104). Cary does not approve of the idea of the assimilation into white culture by neglecting the value and the unique features of black culture, neither will she regard it as a shame to absorb the elements of white culture into black culture. Both white culture and black culture should be integrated as a whole in a healthy way, thus making contributions to enrich American culture.

4.3.3 The Role as a Black Teacher and a Crossover Artist

Fifteen years later, Cary came back to St. Paul's to teach because "I'd wanted to revisit the place that had so disturbed me in my overserious youth; to encourage kids who might feel similarly; and to learn from them" (*BI* 232). When one of her classmates wondered whether it was worthwhile to come back to St. Paul's to teach, she smiled, "but I don't feel that there's anything wrong in giving it here, too. It is like admitting who I am. I came here, and I went away changed. I've been fighting that for a long time, to no purpose. I am a crossover artist, you know, like those jazz musicians who do pop albums, too" (*BI* 232-33). She came back because she knew the great significance of working as a teacher and acting as "a crossover artist." Working as a teacher and a trustee offered Cary a third space and a marginal space, both of which enabled her to know more about the white world and the black world, and to strike a balance between these two worlds, to "elude the politics of polarity" (Bhabha, "Cultural Diversity and Cultural Differences" 209), and to articulate the hybridity of cultures. She would make an effort to promote the mutual understanding between the white and the black students, with a focus on helping black students liberate themselves from the cage imposed on them both by the white society and by themselves, helping them integrate themselves into the nation of America as a whole.

Examining her life in St. Paul's from a new perspective, the meaning of the past experiences seemed to be different. Cary used to have mistrust in both the white teachers and black teachers, thinking that white teachers had prejudice against black students and that black teachers were disloyal to their race. For instance, she had been wary of John Walker, "the first black teacher at St. Paul's, its first black trustee, and the first black Bishop of the Washington, D.C." (*BI* 6). She was not sure whether "the small man with the tiny eyes was traitor or advocate" (*BI* 5). However, fifteen years later, "the faculty that had appeared to my teenaged eyes as a monolith of critical white adulthood now revealed itself as a community of idealists, all trying, each according to his or her ability, to help young people" (*BI* 225). She thought the mission of the teachers in the school was to "stuff as much Christian charity into our arrogant charges as possible" (*BI* 225). As a black teacher and a trustee in St. Paul's, Cary understood her mission for her race. Mr. John Walker became her guide and her role model to achieve her goal. "I watched John Walker carefully, the way a desert pilgrim stares at an oasis" (*BI* 229). It was John Walker who "filled [her] with hope for her own racial and spiritual healing, and courage to look black" (*BI* 6). She saw him as a man "who affected people deeply by his presence" and who "spoke wisely…[and] emanated both judgment and compassion" (*BI* 6). Following the path of John Walker, Cary would play the vital role as a "crossover artist," acting as a bridge to connect the two worlds of the black and the white, helping her black student to know what it meant "to be black in America if it did not mean handicap, shame, or denial" (*BI* 229). She would help the young black student "to attain self-conscious manhood, to merge his double self into a better and truer self" (Du Bois 12). Her mission was "to make sure that the blackness, the confidence, the love—were real. I wanted to see if it would wither or waver or waffle. It did not" (*BI* 229).

She was devoted to her job, knowing well about the isolation and the fear of the new black students, trying to be helpful to them. "I felt the zeal of it, the ironic, subversive missionary zeal. I felt the frustration. …Like the other faculty members, I exerted too much pressure on my already stress-filled students" (*BI* 225). She did so because she was eager to liberate the black students from their psychological cage imposed on them both by the white society and by themselves. She wished that the black students would not waste the opportunity as she had done. She tried to encourage them to make full use of the opportunity to develop their potentials and do something meaningful for her race:

And yet, it took all my control to keep from shaking them sometimes, from jacking them up against the wall and screaming into their faces: "Look at what you have here. Buildings, grounds, books, computers, experts, time, youth, strength, ice rinks, forests, radio equipment, observatories. Learn, damn you! Take it in and go out into the world and do something. (*BI* 225)

She told the black students "to try to think of St. Paul's as their school, too, not as a white place there they were trespassing" (*BI* 5) and attempted to let them know that "just as St. Paul's was theirs, because they had attended the school and contributed to it, so too, was American life and culture theirs, because they were black people in America" (*BI* 5). The black students in St. Paul's should free themselves from the burden of history, and should believe that St. Paul's belongs to the black students as well as to the white students, and should be confident that they are the important members of the school, because as part of the school, the black students have also made contributions to the school. Similarly, since the black people have made great contributions to their country in all aspects, they should also consider themselves and should be regarded as citizens of America, but not the marginalized people who are inferior to the others in the American society.

4.3.4 Cary's New Interpretation of Folk Stories

Homi Bhabha is conscious of "the dangers of fixity and fetishism of identities within binary colonial thinking, arguing that 'all forms of culture are continually in a process of hybridity' " (Meredith 2). In the process of liminal negotiation, cultural values keep changing, just as Bhabha argues, "it is in the emergence of the interstices—the overlap and displacement of domains of difference—that the intersubjective and collective experiences of *nationess*, community interest, or cultural value are negotiated" (Bhabha 2). Bell hooks argues for the advantages brought about by the marginal space: "Spaces can tell stories and unfold histories. Spaces can be interrupted, appropriated, and transformed through artistic and literary practice" (*Yearning*: *Race, Gender and Cultural Politics* 152).

Cary found a new meaning in her great-grandfather's stories about "trusting no man" and the woman slipping out of her skin. When still a student in St. Paul's, she resorted to the folk stories for comfort and explanation of her difficult condition. She learned from the stories that she should "be well-mannered, big-hearted, defiant," and that "at the center of all my posing, I would remain alone. I would trust no man" (*BI* 132). When recalling those stories, the adult Cary found it hard to "find the words to say it outright: that Pap was wrong. His stories taught me fear and shame and secrecy" (*BI* 236). As a crossover artist, Cary was open-minded enough to interrogate the meaning of the traditional folk stories. "The borderline engagements of cultural difference may as often be consensual as conflictual; they may confound our definitions of tradition and modernity; realign the customary boundaries between the private and the public, high and low; and challenge normative expectations of development and progress" (Bhabha, *The Location of Culture* 2). Cary found it necessary "to evolve within that tradition [of storytelling] by revising loaded stories whose intended meaning might not be the best for the determination of the black woman's identity" (Gonzalez 131).

However, it does not mean that she would throw away the stories because she knew "without the stories and the songs, I am mute" (*BI* 237), but that she found she could interpret the stories from a new perspective. On the one hand, Cary considered her heritage of black culture as the root of her identity. "Nowhere else will I get the rhythm of these stories, the ghosts and their magic" (*BI* 236). But on the other hand, she can also learn things from white culture:

> A white American education will never give them [the black folk stories] to me; but it can— if I am graced, if I do not go blind in the white light of self-consciousness, if I have guides before me and the sense to heed them—it can help me to see the stories, growing like a vine out of the cane fields, up out of unmarked graves, around my soul. It can help me search out the very history it did not teach me. "Let us learn those things here on earth," proclaims the school motto, "the knowledge of which will continue into the heavens." (*BI* 237)

Education in St. Paul's gave her an opportunity to gain new insight into the hybridity of cultures. "St. Paul's gave me new words into which I must translate the old. But St. Paul's would keep me inside my black skin, that fine, fine membrane that was meant to hold in my blood, not bind up my soul. The stories show me the way out. I must tell my daughter that" (*BI* 237). As Bhabha points out:

> The intervention of the Third Space of enunciation…makes the structure of meaning and reference an ambivalent process…Such an intervention quite properly challenges our sense of the historical identity of culture as a homogenizing, unifying force, authenticated by the

original Past, kept alive in the national tradition of the People. (Bhabha, *The Location of Culture* 37)

Bhabha argues that "all forms of culture are continually in a process of hybridity" (qtd. in Meredith 2). Cary expressed her idea similarly:

> I did not ask for the stories, but I was given them to tell, to retell and change and pass along. (Each one teach one, pass it on, pass it on.) I was given them to plait into my story, to use, to give me the strength to take off my skin and stand naked and unafraid in the night, to touch other souls in the night. (*BI* 237)

When she was still a student in St. Paul's, if the story of the flying woman stepping out of her skin "warns her of the dangers of crossing boundaries" (Gonzalez 128), fifteen years later, Cary endowed the story a new rich meaning. The story of "Skin, skin, ya na know me?" was transformed into the story of a free flying woman who did not have to fear her skin. She imagined that the flying woman gained freedom to fly out into the darkness and joined those who "are there already, calling, welcoming" (*BI* 237), enjoying her freedom without fearing being discovered by her husband. Cary imagined how she could enjoy her full freedom:

> Then I can go to my own room where the window is open to the black night and fly out unafraid to meet the darkness. I can fly out at dark to rub against the open sky... At dawn I will alight on my sill. I can slip into my smooth black skin. It will welcome me... I will return again and again to the sky. The skin will grow wrinkled... but my husband will not salt it. My skin will know me, and I will not have to fear my skin. (*BI* 237)

Cary was looking forward to the day when people are likely to cross the racial divide, when it is "possible for a man to be both a Negro and an American, without being cursed and spit upon by his fellows, without having the doors of opportunity closed roughly in his face" (Du Bois 13), when the color of skin will not become a burden for the black people, when people of different races will respect their cultures and learn from other cultures, when people will have mutual trust in each other. She was looking forward to the day when "Izzy will jump of her own will when her legs have grown strong enough to absorb the shock; she will not lie on the ground...crippled by distrust," when Izzy will "paint, dance, read, sing, skate, write, climb, fly" (*BI* 237-38).

The book's title "black ice" is profound in meaning. Critics have interpreted it in different ways. For Jeanne Braham, black ice symbolizes "the trap and danger St. Paul's represents for young Cary"; for Jacqueline Trescotte, "it is a metaphor for the protagonist's adopted personality"; for Phillip Lopate, black ice refers "to the icy self-control demanded by the situation of being a token or model minority student, and the anger it generated underneath" (qtd. in Conzalez 132). In my opinion, the meaning of black ice varies with time. When Cary was a student, black ice is a metaphor for her psychological and spiritual cage of isolation from both the whites and the blacks, and her gloomy and reserved attitude towards her environment. But the adult Cary viewed it with a new perspective. Black ice means the Third Space to bridge the racial divide between white and black cultures, which will enable the earth to "stretch smooth and unbroken like grace" (*BI* 238). By skating on the black ice which provided possibilities for them to cross the racial divide, the young black people would "have their share" of the nation of America (*BI* 238).

Chapter Five

The Narrative Strategies in the Three Autobiographies

5.1 The Influence of Main American Literary Thoughts on the Autobiographies of Hurston and Angelou

5.1.1 Modernism in *Dust Tracks on a Road*

The 1940s witnessed the new development of black autobiographies. Langston Hughes published *The Big Sea* in 1940 and Richard Wright published his *Black Boy* in 1945. Many black women used the writing of autobiographies as a vehicle to assert their identity and self-acceptance. Examples were Hurston's *Dust Tracks on a Road*, Mary Church Terrell's *A Colored Woman in a White World* and Laura Adams's *Dark Symphony*. Influenced by the spirit of the Harlem Renaissance, a period of "a fertile flowering of black art, music and voice in the 1920s and 1930s" (Butterworth 248), the black autobiographers expressed a new sense of racial pride. Many black men wrote their autobiographies in the protest mode, a dominant mode of writing in the 1930s. Both male and female autobiographers treated racial issues as the main themes. According to Braxton, "the 1940s also saw the rise of modernism in black autobiography—a great change had occurred, both in the spirit of the autobiographers and the form of their works" (Braxton 139). Hurston's *Dust Tracks on a Road* has also reflected some characteristics of modernism.

The Modernism Movement began at the end of the 19th century and it was influenced by the avant-garde movement that originated in France. Modernism re-examines every aspect of human existence, from commerce to philosophy, including arts, literature, architecture, religious faith, social organization and daily life, etc. It tries to find out the reasons that hold back progress, and replace it with new ways. As a main literary thought, it is closely related to the philosophical thoughts of Arthur Schopenhauer, Friedrich Nietzsche, Henri Bergson and Martin Heidegger, and modern psychological theories developed by psychologists such as William James and Sigmund Freud. American modernism was introduced mainly by the pioneer female writer Gertrude Stein. It reached its peak in the 1920s. The major representative writers were the Lost Generation writers such as Ernest Hemingway, Dos Passos, Francis Scott Fitzgerald, Thomas Wolfe. After World War I, the young writers were deeply disappointed with the American society and felt betrayed, helpless and lost because the traditional values could not help them adapt themselves to the cruel reality. They abandoned the conventional values and felt alienated from the new industrialized world. In their writing they expressed their alienation, pessimism and despair by employing new modernist writing techniques.

Among them, Dos Passos (1896-1970) is known for his unique writing skills and an experimental approach to form. His skills are fully embodied in his masterpiece *U.S.A.* (1937), a trilogy comprising the novels *The 42nd Parallel* (1930), *1919* (1932), and *The Big Money* (1936). In the novels, Dos Passos employed modernist techniques to portray the first three decades of the 20th century. As a painter himself, Dos Passos was greatly influenced by the avant-garde movement and created his unique style by merging different elements of Impression, Expressionism and Cubism. In his *U.S.A* trilogy, he gave up traditional writing skills and created nonlinear narration by employing a collage of techniques, which consists of four different genres. Firstly, Passos resorted to the device labeled as "Camera Eye," and wrote autobiographical episodes of a stream of consciousness. Secondly, he used fictional narratives to tell stories of 12 fictional characters. Thirdly, he employed the device of "Newsreel," which is made up of the collages of newspaper clippings and headlines, fragments of pop songs and political speeches. Lastly, he wrote biographical sketches of those prominent figures from the early 1900s to 1920s, aiming to express the historical background (Yang 269-70). As one of the prominent figures in the Harlem Renaissance Movement, Hurston is greatly influenced by modernism and it is also shown in her autobiography *Dust Tracks on a Road*.

In the book, Hurston subverted the conventional form of autobiography and adopted the similar skills of Passos. Similar to the form of Passos's *U.S.A.*

trilogy, Hurston also merged different genres in her autobiography, traditional chronological narration of her childhood, a series of essays centered on different topics, folk stories, etc. As has been stated in Chapter Two of this book, *Dust Tracks on a Road* can be divided into two parts, with the first part describing her hometown Eatonville, her happy childhood and her mother's death in chronological order. She mentioned twelve prophetic visions, which were originally intended to be a coherent clue to explain her life, but they failed to shape the book coherently because Hurston seemed to forget them in her later narration. The second part of the book is composed of several chapters which are devoted to the discussion of some topics such as her research, her attitudes towards books, race, friendship, love, religion. As Claudine Raynaud points out, "the horizontal chronological progression gave way to a vertical organization, une topique, a series of 'commonplaces' " (113). In some sense, the book is like a collage of "competing discourses—folkloric material, tall tales, residual structure from the spiritual autobiography—which finally dissolve into 'scattering remarks' " (Raynaud 131).

Besides, *Dust Track on a Road* is a text in which Hurston modulates between standard English and black dialect, and in which the oral performance intermingles with the written text. "Hurston's narrative voice relies ostensibly on standard English, but the tone belongs to a colloquial, oral storytelling voice" (Pierre Walker 390). As Pierre Walker states, the autobiography "is, at the same time, neither bird nor beast and both bird and beast" (390).

Modernism has not only exerted an influence on Hurston's autobiography in her employment of the modernist writing skills, but also on her illustration of the concept of self. In the autobiographical writing, the autobiographers are expected to shape a unified self. According to Jelinek,

> although most critics no longer expect autobiographies to adhere stylistically to a precise progressive narrative, nonetheless a unified shaping is considered ideal. That unity should be achieved by concentrating on one period of the autobiographer's life, the development of his life according to one theme, or the analysis of this character in terms of an important aspect of it. The autobiographer is expected to "gather the different elements of his personal life and organize them into a single whole," to begin his life study "with the problem already solved." (Jelinek 5)

As Pierre Walker points out, according to Cartesian or Enlightenment philosophy, there exists a stable, coherent self and the individual is a single, autonomous and homogeneous unity. In Cartesian or Enlightenment paradigm, the unity of the individual and the unity of the story should go together (Pierre Walker, "Zora Neale Hurston and the Post-modern Self in *Dust Tracks on a Road*" 388).

But in *Dust Tracks on a Road*, Hurston adopted deceptive narrative strategies to resist the unity of the self and refused to give "a focused projection of the autobiographical persona" (Walker, "Zora Neale Hurston and the Post-Modern Self in *Dust Tracks on a Road*" 387). As Maya Angelou states, "it is difficult, if not impossible, to find and touch the real Zora Neale Hurston" (Angelou, "Forward" xi-xii). Instead, what is embodied in the autobiography is a repressed individual who is lacking in consistency, coherence and unity. Firstly, readers find it hard to know the personality of the autobiographer because Hurston doesn't provide enough information about her personal life. Even if there are descriptions about her own life, they are full of evasions, even distortions. Lionnet points out that Hurston exemplifies "the 'paradoxes of her personality' by revealing a fluid and multidimensional self that refuses to be framed or packaged for the benefit of those human, all-too-human mortals" (Lionnet 387). In my opinion, Hurston tries to avoid the description of a unified self, partly influenced by modernist thought. According to Yang Renjing, "American modernist literature emphasizes the value and freedom of individuals, and likes to express a self which embodies the uncertainty of life and the inhibition of the individuals by the society" (67). In her autobiography, Hurston expressed an alienated self and a repressed self, who found it difficult to strike a balance between the black world and the white world. In order to gain the dual readership, Hurston had to repress her real self. By reading the autobiography, readers will find that the individuality of the black people are severely inhibited by the white society. Even Hurston with such an optimistic personality could not free herself from the deep-rooted influence of the repression imposed on the black people by the dominant white society.

5.1.2 Realism and Other Narrative Skills in *I Know Why the Caged Bird Sings*

In the following part, I will mainly focus on Angelou's first autobiography *I Know Why the Caged Bird Sings*, centering on the influence of realism on the autobiographical proses, the mixture of fact and fiction, the use of the dialogue, metaphor, and self-parody in the book, etc.

Angelou published her autobiography *I Know Why the Caged Bird Sings* at the end of the 1960s, "one of the most turbulent times in modern American history" (Sickels 19), when the Civil Rights Movement, the Feminist Movement and the Black Arts Movement influenced the era greatly. Angelou's autobiography was greatly affected by the special social background and main literary thoughts of the 1960s. In her autobiography, Angelou adopted the approach of realism to embody the condition of both the specific historical moment in which the book was set and the specific historical moment in which it was written. She incorporated her attitudes to the Civil Rights Movement, the Feminist Movement and the Black Arts Movement into the description of a typical segregated southern village, Stamps, Arkansas in the 1930s. When Angelou wrote the autobiography, she said

> I wasn't thinking about so much about my life or identity. I was thinking about a particular time in which I lived and the influences of that time on a number of people. I kept thinking, what about that time? What were the people around young Maya doing? I used the central figure—myself—as a focus to show how one person can make it through those times. (Tate 6)

After the American Civil War, three constitutional amendments—the 13th Amendment, the 14th Amendment and the 15th Amendment—put an end to slavery, gave the African Americans citizenship and granted black males the right to vote respectively. In spite of the passage of those amendments, the African Americans still suffered racial discrimination and were deprived of their civil rights. The whites imposed racial segregation by law. The Jim Crow system that emerged out of the post-Reconstruction South worsened the discrimination and oppression. Segregation was part of their life. Blacks and whites went to different schools and churches, used separate public restrooms, swam in different pools, had their meals in different restaurants. The Jim Crow system remained virtually intact into the mid-1950s. African Americans kept struggling for their civil rights. On December 1, 1955 in Montgomery, Alabama, Rosa Parks—the mother of the Civil Rights Movement—refused to give her seat on a public bus to white passengers and was detained. The incident led to the organization of the Montgomery Bus Boycott, which ushered in a new era of the Civil Rights Movement in the United States. Martin Luther King, Jr., a young Baptist minister, organized the boycott and the protest made Martin Luther King a national figure. He played an influential role in the advancement of civil rights using nonviolent

civil disobedience. In 1963, he delivered his famous speech "I Have a Dream."
On December 10, 1964, Dr. Martin Luther King, Jr. was awarded the Nobel
Peace Prize. The Civil Rights Movement made great achievements with sit-ins
and marches. The efforts of the African Americans led to the passage of the most
important legislative achievements—the Civil Rights Act of 1964, which banned
discrimination based on "race, color, religion, or national origin" in employment
practices and public accommodations.

However, as the Civil Rights Movement went on and made great
achievements, African Americans were fiercely and viciously attacked. The
society was exposed to great violence. Bombings, lynchings and beatings could
be seen everywhere. On November 22,1963, President John F. Kennedy was
assassinated, which caused more violent riots. Many African Americans sacrificed
their lives to fight for their rights. In 1965, Malcolm X, a black nationalist, was
assassinated. On April 4, 1968, Martin Luther King was also assassinated. The
whole nation was plunged into fury and grief. Maya Angelou, who also took an
active part in the Civil Rights Movement, was stunned and devastated by their
deaths because both Malcolm X and Martin Luther King were her close friends.
In the early 1960s, she got to know Malcolm X in Accra and they became close
friends. In 1965, she helped him to build the organization of Afro-American Unity.
Shortly afterwards, Malcolm X was assassinated. Devastated by his death, she
moved back to Los Angeles to begin her writing career. In 1968, she was invited
by her friend Martin Luther King to organize a march, but before she was ready
for it, he was assassinated coincidently on her 40th birthday. Devastated again,
she was encouraged by her friend James Baldwin and Judy Feiffer to write her
autobiography *I Know Why the Caged Bird Sings*, which gained her international
recognition after it was published in 1969. As Gillespie states, "if 1968 was a year
of great pain, loss, and sadness, it was also the year when America first witnessed
the breadth and depth of Maya Angelou's spirit and creative genius" (Gillespie et
al. 98).

Meanwhile, in the 1960s in the U.S., the Feminist Movement was driven
by the economic and societal changes. At that time, women still suffered gender
discrimination in almost every aspect of social life. The goal of the Feminist
Movement was to dismantle the inequality in workplace and overthrow patriarchy.
The Civil Rights Movement also inspired the feminist leaders. Many black women
were devoted to the liberation of black women, although many of them had no
opportunity to play the leadership roles. In addition, the Black Arts Movement

played a key role in influencing the works of many African American writers. The Black Arts Movement

> described a set of attitudes, influential from 1965 to 1976, about African-American cultural
> production, which assumed that political activism was a primary responsibility of black
> artists. It also decreed that the only valid political end of black artists' efforts was liberation
> from white political and artistic power structure. (Nash 190)

Therefore, when Maya Angelou wrote *I Know Why the Caged Bird Sings*, she was deeply influenced by thoughts of the Civil Rights Movement, the Feminist Movement and the Black Arts Movement. In my opinion, the main reason why Angelou's friends tried to persuade her to write about her childhood was that "the predominant setting for the book—the oppressive Jim Crow South—represents the very bigotry that Angelou [and other African American activists were] fighting against during the Civil Rights Movement" (Sickels 23).

In her book, she narrated the impotence of the blacks under the segregation system in her hometown Stamps, Arkansas, the violence and intimidation that the blacks confronted, the difficult life of the black cotton workers, the discrimination from the whites, for example, from the white dentist and the white girls. As for the segregation, she stated that "in Stamps the segregation was so complete that most black children didn't really, absolutely know what whites looked like" (*CB* 20). By narrating her personal story, Angelou revealed the reality of black children's sufferings. For example, three-year-old Maya and her brother Bailey were sent back to her grandmother Mrs. Annie Henderson. At that time, they regarded themselves the most unlucky children. However, Angelou pointed out that thousands of black children had to confront similar situations. She wrote: "Years later I discovered that the United States had been crossed thousands of times by frightened Black children traveling alone to their newly affluent parents in Northern cities, or back to grandmothers in Southern towns when the urban North reneged on its economic promises" (*CB* 4). Knowing well the harsh life of cotton pickers, Angelou stated that "In later years I was to confront the stereotyped picture of gay song-singing cotten pickers with such inordinate rage that I was told even by fellow Blacks that my paranoia was embarrassing" (*CB* 7). Angelou revealed that the lynchings were part of the life of the black people in the 1930s. To avoid becoming the victim of lynchings, Angelou's uncle Willie was forced to hide himself although he didn't do any harm to anybody. Bailey witnessed the dead body of a victim of the lynching. Just as Braxton points out,

> *Caged Bird* admits harsh and painful aspects of the southern black experience before the civil rights era—the economic oppression and racial violence that Thompson and Hurston either knew little about or chose to ignore. This awareness lends Angelou's lyric imagery the knife-sharp edge of realism, something contributed to black female autobiographical tradition through the Richard Wright school of the 1940s and 1950s. (Braxton 192)

Besides, in the book, inspired by the Feminist Movement, Angelou also showed great concern about the situation of black women. She wrote: "If growing up is painful for the southern black girl, being aware of her displacement is the rust on the razor that threatens the throat" (*CB* 3). When she was 16, encouraged by her mother, she succeeded in obtaining the job as the first Negro driver on the San Francisco streetcars.

In short, in *I Know Why the Caged Bird*, Angelou adopted the method of realism to reveal the grim reality of the black community in the South of the United States in the 1930s, describing the miserable life of the blacks and denouncing the cruelty of the Jim Crow system. Meanwhile, she tried to enhance the blacks' national pride, encouraging black women to be aware of the importance of self-independence, calling on them to fight for their equality and dignity.

Besides, in *I Know Why the Caged Bird*, there is not only description of realism, but also the blending of fact and fiction, and the imaginative and poetic depiction of the surroundings and her feelings.

For example, in the chapter on Dentist Lincoln's refusal to treat Maya's toothache, Angelou blended the fact with fiction. Mrs. Henderson brought little Maya to see the white dentist Lincoln and she was sure that the dentist would help her grandchild, because she had lent him money to keep his building. But to her anger, she was refused by the dentist just because Maya was a black girl. There are two versions about Momma's response to Lincoln's discrimination against black people. The first imaginative version is created by Maya, in which her Momma was brave, powerful, proud and behaved like a queen. She was "ten feet tall with eight-foot arms" (*CB* 162). As Angelou put it, "Momma walked in that room as if she owned it. She shoved that silly nurse aside with one hand and strode into the dentist's office…Her eyes were blazing like live coals and her arms had doubled themselves in length" (*CB* 161). She ordered the dentist to leave Stamps by sundown and forbade him to practice dentistry. This version is just an imaginative story created by Maya, which shows the little girl's rebellious spirit. However, the real version is that Mrs. Henderson just demanded the dentist to compensate her ten dollars as the interest of the money that she had lent to him in the past. This is typical of Mrs. Henderson's subtle resistance to the whites' discrimination against black people.

Besides, the use of dialogue is one of Angelou's stylistic features in her serial autobiographies. In *I Know Why the Caged Bird Sings*, direct dialogues are frequently used to describe the distinctive language used by the main characters. For example, in the same chapter related to Maya's treatment of her toothache, there are some dialogues between Maya's Momma and the white dentist. Momma said: "I wouldn't press on you like this for myself but I can't take No. Not for my grandbaby…" (*CB* 160), Dentist Lincoln said: "Annie, my policy is I'd rather stick my hand in a dog's mouth than in a nigger's" (*CB* 160). From the vivid description of the dialogue, readers will be deeply impressed by the white dentist's ungratefulness and his deep-rooted discrimination against black people. Another example is the renaming of Margaret by the white woman Mrs. Cullinan. "You mean Margaret, ma'am. Her name's Margaret" (*CB* 91). "That's too long. She's Mary from now on" (*CB* 91). This episode shows that the white people didn't treat the black people as human beings who should also be respected. They called the blacks whatever they liked, such as "niggers, jigs, dinges, blackbirds, crows, boots and spooks" (*CB* 91).

In the autobiography, Angelou also employed other writing techniques such as the use of metaphor, the comic irony and self-parody. Angelou's skillful use of comic irony and self-parody helps her achieve a sense of universality in her autobiographical writings. For example, in *I Know Why the Caged Bird Sings*, Angelou employed the device of self-parody to narrate Maya's embarrassment on the Easter Day when she forgot the lines of the poem and told of Uncle Wilie's hiding in an empty bin for fear of becoming the victim of lynchings in an ironic way.

5.2 Unreliability and Dual Readership in *Dust Tracks on a Road*

Unreliable narration in autobiography is an important issue in the study of autobiography. Wayne C. Booth proposes the concept of unreliable narration in his

The Rhetoric of Fiction, "for lack of better terms, I have called a narrator reliable when he speaks for or acts in accordance with the norms of the work (which is to say, the implied author's norms), unreliable when he does not" (158-59). His definition aroused heated discussion among many western narratologists such as James Phelan, Shlomith Rimmon-Kenan, Susan S. Lanster, among whom Phelan and Martin also gave their definition of unreliable narration. In the dissertation of Xu Dejin, he defines unreliability in autobiography based on Phelan and Martin's definition of reliability in the following way:

> A Homodiegetic narrator is "unreliable" in autobiography when she/he offers an account of some event, person, thought, feeling, fact or any other object that either deviates from the textual norm (textual logic) leading to internal contradiction (hence unreliable in the textual world), or is not in accordance with what it refers to in the extratextual world (hence unreliable when measured against the "real" world). (Xu Dejin 26)

Xu Dejin analyzes the difference of unreliability between fiction and autobiography and draws the conclusion that there exist three types of unreliability in autobiography—"(1) the textual unreliability that corresponds to the one in fiction; (2) the extratextual unreliability that is exclusive to nonfictional autobiography proper; and (3) intertextual unreliability that is inferred from the inconsistencies between two autobiographies by the same autobiographer about the same period of life" (Xu Dejin 27).

Liu Jiang furthers the study on unreliability of autobiography based on the study of Xu Dejin. He classifies unreliability of autobiography into two types: unconscious unreliable narration and conscious unreliable narration, the latter of which is composed of three types of narration: (1) extratextual referent unreliable narration which is caused by the wrong or distorted description of facts; (2) anti-the-genre-of autobiography unreliable narration by using the rhetoric narration of fiction; (3) intertexual unreliable narration.

I will illustrate unreliable narration in *Dust Tracks on a Road* based on Liu Jiang's analysis. According to Hurston's biographer Robert Hemenway, *Dust Tracks on a Road* "presents an image of its author that fails to conform with either her public career or her private experience" (ix). The text is full of paradoxes and inconsistencies. In this autobiography, the unreliability mainly lies in its extratextual referent unreliable narration.

Firstly, in *Dust Tracks on a Road*, Hurston deliberately avoided descriptions about her private life, including her birth date and her marriage life. Her birth date is always an issue that arouses readers' interest. It is beyond readers' expectation that she refused to reveal her birth date even in her autobiography. All her life, Hurston seemed to be trying hard to disguise her true birth date, mentioning variously the year of 1898, 1899, 1900, 1901, 1902 and 1903 on public documents (Hemenway, "Introduction" xi). It remained an enigma until Professor Cheryl Wall of Rutgers University proved that she was born on January 7, 1891 according to the study of 1900 census records for Eatonville, Florida (Hemenway, "Introduction" xi). Although Hurston avoided the issue of her birth date in *Dust Tracks on a Road*, she tried to impress the readers that she was only a teenager when she enrolled in the high school of Baltimore's Morgan Academy in 1917. When she entered Barnard College, she still appeared to be "a young, untried coed, an illusion *Dust Tracks* tries hard to maintain" (Hemenway, "Introduction" xii).

Readers expect to know the feelings and marriage in a woman's autobiography, but in this sense Hurston's autobiography will disappoint its readers, because she didn't write in detail about her love, and even forgot to mention the name of her first husband, as if the marriage didn't mean much to her. As for her second marriage, she didn't even mention it at all. As Elizabeth Fox-Genovese argues, "Hurston's autobiography singularly lacks any convincing picture of her own feelings" ("My Statue, My Self: Autobiographical Writing of Afro-American Women" 78-79). In the chapter "Love," which is more like an essay, she portrayed her experience of feelings in an amusing tone. She wrote, "love is a funny thing; love is a blossom. If you want your finger bit, poke it at a possum" (*DT* 265). She warned the readers to "pay no attention to what I say about love, for as I said before, it may not mean a thing. It is my own bathtub singing. ...So pay my few scattering remarks no mind as to love in general. I know only my part" (*DT* 265).

Hurston's unreliable narration also occurs when she wrote about racial problems. According to Hemenway, "*Dust Tracks* sacrifices truth to the politics of racial harmony" ("Introduction" xiii). When she talked about the life in Barnard, she stated that "I have no lurid tales to tell of race discrimination at Barnard" (*DT* 169). "The Social Register crowd at Barnard soon took me up, and I became Barnard's sacred black cow" (*DT* 169). Hurston tried to convey that she didn't suffer racial discrimination at Barnard. But according to her biographer Hemenway, the condition was far more complicated. "Her private letters show

that she was ordered not to attend the Barnard Prom held at the Ritz Hotel…
We also know that Hurston's classmates mocked her French pronunciation and
laughed at her recitations." (Hemenway, "Introduction" xiii)

Unreliable intertexual narration also abounds in the text of *Dust Tracks on
a Road*. Her relatively conservative political attitude is not in accordance with
her radical bombardment towards the western imperialism in Asia. Hurston's
ambiguous attitude towards racial problems has aroused controversial discussion.
Her ambivalent statement about racial problems irritated the black readers. "So
Race Pride and Race Consciousness seem to me to be not only fallacious, but
a thing to be abhorred. It is the root of misunderstanding and hence misery and
injustice" (*DT* 326). "So Racial Solidarity is a fiction and always will be" (*DT*
329).

To conclude, readers find it frustrating to understand the real intention of the
author. As a matter of fact, the conscious unreliable narration is just a narrative
strategy that Hurston deliberately adopts to confront the complicated outside
world around her.

I will discuss the dual readership in *Dust Tracks on a Road* in the following
part. When discussing the narratology of autobiography, Xu Dejin analyzes the
relationship between the reader and the author in autobiography as opposed to
fiction. He classifies readers of autobiography into "unaware audience/reader" and
"aware audience/reader" (to appropriate Angelou's term). He argues that in the
narratology of autobiography, the narrator plays the double roles of the implied
author and narrator. As a result, the "authorial audience"—the "hypothetical
ideal audience for whom the author designs the work" (Phelan 140) and the
"narrative audience"—the "imaginary audience for which the narrator is writing"
(Rabinowitz 127) converge into one, what he calls "unaware audience/reader"
(Xu 22). According to Xu, the "unaware audience" in autobiography "believes
the story of a given autobiography to be in keeping with the 'real' world and
is unaware of the discrepancies between the textual story and the real personal
experiences referred to" (Xu 22), whereas the "aware audience/reader" is
competent enough to compare the textual world with the extratextual world" (Xu
22).

I will use Xu's concept of "unaware audience" to illustrate the relationship
between the author and the reader in *Dust Tracks on a Road*, where the author
writes for two different groups of readers and tries to mediate a dual readership—
both the white bourgeois readers and the highly-educated black readers.

"Presumably she [Hurston] expected to be read by New York intellectuals, black and white. And, presumably, she was not about to trust them with her private self" (Fox-Genovese, "My Statue, My Self: Autobiographical Writing of Afro-American Women" 194). It is just because of the complicated dual readership that Hurston's autobiography is full of ambiguous and contradictory ideas and ambivalent attitudes towards racial problems and other political issues. That is the very reason why the autobiography is lacking in direct self-disclosure.

By 1942, as "the most prolific black woman writer in America," Hurston had published three novels and two books of folklore, which had won her great commercial success. When talking with her publisher Bertram Lippincott about her plan for a new book in 1941, she was advised to write an autobiography. She objected but Lippincott "proposed that it be the first volume of a multivolume work" (Hemenway, *A Literary Biography* 275). Although she admitted that "I did not want to write it at all, because it is too hard to reveal one's inner self," she accepted the proposal reluctantly. Considering Hurston's personality, it is hard to believe that she would be manipulated by her publisher about the development of her writing career. However, Hurston was put in a dilemma which most of the black writers in the 1930s and 1940s had to confront—they had no economic security and had to depend on patronage from the whites. As Hemenway argues, "her [Hurston's] struggle for survival as a writer represents the struggle of a whole generation of pre-1960s black artists. Her autobiography illustrates the special kinds of pressures faced by black writers of the 1930s and 1940s" (Hemenway, "Introduction" xv).

Hurston, as a southern black woman, had to confront more complicated conditions because there were both racial and sexual pressures. When writing the book, she was keenly aware of the importance of her targeted readers—most of whom were her white patrons such as Mrs. R. Osgood Mason, Katherine Merson, Fanny Hurst and Carl Van Vechten. Meanwhile, she knew that her autobiography would surely attract the attention of the Afro-American intelligentsia such as Du Bois, Alain Locke, Richard Right and Ralph Ellison. Although Hurston was a New Negro of the Harlem Renaissance, she "resisted situating herself within the boundaries set out by Locke and Du Bois" (Rembold 42). Locke advocated the concept of "art for art's sake," while Du Bois advocated "art as propaganda" (Rembold 41). "Hurston's knowledge of black folklore and idiom had taught her that popular culture did not need to be interpreted into a 'higher' art form that adopted Western culture's standards" (Rembold 42). So, when writing the autobiography, she must have been trying to "mediate a mainstream white readership with a readership from the Afro-American intelligentsia" (Rembold 43). After her autobiography was published, it turned out to be a commercial success and won the Anisfield-Wolf Award for its contribution to relieving race relationships. Though warmly welcomed by the white audience, the autobiography was severely criticized by the black readers as pandering to a white mainstream readership (Rembold 42).

At the beginning of the text, Hurston bore in her mind a white reader who has no knowledge about black culture. She often used the pronoun "you" to show her awareness of the reader in her mind, "so you have to know something about the time and place where I came from, in order that you may interpret the incidents and directions of my life" (*DT* 3). "Eatonville is what you might call hitting a straight lick with a crooked stick" (*DT* 3). When telling the story, she gave patient explanations to the white reader about the way Negro speaks. When she asked for a black saddle horse, her father flew into a rage and said: "Lemme tell you something right now, my young lady; you ain't white" (*DT* 38). Then "you ain't white" is explained as "a Negro saying that means 'Don't be too ambitious. You are a Negro and they are not meant to have but so much'" (*DT* 39).

Bearing the white readers in her mind, knowing what the readers are interested in, she attached much importance to the introduction about black culture in Eatonville and her experience in collecting black folklores in different places.

When writing about her experience in Barnard, she didn't record any discrimination she suffered. What she remembered was the help from the whites.

When talking about friendship, she showed her gratefulness to Fannie Hurst and Ethel Waters and she said "both of them meant a great deal to me in friendship and inward experience" (*DT* 238). In the excised appendix, she showed her gratitude to many people, including her Godmother Mrs. R. Osgood Mason, Carl Van Vechten, and so on.

Throughout the autobiography, Hurston addresses not only the white bourgeois readers, but also the black intelligentsia, trying to mediate between the two groups of readers. In his dissertation, Robert Rembold makes a comparison between *Dust Tracks on a Road* (1942) and Hurston's manuscripts, and points out that the text is "a site mediating between the voices of the writer, the editor and two readerships" (Rembold 78). Hurston's discussions about democracy, justice, race construction and the impact of Jim Crowism are all addressed to both white and black readers.

For example, in the chapter "My People, My People" in Appendix, she is addressing both the black and white readers, her statements full of inconsistencies and contradictions. She wrote:

> Last but not least, My People love a show. We love to act more than we love to see acting done. We love to look at them and we love to put them on, and we love audiences when we get to specifying. That's why some of us take advantage of trains and other public places like dance halls and picnics. We just love to dramatize. (*DT* 304).
>
> Now you've been told, so you ought to know. But maybe, after all the Negro doesn't really exist. What we think is a race is detached moods and phases of other people walking around. What we have been talking about might not exist at all…God made everybody else's color. We took ours by mistake. The way the old folks tell it, it was like this, you see. (*DT* 304).

In the first paragraph, she tells the white readers about the Negroes' passion for dramatizing, feeling proud of her people's ability in art. Black readers themselves will not deny the fact. In the second paragraph, she seems to be addressing both white and black readers, attempting to deconstruct people's stereotyped concept of race.

According to Hemenway, "throughout the book a tension exists between the need to further racial equality, a fear of alienating the white audience, and the drive to celebrate Afro-American esthetic practice" ("Introduction" xv).

5.3 Narrative Perspective in *I Know Why the Caged Bird Sings*

Narrative perspective is an important issue in fictional narrative studies. Many critics such as Gerard Genette and Seymour Chatman have discussed it on the discourse level and on the story level respectively, while Shen Dan points out the dual role of narrative perspective on both levels of story and discourse. (Xu Dejin 101). According to Xu Dejin, narrative perspective is also an important strategy of self-representation in autobiography. (Xu 101) I will make an analysis of Angelou's dexterous manipulation of two viewpoints: from the angle of vision of "the narrating self (i.e., the narrator's retrospective point of view)" and from the viewpoint of "the experiencing self (i.e., the character I's point of view when experiencing the events in the past)" (Xu 103). While being interviewed by Claudia Tate, Angelou talked about the importance of preserving the distance of the experiencing self and the narrating self:

> While writing, I have to be apart from the story so that I don't fall into indulgence. Whenever I speak about the books, I always think in terms of the Maya character. When I wrote the teleplay of *I Know Why the Caged Bird Sings*, I would refer to the Maya character so as not to mean me. It's damned difficult for me to preserve this distancing. But it's very necessary. (Tate 3)

To keep the distance between the experiencing self and the narrating self, the autobiographer uses different strategies such as shifting from the past tense to the present tense, using some signaling words such as "I don't know" (*CB* 128), "I don't remember" (*CB* 4), "I don't think" (*CB* 78, 98), using words signaling time such as "Years later" (*CB* 4), "It didn't occur to me for many years" (*CB* 78).

In the prefatory opening chapter, the story is first narrated by young Maya, the experiencing self, revealing the feelings of displacement as a southern black girl in the 1930s. In Easter Sunday's recital, standing before "the children's section of the Colored Methodist Episcopal Church" (*CB* 1), young Maya forgot the lines of the poem, because she was thinking about the dress she was wearing, which was something more important to her. She had expected that the dress would turn her into "one of the sweet little white girls" (*CB* 1), but she was so disappointed about it that she failed to remember the lines of the poem: " 'What you looking at me for? / I didn't come to stay […]' " (*CB* 1). She experienced such bitter disillusion and such an embarrassing occasion that she fled the church, running, urinating and crying. At the end of the chapter, the narrating self gives her retrospective point of view, showing that young Maya is a symbolic representative of the black girls growing up in the South of America. The present tense is used here to indicate that the narrating self is reflecting on the experience of young Maya and makes the general commentary that "if growing up is painful for the southern black girl, being aware of her displacement is the rust on the razor that threatens the throat. It is an unnecessary insult" (*CB* 3). According to Xu Dejin, the present tense commentary here serves as "a cue for readers to take to help them get a fuller understanding of the meaning of subsequent personal stories related" (Xu 180), revealing that "awareness on the part of both the narrator and protagonist here thus becomes an essential means of survival in the life of a Southern black girl" (Xu 181). Readers will predict the displacement and the pain that young Maya would confront during the process of growing up and how she managed to survive as an independent girl. Just as Angelou points out, "all my work, my life, everything is about survival. All my work is meant to say, 'You may encounter many defeats, but you must not be defeated.' " (Tate 7). At the end of the autobiography, fully aware of the oppression that black girls suffered, the adult narrator again makes the conclusion that "the black female is assaulted in her tender years by all those common forces of nature at the same time that she is caught in tripartite crossfire of masculine prejudice, white illogical hate and Black lack of power" (*CB* 231). The narrating self also points out the gender prejudice that black women suffered and the necessity of changing the attitude towards them: "The fact that the adult American Negro female emerges a formidable character is often met with amazement, distaste and even belligerence. It is seldom accepted as an inevitable outcome of the struggle won by survivors and deserves respect if not enthusiastic acceptance" (*CB* 231).

In this autobiography, the past tense is predominantly used to narrate the story of young Maya, but the present tense is used to keep the distance between the experiencing self and the narrating self so that the story of young Maya is more convincing and is able to achieve universal meaning.

The autobiographer also uses some words related to time to keep the distance between the experiencing self and the narrating self. When telling about the experience of being sent back to her grandmother at the age of three because of her parents' divorce, young Maya impressed upon readers her trauma caused by her parents' abandonment. At that time, young Maya and her brother Bailey regarded themselves as the most unlucky children. However, "*Years later* I discovered that the United States had been crossed thousands of times by frightened black children traveling alone to their newly affluent parents in northern cities, or back to grandmothers in southern towns when the urban North reneged on its economic promises" (*CB* 4, emphasis mine). Therefore, according to adult Angelou, the narrating self, thousands of black children shared similar painful experiences. Young Maya and Bailey were only two of them.

Mrs. Flowers, who threw young Maya her first life line, was one of the black women she admired. When Mrs. Henderson had a conversation with Mrs. Flowers, young Maya felt ashamed of her grandmother's poor pronunciation and "ignorance." But adult Angelou, the narrating self, who had now fully realized the importance of sisterhood among black women, gave the retrospective narration: "*It didn't occur to me for many years* that they were as alike as sisters, separated only by formal education" (*CB* 78, emphasis mine).

Some critics classify Angelou's *I Know Why the Caged Bird Sings* as autobiographical fiction because she challenged the writing of autobiography as that of literature. While writing, she deliberately adopted some fiction-writing techniques such as arranging plot, setting, dialogue to achieve the effect she expected. Maya Angelou's skillful manipulation of the two narrative perspectives also serves as one of the strategies to achieve the goal. When keeping the distance from the narrating self, the experiencing self narrates her stories as if she were the protagonist in the novel. Readers are deeply attracted by the stories of the young southern girl and will be only interrupted by the occasional retrospective analysis of the narrating self, which interacts with the experiences of young Maya, reinforcing each other and effectively revealing the thematic concerns of the autobiographer.

5.4 The Quest for Black Oral Traditions

Employing techniques of oral tradition is typical of African-American literature, not only in poetry, short fiction and novels, but also in the writing of autobiographies, because "oral tradition offers continuity of voice as well as its liberation" (Jones 179). As Gayl Jones puts it, "the voices of the less powerful group, 'the other,' always must free themselves from the frame of the more powerful group, in texts of self-discovery, authority, and wholeness" (192). As a result, the African-American writers find their own means to articulate their unique voices and to define themselves by breaking away from the Western literary tradition and resorting to the forms of oral tradition. Gayl Jones points out that

> the relationship of the African-American writer to this oral tradition makes his writing a vital part of world literary history, in which writers mine the rich veins of their oral heritages as they move from imitation to creation, from presentation to invention, and from being destroyers of old forms to creators of new ones. Oral traditions provide the terrain through which many writers have searched and wandered until they have been surprised by the blooming orchid, then called out in their own clear voices, as Zora Neale Hurston's Janie might call out, for others to come and see. (Jones 190)

Gayl Jones' book, *Liberating Voices*: *Oral Tradition in African American Literature*, illustrates the oral techniques embodied in African-American literature, including poetry, short fiction and novels, for example, the use of dialect in Hurston's *Their Eyes Were Watching God*, blues and jazz structures in Anne Petry's "Solo on the Drums," folk speech in Sterling Brown's "Uncle Joe." Genevieve Fabre also points out the significance of black oral tradition, believing that the literary "vernacular" form of black autobiography "can help define Afro-American cultural uniqueness and difference, define the claims and commitments, the new premises which have to be distinct from the ones set by the mainstream literary establishment" (Fabre 102).

In the following part, I will illustrate the use of oral techniques in Hurston's *Dust Tracks on the Road*, Angelou's *I Know Why the Caged Bird Sings*, and Cary's *Black Ice*.

5.4.1 Signifying in *Dust Tracks on a Road* as a Speakerly Text

5.4.1.1 The Trope of Signifying in *Dust Tracks on a Road*

Dust Tracks on a Road succeeds in obtaining the recognition of the white readers owing to its contribution to improvement of race relations. However, as is known to us, it was severely criticized by the black critics because of its evasions of the racial problems. Harald Preece even regards the book as "the tragedy of a gifted, sensitive mind, eaten up by an egocentrism fed on the patronizing admiration of the dominant white world" (qtd. in Hemenway, *Zora Neale Hurston—A Literary Biography* 289). The black critics give the book such negative criticism because they don't understand Hurston's cultural view, and they "have failed to apprehend the politics of its author's identification with southern black culture and the linguistic strategies by which black women writers have affirmed their literary autonomy even at the expense of literal authenticity" (Andrews, "African-American Autobiography Criticism: Retrospect and Prospect" 209). They have misunderstood her because they haven't realized that Hurston is employing the Afro-American trope of signifying in her autobiography. I agree with Claudine Raynaud's augument that "as Hurston is 'lying,' is telling stories about herself, she can be seen as 'signifying' upon an autobiographical practice whose truth discourse she is forced to parody, or at least allude to" (128). In Angelou's *I Know Why the Caged Bird Sings*, she writes about her grandmother's caution, which involves the use of the trope of signifyin(g) in the black people's daily life:

> We have a saying among Black Americans which describes Momma's caution. "If you ask a Negro where he's been, he'll tell you where he's going." To understand this important information, it is necessary to know who uses this tactic and on whom it works. If an unaware person is told a part of the truth…he is satisfied that his query has been answered. If an aware person… is given an answer which is truthful but bears only slightly if at all on the question, he knows that the information he seeks is of a private nature and will not be handed to him willingly. Thus direct denial, lying and the revelation of personal affairs are avoided. (*CB* 164-65)

In black folklores, there is a story about the Monkey, the Lion and the Elephant, who are friends as well as enemies. The Monkey is the weakest among them, but he is clever enough to deal with the subtle relationship among them. The trickster Monkey gave some information about the Elephant to the Lion, which was taken literally by the Lion. As a result, the Lion was fooled by both the Monkey and the Elephant. The Monkey employs the strategy of what Gates defines as "Signifyin(g)," the most crucial rhetoric strategy of African-American vernacular tradition. Thus the Monkey is named "the Signifying Monkey," which "is the figure of a black rhetoric in the Afro-American speech community" (Gates 53). Henry Louis Gates defines "signifyin(g)" as "the black trope of tropes, the figure for black rhetorical figures" (Gates 51). Gates cited Roger D. Abrahams' definition of the word "Signifyin(g)":

> Signifying seems to be a Negro term, in use if not in origin. It can mean any of a number of things; in the case of the toast about the signifying monkey, it certainly refers to the trickster's ability to talk with great innuendo, to carp, cajole, needle, and lie…Also it can denote speaking with the hands and eyes, and this respect encompasses a whole complex of expressions and gestures. (Gates 54)

According to Abrahams,

> signifyin(g) is a "techinique of indirect argument or persuasion," "a language of implication," "to imply, goad, beg, boast, by indirect verbal or gestural means." … The Monkey, in short, is not only a master of technique…he is technique, or style…he is the great Signifier. In this

sense, one does not signify something; rather, one signifies in some way. (Gates 54)

According to Gates, signifyin(g) "means in black discourse modes of figuration themselves" (Gates 52). He points out that "the black rhetorical tropes, subsumed under Signifyin(g), would include marking, loud-talking, testifying, calling out (of one's name), sounding, rapping, playing the dozens, and so on" (Gates 52).

As a folklorist, Hurston knows well the strategy of signifyin(g). When writing *Dust Tracks on a Road*, when confronting her subtle relationship with the white audience, it is not surprising that she would employ the strategy to play with her white audience. According to Fox-Genovese, "there is nothing in *Dust Tracks* to suggest that Hurston trusted her readers. She never precisely identifies them, although she cultivates an arresting mixture of the urbane intellectual and the *enfant terrible*" ("My Statue, My Self: Autobiographical Writing of Afro-American Women" 194). In *Mules and Men*, she proposes a strategy to deal with the relationship between the white reader and the black writer:

> The theory behind our tactics: "The white man is always trying to know into somebody else's business. All right, I'll see something outside the door of my mind for him to play with and handle. He can read my writing but he sho' can't read my mind. I'll put this play toy in his hand, and he will seize it and go away. Then, I'll say my say and sing my song." (qtd. in Raynaud 114-15)

In *Dust Tracks on a Road*, Hurston introduces to her white readers some materials to read, but at the same time, the audience is left something to play with. What she offers to the audience is just "a coded system of signs, arbitrary in reference" (Gates, *Figures in Black Words, Signs, and the "Racial" Self* 123), which is full of implications, full of "burdensome ironies" (123). Her autobiographical text is a discourse of figuration rather than a discourse of information (Raynaud 128). "In attempting to cope with the powerlessness and vulnerability of the racial self, blacks have employed language strategies, particularly artifice and concealment, in their relationships with white America" (McKay, "The Narrative Self: Race, Politics, and Culture in Black American Women's Autobiography" 181). "Signifyin(g)" is one of the strategies employed by Hurston to deal with her complicated and subtle relationships with her publisher, the white and black audience. On the one hand, she writes about the life of blacks in Eatonville, the life when she collected the black folklores and the richness of black culture; on the other hand, she bears in mind the expectations of her readers and the editorial demands. She gives the white readers explanations and interpretations, but there is still something whose implied meaning is beyond the white readers' reach (Raynaud 128). "In a way, Hurston casts the white reader in the role of the Lion" (Raynaud 128), while she assumes the role of the "signifyin(g)" Monkey. As Raynaud puts it, "Hurston's obliqueness, her obvious omissions, her ability to 'lie,' find in 'signifying' a model, a justification, a culturally viable practice as well as a way out of the pressure imposed by her editor and of the demands of the autobiographical mode" (Raynaud 128).

Behind the hide-and-seek game, what Hurston really wants to express is the richness, strength, diversity and vitality of black culture by describing it around the Caribbean and the areas of the South. Believing that black culture is "a complex communication code that could protest subjection without being overt," and that "popular culture did not need to be interpreted into a 'higher' art form that adopted western culture's stands" (Rembold 42), she resorts to the strategy of "signifying" to disguise the truth: her passionate love for black culture and her devotion to the celebration of the richness and strength of Afro-American esthetic practice.

5.4.1.2 *Dust Tracks on a Road* as a Speakerly Text

Many critics criticize Hurston's *Dust Tracks on a Road* for her negligence of racial problems. In fact, as an anthropologist and folklorist, she cherishes a passionate love for the culture of her race, never forgetting to take on the responsibility of representing the richness and diversity of black culture and the real blackness of the black community not only in her novels such as *Their Eyes Were Watching God*, but also in her autobiography *Dust Tracks on a Road*. To achieve this goal, Hurston makes full use of black oral tradition and employs her unique rhetorical strategy to write her works as speakerly texts. In *The Signifying Monkey—A Theory of Afro-American Literary Criticism*, Gates makes a detailed analysis of Hurston's novel *Their Eyes Were Watching God*, viewing it as the first example in the tradition of "the speakerly text."

According to Gates, by the speakerly text, he means "a text whose rhetorical strategy is designed to represent an oral literary tradition, designed 'to emulate the phonetic, grammatical, and lexical patterns of actual speech and produce the illusion of oral narration" (Gates, *The Signifying Monkey* 181). In the speakerly text, "all other structural elements seemed to be devalued…because the narrative strategy signals attention to its own importance, an importance which would seem to be the privileging of oral speech and its inherent linguistic features" (181). It seems to be "imitating one of the numerous forms of oral narration to be found in classical Afro-American vernacular literature" (181). Gates argues that the use of direct speech—the voice of the black oral tradition, and the use of free indirect discourse—"the rhetorical analogue to the text's metaphors of inside and outside," are two important narrative strategies in Hurston's *Their Eyes Were Watching God*. Both elements are essential to the representation of the protagonist's quest for becoming a speaking black subject.

In my opinion, Hurston's *Dust Tracks on a Road* can also be considered as a spearkerly text, in which Hurston depicts the heritage of black oral tradition by using the same rhetoric strategies, turning herself into a speaking black subject, speaking not only for her personal self, but also for the racial self. As Gates puts it,

> the narrative voice Hurston created, and her legacy to Afro-American fiction [including her autobiography], is a lyrical and disembodied yet individual voice, from which emerged a singular longing and utterance, a transcendent, ultimately racial self, extending far beyond the merely individual (Gates 183).

According to Gates, Hurston's detailed depiction of her mother's death is symbolic in meaning, revealing the "notion of the articulating subject" (Gates 183). Hurston remembered the scene when her mother was dying. "Her mouth was slightly open, but her breathing took up so much of her strength that she could not talk. But she looked at me, or so I felt, to speak for her. She depended on me for a voice" (*DT* 86-87). In the autobiography, Hurston, as the speaking subject, takes on the responsibility of uttering her mother's voice.

Firstly, Hurston uses direct speech to represent the voice of black oral tradition. In the first several chapters depicting her childhood spent in the all-black Eatonville, for example, she uses direct speech to describe the plot related to the Christmas present.

> —"I want a fine black riding horse with white leather saddle and bridles," I told Papa happily.
>
> —"You, what?" Papa gasped. "What was dat you said?"
>
> — "I said, I want a black saddle horse with…"
>
> — "A saddle horse!" Papa exploded. "It's a sin and a shame! Lemme tell you something right now, my young lady; you ain't white. Riding horse! Always trying to wear de big hat! I

don't know how you got in his family nohow. You ain't like none of de rest of my young'uns."
—"If I can't have no riding horse, I don't want nothing at all," I said stubbornly with my mouth, but inside I was sucking sorrow. My longed-for journey looked impossible. (*DT* 38-39)

Through the use of direct speech, Hurston represents the voice of black vernacular tradition. The dialogue between Hurston and her father shows that the history of slavery has exerted an everlasting traumatic influence on the blacks, while Hurston, growing up in the first incorporated all-back town in America, with no memory of the past and no burden of the painful history, fully enjoyed the richness of black culture and the freedom encouraged by her mother. When Hurston was criticized by her father, she shifted to direct speech, showing her mother's positive influence on her disposition, "Zora is my young' un, and Sarah is yours. I'll be bound mine will come out more than conquer. You leave her alone. I'll tend to her when I figger she needs it" (*DT* 21). Considering her mother's way of educating children, readers will not be surprised that the black girl would cherish such an incredible dream of riding a black horse with a white leather saddle and bridles.

Meanwhile, Hurston employs the free indirect discourse to "remove the distinction between repeated speech and represented events" (Gates 208). For Hurston, "free indirect discourse attempts to represent 'consciousness without the apparent intrusion of a narrative voice,' thereby 'presenting the illusion of a character's action out of his [or her] mental state in an immediate relationship with the reader' " (Gates 209). Claudine Raynaud points out, "the advantage of this technique is to bring the reader back to the moment of enunciation and, thus, to restore the immediacy of the utterance, while the controlling presence of the narrator is still felt in the verb tenses and the pronouns" (Raynaud 118).

In the autobiography, Hurston uses free indirect discourse to utter the voice for her self, her mother and the whole black community. For example, when talking about her parents' different attitudes towards the education of the children, Hurston shifts to free indirect speech:

We had a big barn, and a stretch of ground well covered with Bermuda grass...Mama contended that we had plenty of space to play in...*If she had her way, she meant to raise her children to stay at home.* She said that there was no need for us to live like no-count Negroes and poor-white trash—too poor to sit in the house—had to come outdoors for any pleasure, or hang around somebody else's house. *Any of her children who had any tendencies like that must have got it from the Hurston side. It certainly did not come from the Potts.* Things like that gave me my first glimmering of the universal female gospel that all good traits and leanings come from the mother's side.

Mama exhorted her children at every opportunity to "jump at de sun." *We might not land on the sun, but at least we would get off the ground.* Papa did not feel so hopeful…My mother was always standing between us. She contends that I was imprudent and given to talking back, but she didn't want to "squinch my spirit" too much for fear that I would turn out to be a mealy-mouthed rag doll by the time I got grown. Papa always flew hot when Mama said that…He predicted dire things for me. *The white folks were not going to stand for it. I was going to be hung before I got grown. Somebody was going to blow me down for my sassy tongue. Mama was going to suck sorrow for not beating my temper out of me before it was too late. Posses with ropes and guns were going to drag me out sooner or later on account of that stiff neck I toted…* (*DT* 20-21, emphasis added).

In these two paragraphs, Hurston first uses words like "Mama contended that…" "she said that…" "He predicted…", then she abandons these introductory verbs and gradually and naturally shifts to free indirect speech (see the sentences emphasized). By employing free indirect discourse, Hurston firstly tries "to emulate the phonetic, grammatical, and lexical patterns of actual speech" of the black community (Gates 181), imitating the actual language used by the blacks in Eatonville such as Hurston's father and mother. Secondly, Hurston uses the strategy to represent "the power of village voice, the strength of popular sayings, the force of those generalizations which constitute the knowledge of the community" (Raynaud 117). For example, Hurston's mother's words convinced her of the universal female gospel that "all good traits and leanings come from the mother's side" (*DT* 20). Thirdly, the use of free indirect discourse seems to be representing the consciousness and the mental state of the people in the black community. Actually, Hurston serves as the speaker for her mother's voice that children should seize every opportunity to enjoy the freedom to "jump at de sun," which would exert a great influence on Hurston's future development, while her father's anxiety about her ambition and her arrogance represents the consciousness of many other members of the black community, which reveals the black community's trauma brought about by the history of slavery.

In conclusion, in her autobiography, Hurston uses both direct speech and free indirect discourse to emulate and represent the speaking voice of black oral tradition. The speakerly diction "aspires to resolve the tension between standard English and black vernacular" (Gates 215). Hurston writes the speakerly texts so that the "discourse rendered through direct, indirect, or free indirect means may partake of Hurston's 'word-pictures' and 'thought-pictures'," which are defined by Hurston as "the nature of Afro-American spoken language" (Gates 215). According to Gates,

> Hurston realized a resonant and authentic narrative voice that echoes and aspires to the status of the impersonality, anonymity, and the authority of the black vernacular tradition, a nameless, selfless tradition, at once collective and compelling, true somehow to the unwritten text of a common blackness. For Hurston, the search for a telling form of language, indeed the search for a black literary language itself, defines the search for the self. (Gates 183)

Hurston uses her rhetoric strategies in almost all her works: in her fiction, her autobiography as well as her books of folktales such as *Mules and Men* (1935).

5.4.2 The Blues Aesthetics in *I Know Why the Caged Bird Sings*

Of the elements of black oral tradition, the blues has a profound influence on Angelou's *I Know Why the Caged Bird Sings* both in form and content. The blues is a music form descending from the Negro spiritual. Houston A. Baker Jr. states that "with the birth of the blues, the vernacular realm of American culture acquired a music that had 'wide appeal because it expressed a toughness of spirit and resilience, a willingness to transcend difficulties…' " (Baker 11). According to Ralph Ellison,

> the blues is an impulse to keep the painful details and episodes of a brutal experience alive in one's aching consciousness, to finger its jagged grain, and to transcend it, not by the consolation of philosophy but by squeezing from it a near-tragic, near-comic lyricism. As a form, the blues is an autobiographical chronicle of personal catastrophe expressed lyrically. (qtd. in Barnwell 219)

For the blacks, the blues becomes a weapon to express their painful personal experiences intermingling with the disastrous fate of the whole black race in the white-dominated America. When discussing the importance of the blues for the blacks, Cherron A. Barnwell points out that

> its polyphonic rhythms, loud and brass timbres accent the history of black America's
> uprooting encounters and cultural ransacking. The whoops and hollers scream out the pain
> of being the nation's exploited laborers who have been denied the right to possess even the
> vestiges of ransacked ancestral cultures. (Barnwell 221)

Some critics have noticed the relationship between the blues and black autobiography. Elizabeth Schultz points out that "in its development, all black autobiography might be compared to the development of the blues" and that "black autobiography in general, however, like the blues, expands the solo; the voice of the single individual retains the tone of the tribe" (Schultz 82). In a sense, Maya Angelou is a blues artist as she lyrically narrates the story of young Maya, whose personal suffering and triumph represent the fate of the whole black race.

Right at the beginning of the prelude chapter, young Maya was trying to recite the poem in the blues: "What you looking at me for? /I didn't come to stay [...]/ "What you looking at me for? /I didn't come to stay [...]" Young Maya seemed to be inviting readers to sing the blues together. The forgotten line is whispered to her by the minister's wife, "I just come to tell you, it's Easter Day." If readers are familiar with the poem, they will naturally join the singing of the blues with young Maya. Invited by young Maya, readers will be attracted by her story, trying to find out the reason why she forgets the lines. Maya said: "I hadn't so much forgot as I couldn't bring myself to remember. Other things were more important" (*CB* 1). What is more important to her? The reason is that she was bitterly disappointed at her dress because the dress donated by the white failed to turn her into a sweet white girl. It can be inferred that young Maya is tortured by her severe self-hatred, and she is keenly aware of her displacement. However, despite the embarrassing and humiliating situation, young Maya managed to find out a way to relieve herself of the anxiety and pressure by running out of the church, peeing, crying and laughing. In a sense, she triumphs spiritually. "I laughed anyway, partially for the sweet release; still, the greater joy came out not only from being liberated from the silly church but from the knowledge that I wouldn't die for a busted head" (*CB* 3). To some degree, young Maya is singing a blues of transcendence full of pains and triumphs because Maya's blues "expressed a toughness of spirit and resilience, a willingness to transcend difficulties..." (Baker 11).

At the end of the opening, the adult Angelou made her general commentary: "If growing up is painful for the southern black girl, being aware of her displacement is the rust on the razor that threatens the throat" (*CB* 3). It implies that the displacement that young Maya experienced is typical of the experiences of all the black girls growing up in the 1930s in the South of America. Young Maya is a symbolic representative of the girls in the black community. The autobiography is just like a blues in which the voice of young Maya blends with that of the black community.

On the graduation day, young Maya and the proud graduating class of 1940 experienced complicated feelings, from joyful expectation of the graduation ceremony to the disillusion of their hopes and dreams, from emotional despair to spiritual triumph. The graduating students and their parents were originally full of joys and hopes for their future. However, the white man Donleavy delivered a spirit-killing speech, which threw the blacks into despair and anger. Directed by Little Henry Reed, one of the top students, all the black people sang their blues songs, which enhanced the national pride and unity. Henry Reed turned to the blacks and sang the blues, the Negro national anthem: "Lift ev'ry voice and sing/ Till earth and heaven ring/ Ring with the harmonies of Liberty" (*CB* 155). Then, all the blacks, including the mothers, fathers, teachers, small children, joined in the hymn of encouragement, "Stony the road we trod/ Bitter the chastening rod/ Felt in the days when hope, unborn, had died/ Yet with a steady beat/ Have not our weary feet/ Come to the place for which our fathers sighed?" (*CB* 155) For the first time, young Maya understood the meaning of the profoundly dignified blues voice, "we have come over a way that with tears / has been watered/ We have come, treading our path through/ the blood of the slaughtered" (*CB* 56). By singing the blues, the black people regained their strength and racial pride, "we were on top again. As always, again, We survived… I was a proud member of the wonderful, beautiful Negro race" (*CB* 156). According to Barnwell, the poems quoted above are in the form of primitive blues, which "reflects the social and cultural problems plaguing African American life" and at the same time "celebrate social transcendence rather than spiritual or religious transcendence" (229).

As a blues priestess herself, Angelou is keenly aware of the significance of blues artists for enhancing the national spirit for the black community. She wrote:

Oh, Black known and unknown poets, how often have your auctioned pains sustained us?
Who will compute the lonely nights made less lonely by your songs, or by the empty pots

made less tragic by your tales?

If we were a people much given to revealing secrets, we might raise monuments and

sacrifice to the memories of our poets. …We survive in exact relationship to the dedication

of our poets (include preachers, musicians and blues singers). (*CB* 156)

In fact, in all Angelou's serial autobiographies, she serves as a black poet/ blues priestess and employs blues aesthetic to "dramatize her life as stories about surviving displacement with pride and dignity" (Barnwell 231) and about struggles for self-fulfillment and self-assurance.

5.4.3 Storytelling Tradition as a Healing Therapy in *Black Ice*

Storytelling is one of the most important traditions for the black people, which has become an inseparable part of their life and merged into the soul of the black people. Susan Willis states that "the strongest influence on the development of black women's narratives derives from the storytelling tradition" (15). Susan Willis concludes that unlike the storytelling tradition in Europe, "everyone in the southern black community participates in storytelling and story listening," that "there is no separation between the teller and text" (Willis 15). Being regarded as "the others," the blacks "look to their own folklores and oral modes for forms, themes, tastes, conceptions of symmetry, time, space, detail and human values" so that they are likely to "liberate their voices from the often tyrannic frame of another's outlook" (Jones 192). Cary M. Kenyon considers the storytelling of the black community as a healing therapy when the black people are confronted with the hostile world. She argues that

storytelling (and storylistening) is not merely a method for solving particular problems that

crop up in our lives, but has an importance and integrity all its own, as a means to personal

wholeness. In this sense, it is a spiritual activity. Through it, we become more of who we

are—"more authentic and more alive" (Atkinson, 1995, 51)—and discover and celebrate our

personal, ordinary wisdom. (Kenyon and Randall 2)

In *Black Ice*, Cary also employs storytelling as a means to console herself when she was in helpless confusion, constant fear and alienation in St. Paul's. The tradition of storytelling becomes a weapon of struggling for her personal wholeness. As Gonzalez puts it:

> Lorene Cary's journey into social ethnic integration is parallel to her journey into the integration of her selves towards personal wholeness. And to that personal wholeness undoubtedly contributes the African-American tradition of storytelling passed down from her forebears, from what Gary Kenyon terms a "therapoetic perspective." (Gonzalez 131)

In *Black Ice*, two folk stories told by her great-grandfather permeate through the whole autobiography. In some sense, the storytelling is the clue to the organization of the book and the key to the understanding of Cary's exploration of crossing the racial divide. Whenever she felt lonely and alienated from the others, she would recall the two folk stories, one about the flying black woman stepping outside of her skin to wander in the woods at night, another about the little girl Izzy who jumped and fell down because of trusting her father's words. Although the meaning of the stories seemed to be changing with the passing of time, they always gave Cary comfort. Fifteen years later, she recalled the night when she used the stories to console herself. "I recalled my great-grandfather's stories that I had used for comfort that night when I'd sat out on the ice" (*BI* 236). At that time, the story of Izzy offered her the explanation of her puzzling condition and taught her the attitude towards the outside world. "I remembered Izzy and fashioned for myself the perfect pose. That was it. That was what I'd been trying to remember these months at St. Paul's School, the pose: I would be well-mannered, big-hearted, defiant, and because a pose cannot resist great intimacy… I would remain alone. I would trust no man" (*BI* 132). The stories meant a lot to her, because "without the stories, I'd have nothing to explain the cacophony in my head in the indigo New Hampshire night" (*BI* 236). She is keenly aware of the importance of the folk stories for her personal wholeness. "Nowhere else will I get the rhythm of these stories, the ghosts and their magic…Without the stories and the songs, I am mute" (*BI* 237). Fifteen years later, she had a new understanding of the heritage of the folk stories. "I didn't ask for stories, but I was given them to tell, to retell, and change and pass along…I was given them to plait into my story, to use, to give me the strength to take off my skin and stand naked and unafraid in the night, to touch other souls in the night" (*BI* 237). For Cary, storytelling is a healing therapy with which she knows how to get through the difficult condition as a black student in the white dominated world. As she became more experienced and gained keener insight into social life, she helped to enrich and give new meanings to the storytelling tradition.

Conclusion

In the previous chapters, the development and characteristics of both black male and female autobiographies are reviewed in detail. By focusing on the black women's autobiographies of Zora Neale Hurston, Maya Angelou and Lorene Cary, I try to examine how black women have created the unique tradition of black women's autobiographies by both inheriting and revising the tradition of black autobiography, what breakthroughs they have made for black women's autobiographical writing, and how they have enlarged the scope of black autobiography as a genre.

Black women resort to the instrument of autobiographical writing to define "the black female self in black terms from a black perspective" (Blackburn 147), trying to establish their identity under the pressure of "black male sexism, white female racism and white patriarchal authority" (McKay, 1998, 97). As a result, each black woman's autobiography is unique and personal, with a different perspective of herself, her community and the society, with different attitudes towards the past and the future. Some of them such as Angelou condemn slavery and racial discrimination fiercely, revealing the sufferings and the impotence of the black people; some of them express their pride in their blackness, focusing on the strength of their community; some of them such as Hurston avoid confronting the racial problems directly; and some others such as Lorene Cary focus on the negative effects of the past on the psychology of the blacks. Despite the uniqueness of different black women's autobiographies, they should not be treated only as personal stories about the life of some individual black women, because they share the common traits of black women's autobiographies, influencing and interacting with each other. All those individual and unique writings about their personal experiences derive "from the historical experience of being black and female in a specific society at a specific moment and over succeeding generations" (Fox-Genovese, "To Write My Self—The Autobiographies of Afro-American Women" 161). Therefore, they should be examined within the general framework and the specific context of both as black autobiography and black women's literature.

On the one hand, the black women autobiographers inherit the tradition of the black autobiography, emphasizing the exploration of themes such as its political consciousness—the violence and degradation suffered by the blacks, the racial problems, the importance of the combination of personal and racial self, the strength of the black community and the pursuit of freedom. In the autobiographies of Hurston, Angelou and Cary, the autobiographers never forget that they are members of their black community, which is always a source of their spiritual power for them. Emphasizing the strength of the black community is typical of the narration of Angelou's hometown Stamps and Hurston's hometown Eatonville. Stamps is described as a place where black people living in the segregated town suffer from violence and impotence, while the all-black Eatonville is the paradise for the black people to enjoy their freedom and autonomy. In spite of the difference between Stamps and Eatonville, both of them remain the source of Angelou's and Hurston's spiritual power. Similarly, in *Black Ice*, Cary still derives her strength from her community, from the oral tradition of black culture—storytelling. The folk stories passed on to her by her great-grandfather serve as a healing therapy for her whenever she feels alienated from the outside world.

On the other hand, black women use autobiographical writing as a vehicle to revise some of the traditions of black autobiographies, for example, correcting the stereotyped images of black women—from the image of victims to the image of women full of dignity and self-respect, or revising the forms of black autobiography in various ways. Black women's autobiographical writing is a process of revision and transcendence—a process of inheriting and revising the tradition of black autobiography.

Among the three autobiographies mentioned above, Hurston's *Dust Tracks on a Road* is the most typical one that has "stepped outside of the boundaries of conventional patterns in black autobiography" (McKay, "The Autobiographies of Zora Neale Hurston and Gwendolyn Brooks: Alternative Versions of the Black Female Self" 264) and has revised the tradition of black autobiography. Hurston, the most enigmatic woman at that time, subverts the conventional forms and contents of black autobiography and tries every means to hide her personal self behind the racial self represented by the people in the community of Eatonville. Her book seems to be very ambiguous and confusing, which leads to the disappointment and complaints from the readers, with her real intention hidden behind the "dust tracks." In fact, the title of the autobiography "Dust Tracks on a Road" itself reveals that the text is not one through which the readers can read her mind clearly and easily. Rather, readers should read her mind between the lines. In fact, through the writing of *Dust Tracks on a Road*, Hurston seems to be revising the genre of black autobiography both in themes and form. In terms of its themes, Hurston revises the stereotyped understanding of some important concepts such as the ideas of race, slavery and selfhood. Concerning its narrative skills, Hurston, as a devoted folklorist, knows well about the Negro way of speaking and employs "the black trope of the tropes"—signifyin(g) as her primary narrative strategy to play a hide-and-seek game on her dual readership. By using the strategy of signifyin(g), Hurston turns her autobiography into "a speakerly text," designed "to emulate the phonetic, grammatical, and lexical patterns of actual speech and produce the illusion of oral narration" (Gates, *The Signifying Monkey* 181). On the one hand, the strategy of signifyin(g) helps Hurston reveal the richness and vitality of black culture; meanwhile, it is also a strategy of survival for the blacks in the white dominated society. It is also subtle resistance to the dominated white culture. In effect, by breaking away "from certain imposed, widely accepted conventions" (Fabre 102) and thus revising the tradition of black autobiography, Hurston has created an autobiography which can be compared to a kaleidoscope, for which readers can give different interpretations. For different readers, the autobiographical text signifies different meanings, that is, readers can define it from different perspectives. How they will interpret it depends on whether they are "aware audience" or "unaware audience." In my opinion, however, no matter how readers read the text, they should always bear in mind Hurston's identification with her black community and her passionate love for black culture.

In *I Know Why the Caged Bird Sings*, Angelou elaborates how a black female can manage to survive in the southern United States in the 1930s, exploring what it means to grow up as a black female who is keenly aware of her displacement and isolation, and how the caged bird explores the cage and eventually manages to free herself from it successfully. The autobiography can be regarded as the paradigm of black autobiography as well as the paradigm of black women's autobiographies. In the autobiography, Angelou explores the crucial themes in black autobiography such as racial problems, racial pride, the power of words, and the traditional issues in black women's autobiography such as focusing on the strength of women, the importance of black female bonding and the consciousness of self-independence and self-fulfillment. Besides, Angelou also revises the black women's autobiography by making full use of the special form of cross-genre serial autobiographies. Besides, Angelou employs the fiction-writing skills, among which the most important ones are techniques effectively used by Angelou such as imagination, humor, comic irony and self-parody. Aiming to write her autobiographies as literature, Angelou has achieved the universal meanings in her serial autobiographies, especially in her first volume *I Know Why the Caged Bird Sings*: It has become a text in which not only the black women's experiences are examined, but the conditions of human beings are also explored.

In *Black Ice*, Cary dwells on the destructive psychological effect of the history of slavery on herself as one representative of the black students in the white dominated school of St. Paul's. This autobiography has also contributed to the revision of the tradition of black autobiography owing to its new efforts to explore the possibility of crossing the racial divide. Like Hurston, Cary is trying to examine the hybridity of black culture, believing that black culture is likely to be integrated into American culture. In some sense, her exploration echoes Hurston's idea of cultural fluidity and diversity. When Hurston wrote her autobiography, the idea of integration of black culture into American culture brought about harsh criticism from her black peers, but when Cary wrote *Black Ice*, the idea seems to be acceptable, because it is a truth that black culture has become part of American culture as a whole. Meanwhile, Cary also furthers Angelou's exploration of how black women managed to transcend the stereotyped image as victims in the white society and to claim their positive self instead of becoming the victims of their hostile environment. In the autobiography, readers are informed how young Cary realizes her self-autonomy and self-fulfillment and how she manages to become a member of the Americans by crossing the racial divide successfully.

Meanwhile, no matter whether black women's autobiographies are considered as part of black autobiography or as part of black women's literature, they are the instrument used by black women to quest for their freedom of storytelling. As William L. Andrew puts it, "the history of Afro-American autobiography is one of increasingly free storytelling" ("A Poetics of Afro-American Autobiography" 89). Black women use the weapon of autobiographical writing to tell the unique black women's experiences, to show their ceaseless quest for freedom, for the ways of self-expression and self-definition. They use autobiographical writing as a discourse to change their condition of muteness and to utter their voice. Meanwhile, just as Andrews argues, "the burden of black autobiography is to tell freedom, not just tell about freedom… Telling freedom can involve demonstrating one's liberation from any outworn or restrictive form of thinking or writing" (90), black women autobiographers such as Hurston, Angelou and Cary employ their unique narrative strategies freely to claim their positive black female self, to shoulder their responsibility of revising the literary canon, to make contributions to the flourishing of black women's literature. Since black women use the writing of autobiography as a weapon for self-definition and self-assurance, for rewriting their stereotyped images and recording their unique surviving reality, their writing has given a new dimension to African-American autobiographical tradition. Black women's autobiographies become an indispensable part of black autobiography and black women's literature, making unique and influential contributions to both genres.

Works Cited

Andrews, William L., *To Tell a Free Story*: *The First One Hundred Years of Afro-American Autobiography*, Urbana: Illinois University Press, 1986.

—. "Toward a Poetics of Afro-American Autobiography." *Afro-American Literary Study in the 1990s*, eds. Houston A. Baker Jr. and Patricia Redmond, Chicago: The University of Chicago Press, 1989. 78-93.

—. "African-American Autobiography Criticism: Retrospect and Prospect." *American Autobiography—Retrospect and Prospect*, ed. Paul John Eakin, Wisconsin: The University of Wisconsin Press, 1991. 195-215.

Angelou, Maya. "Foreward." *Dust Tracks on a Road*, by Zora Neael Hurston. New York: Harper-Perennial, 1991. vii-xii.

—. *I Know Why the Caged Bird Sings*, Now York: Random House, 1993.

—. *Poems*, New York: Random House, 1997.

—. *Gather Together in My Name*, New York: Random House, 1993.

Baker, Houston A., Jr. *Blues, Ideology, and Afro-American Literature*: *A Vernacular Theory*. Chicago: University of Chicago Press, 1984.

Balée, Susan. "Autobiography: General Essay." *The Oxford Encyclopedia of American Literature, Volume 1*, ed. Jay Parini, Oxford: Oxford University Press, 2004. 92-104.

Barnwell, Cherron A.. "Singin' de Blues, Writing Black Female Survival in *I Know Why the Caged Bird Sings*." *Critical Insights*: *I Know Why the Caged Bird Sings*. Ed. Mildred R. Mickle. Pasadena: Salem Press, 2009. 219-36.

Bhabha, Homi K.. *The Location of Culture*, New York: Routledge. 1994.

—. "Cultural Diversity and Cultural Differences." *The Post-Colonial Studies Reader*. Eds. Bill Ashcroft, Gareth Griffiths and Helen Tiffin. New York: Routledge. 1995. 206-09.

Blackburn, Regina, "In Search of the Black Female Self: African-American Women's Autobiographies and Ethnicity." *Women's Autobiography*: *Essays in Criticism*, ed. Estelle C. Jelinek, Bloomington: Indian University Press, 1980.

Bloom, Harold, Ed., *Maya Angelou's I Know Why the Caged Bird Sings*, New York: Infobase Publishing, 2009.

Boaduo FRC, Adu-Pipim, and Daphne Gumb. "Classification: Colonial Attempts to Fracture Africa's Identity and Contribution to Humanity." *The Journal of Pan African Studies*, Vol.3, No.9 (June-July 2010): 43-49.

Boas, Franz, *The Mind of Primitive Man*, Rev. edition. New York: Macmillan, 1938.

—. *The Mind of Primitive Man*, New York: Macmillan, 1929.

—. *Race, Language and Culture*, Chicago: University of Chicago Press, 1940.

Bontemps, Arna Wendell. "The Slave Narrative: An American Genre." *Great Slave Narrative*. Boston: Beacon Press, 1969.

Booth, Wayne C. *The Rhetoric of Fiction*. 2nd Ed. Harmondsworth: Penguin Books, 1983.

Braxton, Joanne M., *Black Women Writing Autobiography—A Tradition Within a Tradition*, Philadelphia: Temple University Press, 1989.

—. "Symbolic Geography and Psychic Landscapes: A Conversation with Maya Angelou." *Maya Angelou's I Know Why the Caged Bird Sings*. ed. Joanne M. Braxton. New York: Oxford University Press, 1999. 3-20.

Butterfield, Stephen, *Black Autobiography in America*. Boston: University of Massachusetts Press, 1974.

Butterworth, Susan, "Zora Neale Hurston." *The Oxford Encyclopedia of American Literature, Volume 2*, ed. Jay Parini, Oxford: Oxford University Press, 2004. 247-54.

Christian, Barbara, "Images of Black Women in Afro-American Literature: From Stereotype to Character." *Black Feminist Criticism: Perspectives on Black Women Writers*, New York: Pergamon Press, 1985. 1-28.

Cixous Helene, "The Laugh of the Medusa." *Feminisms—An Anthology of Literary Theory and Criticism*, eds. Robyn R. Warhol and Diane Price Herndl. Rutgers, New Jersey: The State University Press, 1997. 347-51.

Collins, Patricia Hill. *Black Feminist Thought: Knowledge, Consciouness and the Politics of Empowerment*. New York: Routledge, 1991.

Cudjoe, Selwyn R. "Maya Angelou: The Autobiographical Statement Updated." *Reading Black, Reading Feminist*, Ed. Henry Louis Gates Jr., New York: 1990. 272-304.

Danquah, Meri Nana-Ama, "The Incoming Wave: An Introduction." *Shaking the Tree—A Collection of New Fiction and Memoir by Black Women*, Ed. Meri

Nana-Ama Danquah, N.Y.: Norton, 2004. xiii-xxi.

Davis, Olga Idriss, "Theorizing African American Women's Discourse." *Centering Ourselves*: *American Feminist and Womanist Studies of Discourse*, eds. Marsha Houston and Olga Idriss Davis. Cresskill: Hampton Press, 2002. 39-51.

Domina, Lynn, "Autobiography: White Women During the Civil War." *The Oxford Encyclopedia of American Literature, Volume 1*, ed. Jay Parini, Oxford: Oxford University Press, 2004. 111-15.

Du Bois, W. E. B.. *The Souls of Black Folk.* Maryland: Arc Manor, 2008.

Dudley, David L., "African American Life Writing." *Encyclopedia of Life Writing—Autobiographical and Biographical Forms, Volume I*, ed. Margaretta Jolly, Chicago: Fitzroy Dearborn Publishers, 2001. 23-25.

Dunning, Stefanie, K., "Maya Angelou." *The Oxford Encyclopedia of American Literature, Volume 1*, ed. Jay Parini, Oxford: Oxford University Press, 2004. 60-62.

Duran, Isabel, "Angelou, Maya" *Encyclopedia of Life Writing—Autobiographical and Biographical Forms, Volume I*, ed. Margaretta Jolly, Chicago: Fitzroy Dearborn Publishers, 2001. 36-37.

Eakin, Paul John. *Touching the World*: *Reference in Autobiography*. Princeton: Princeton University Press, 1992.

Estes-Hicks, Onita. "The Way We Were: Precious Memories of the Black Segregated South." *Bloom's Modern Critical Interpretations*: *Maya Angelou's I Know Why the Caged Bird Sings*, ed. Harold Bloom. New York: Infobase Publishing, 2009. 65-77.

Fabre, Genevieve. "Response to William L. Andrew's 'Toward a Poetics of Afro-American Autobiography.' " *Afro-American Literary Study in the 1990s*. Eds. Houston A. Baker, Jr. and Patricia Redmond. Chicago: The University of Chicago Press, 1989. 97-104.

Fanon, Frantz. *Black Skin, White Masks*. Trans. Charles Lam Markmann. London: Pluto Press, 2008.

Fox-Genovese Elizabeth. "My Statue, My Self: Autobiographical Writing of Afro-American Women." *Reading Black, Reading Feminist*, Ed. Henry Louis Gates, Jr.. New York: Penguin, 1990. 176-200.

—. "To Write My Self—The Autobiographies of Afro-American Women." *Feminist Issues in Literary Scholarship*. Ed. Shari Benstock. Bloominton: Indiana University Press, 1987. 161-80.

—. "Myth and History: Discourse of Origins in Zora Neale Hurston and Maya Angelou." *Maya Angelou's I Know Why the Caged Bird Sings*. Ed. Harold Bloom. New York: Infobase Publishing, 2009. 29-42.

Friedman, Susan Stanford, "Women's Autobiographical Selves: Theory and Practice." *Women, Autobiography, Theory: A Reader*, eds. Sidonie A. Smith, Julia Watson. Wisconsin: The University of Wisconsin Press, 1998. 72-79.

Gates, Henry Louis, Jr. "Divided Loyalties in Black and White." Rev. of *Black Ice*, by Lorene Cary. The News and Observer Book World 21 April, 1991. http:// www.english. Upeen.edu/~lcary/books/blackice/newsoberserver. html

—. *The Signifying Monkey—A Theory of Afro-American Literary Criticism*. New York: Oxford University Press, 1988

Gillespie, Marcia Ann, Rosa Johnson Butler, and Richard A. Long. *Maya Angelou: A Glorious Celebration*. New York: Random House, 2008.

Gilmore, Leigh. *Autobiographics—A Feminist Theory of Woman's Self-Representation*. New York: Cornell University Press, 1994.

Gonzalez, Susana Vega. "From Black Ice to Black I(s): Lorene Cary's Autobiographical Self." *Revista de Estudios Norteamericanos*. 9 (2003): 123-34.

Greenfield, Sidney M. "Nature/Nurture and the Anthropology of Franz Boas and Margaret Mead as an Agenda for Revolutionary Politics." *Horizontes Antropológicos*, Porto Alegre, ano 7, n. 16, (dezembro de 2001): 35-52.

Gunzenhauser, Bonnie J. "Autobiography: General Survey." *Encyclopedia of Life Writing—Autobiographical and Biographical Forms, Volume I*, ed. Margaretta Jolly. Chicago: Fitzroy Dearborn Publishers, 2001. 75-78.

Hagen, Lyman B. "*I Know Why the Caged Bird Sings*: 'Childhood Revisited'." *Critical Insights: I Know Why the Caged Bird Sings*. Ed. Mildred R. Mickle. Pasadena: Salem Press: 2009. 149-66.

—. *Heart of a Woman, Mind of a Writer, and Soul of a Poet: A Critical Analysis of the Writings of Maya Angelou*. Lanham: University Press of America, 1997.

Hemenway, Robert E., *Zora Neale Hurston: A Literary Biography*, Urbana: University of Illinois Press, 1977.

—. Introduction. *Dust Tracks on a Road*, by Zora Neale Hurston. Ed. Robert Hemenway, Urbana: University of Illinois Press, 1984. ix-xxxix.

—. "Zola Nearle Hurston and the Eatonville Anthropology." *The Harlem Renaissance Remembered*. (1972): 190-214.

Henderson, Mae Gwendolyn, "Speaking in Tongues: Dialogics, Dialects, and the

Black Woman Writer's Literary Tradition." *Changing Our Own Words*, Ed. Cheryl A. Wall. Rutgers: The State University Press, 1989. 16-37.

Hill, Lynda, "Hurston, Zora Neale." *Encyclopedia of Life Writing— Autobiographical and Biographical Forms, Volume I*, ed. Margaretta Jolly, Chicago: Fitzroy Dearborn Publishers, 2001. 449-50.

Hooks, bell, "Black Women: Shaping Feminsit Theory", *Feminist Theory: From Margin to Center*, Boston: South End Press, 1984. 1-15.

—. "Writing the Subject: Reading *The Color Purple.*" *Reading Black, Reading Feminist—A Critical Anthology*, Ed. Henry Louis Gates, Jr., New York: Penguin, 1990. 455-70.

—. *Yearning: Race, Gender, and Culture Politics*, Boston: South End Press, 1990.

—. "Revolutionary Black Women: Making Ourselves Subject." *Postcolonial Criticism*. Eds. Bart Moor-Gilbert, Gareth Stanton and Willy Maley. New York: Addison Wesley Longman Limited, 1997. 215-33.

—. *Feminist Theory: From Margin to Center*. Boston: South End Press, 1984.

Hurston, Zora Neale, *Their Eyes Were Watching God*. Urbana: University of Illinois Press, 1978.

—. *Dust Tracks on a Road.* Ed. Robert Hemenway. Urbana: University of Illinois Press, 1984.

—. "Characteristics of Negro Expression." *Negro: Anthology*, Ed. Hugh Ford. New York: Continuum International Publishing Group, 1996. 24-46.

Jelinek, Estelle C. *The Tradition of Women's Autobiography: From Antiquity to the Present*. Boston: Twayne Publishers, 1986.

Jirousek, Lori, "'That Commonality of Feeling': Hurston, Hybridity, and Ethnography", *African American Review*, Vol. 38, No. 3 (2004): 417-27.

Johnson, Barbara, "Thresholds of Difference: Structures of Address in Zora Neale Hurston." *"Race," Writing, and Difference*, ed. Henry Louis Gates, Jr. Chicago: University of Chicago Press, 1986. 317-28.

Jones, Gayl. *Liberating Voices: Oral Tradition in African American Literature*. New York: Penguin, 1991.

Kamalu, Chukeanyere, *Foundation of African Thought: A World-view Grounded in the African Heritage of Religion, Philosophy, Science & Art*. London: Karnak House, 1990.

Kane, Nazneen. "Frantz Fanon's Theory of Racialization Implications for Globalization." *Human Architecture: Journal of the Sociology of Self-Knowledge*, V. Special Double-Issue (Summer 2007): 353-62.

Kent, George E. "Maya Angelou's *I Know Why the Caged Bird Sings* and Black Autobiographical Tradition." *Kansas Quarterly* 7 (Summer 1975): 72-78.

Kenyon, Gary M., and William L. Randall. *Restorying Our Lives*: *Personal Growth Through Autobiographical Reflection*. Westport: Praeger Publishers, 1997.

Lauret, Maria. *Liberating Literature*: *Feminist Fiction in America*. New York: Routledge Press, 1994.

Lewis, Herbert S."The Passion of Franz Boas." *American Anthropologist* 103. 2 (2001): 447-67.

Lionnet, Francoise, "Autoethnography: The An-Archic Style of *Dust Track on a Road*." *Reading Black*, *Reading Feminist*, Ed. Henry Louis Gates Jr.. New York: Penguin, 1990. 382-414.

Lorde, Audre. *Sister Outsider*. New York: The Crossing Press. 1984.

Lupton, Mary Jane. "Singing the Black Mother—Maya Angelou and Autobiographical Continuity." *Maya Angelou's I Know Why the Caged Bird Sings*. Ed. Joanne M. Braxton. New York: Oxford University Press, 1999. 129-48.

—. *Maya Angelou*: *A Critical Companion*. Westport, Connecticut: Greenwood Press,1998.

McKay, Nellie Y. "The Autobiographies of Zora Neale Hurston and Gwendolyn Brooks: Alternative Versions of the Black Female Self." *Wild Women in the Whirlwind*: *Afro-American Culture and the Contemporary Literary Renaissance*, eds. Joanne M. Braxton and Andree Nicola McLanghlin. New Brunswick: Tutgers University Press, 1990. 264-81.

—. "Race, Gender, and Cultural Context in Zora Neale Hurston's *Dust Tracks on a Road*." *Life/Lines*: *Theorizing Women's Autobiography*, eds. Bella Brodzki, Celeste Marguerite Schenck. New York: Cornell University Press, 1988. 175-88.

—. "Reflections on Black Women Writers: Revising the Literary Canon." *Feminisms—An Anthology of Literary Theory and Criticism*, eds. Robyn R. Warhol and Diane Price Herndl. Rutgers, New Jersey: The State University Press, 1997. 151-61.

—. "The Narrative Self: Race, Politics, and Culture in Black American Women's Autobiography." *Women, Autobiography, Theory*: *A Reader*, eds. Sidonie A. Smith, Julia Watson. Wisconsin: The University of Wisconsin Press, 1998. 96-106.

McMurry, Myra K. "Role-Playing as Art in Maya Angelou's Caged Bird." *Critical Insights*: *I Know Why the Caged Bird Sings*. Ed. Mildred R. Mickle. Pasadena: Salem Press. 2009. 211-18.

McPherson, Dolly A. *Order out of Chaos*: *The Autobiographical Works of Maya Angelou*. London: Virago Press Limited, 1994.

—. "Initiation and Self-Discovery." *Maya Angelou's I Know Why the Caged Bird Sings*. Ed. Joanne M. Braxton. New York: Oxford University Press, 1999. 21-47.

Meer, Sarah. "Slave Narratives." *Encyclopedia of Life Writing—Autobiographical and Biographical Forms, Volume I*, ed. Margaretta Jolly. Chicago: Fitzroy Dearborn Publishers, 2001. 814-15.

Megna-Wallace, Joanne. *Understanding I Know Why the Caged Bird Sings*: *A Student Casebook to Issues, Sources, and Historical Documents*. Westport: Greenwood Press, 1998.

Meredith, Paul. "Hybridity in the Third Space: Rethinking Bi-cultural Politics in Aotearoa / New Zealand." Paper Presented to Te Oru Rangahau Maori Research and Development Conference, 7-9 July, 1998.

Morrison, Toni. "Unspeakable Things Unspoken: The Afro-American Presence in American Literature." *Black Feminist Reader*. Ed. Joy James. Malden, Mass., USA: Blackwell, 2000. 31-32.

Nash, R., William, "Black Arts Movement." *The Oxford Encyclopedia of American Literature, Volume 1*, Ed. Jay Parini. Oxford: Oxford University Press, 2004. 190-95.

Nero, Clarence. "A Discursive Trifecta: Community, Education, and Language in *I Know Why the Caged Bird Sings*." *Critical Insights*: *I Know Why the Caged Bird Sings*. Ed. Mildred R. Mickle. Pasadena: Salem Press, 2009. 237-42.

Newman, Charles, *The Postmodern Aura, The Act of Fiction in an Age of Inflation*. Chicago: Northwestern University Press, 1985.

Olney, James, "Autobiography and the Cultural Moment: A Thematic, Historical, and Bibliographical Introduction." *Autobiography*: *Essays Theoretical and Critical*. Ed. James Olney. Princeton: Princeton University Press, 1980. 3-27.

—. *Metaphor of Self—the Meaning of Autobiography*. Princeton: Princeton University Press, 1972.

Parini, Jay. *The Oxford Encyclopedia of American Literature*. Oxford: Oxford University Press, 2004,

Phelan, James. *Narrative as Rhetoric*: *Technique, Audiences, Ethics, Ideology*.

Columbus: Ohio State UP, 1996.

Popkin, Jeremy D. *History, Historians, and Autobiography*. Chicago: The University of Chicago Press, 2005.

Rabinowitz, Peter. "Truth in Fiction: A Reexamination of Audiences." *Critical Inquiry* 4 (1977): 121-41.

Raynaud, Claudine, "Autobiography as a 'Lying' Session: Zora Neale Hurston's *Dust Tracks on a Road*." *Black Feminist Criticism and Critical Theory*, eds. Joe Weixlmann and Houston A. Baker. Greenwood, Fla.: Penkevill Pub. Co., 1998. 111-38.

Rembold, Robert. *Does Running in the Family Leave Dust Tracks on a Road?—A Traveler's Guide to Inscribing Subjective Ethnicity*. A Doctoral Dissertation. National Library of Canada, 2001.

Schultz, Elizabeth, "To Be Black and Blue: The Blues Genre in Black American Autobiography." *Kansas Quarterly* 7 (Summer 1975): 81-96.

Scott, Lynn Orilla, "Autobiography: Slave Narratives." *The Oxford Encyclopedia of American Literature, Volume 1*, ed. Jay Parini. Oxford: Oxford University Press, 2004. 105-10.

Sickels, Amy. "*I Know Why the Caged Bird Sings*: African American Literary Tradition and the Civil Rights Era." *Critical Insights*: *I Know Why the Caged Bird Sings*. Ed. Mildred R. Mickle. Pasadena: Salem Press: 2009. 19-34.

Smith, Sidonie Anne. "The Song of a Caged Bird: Maya Angelou's Quest After Self-Acceptance." *Southern Humanities Review* 7 (1973): 365-75.

—. *Where I'm Bound—Patterns of Slavery and Freedom in Black American Autobiography*. Westport: Greenwood Press, 1974.

Smith, Sidonie Anne, and Julia Watson. "Introduction: Situating Subjectivity in Women's Autobiographical Practices." *Women, Autobiography, Theory: A Reader*, eds. Sidonie A. Smith, Julia Watson. Wisconsin: The University of Wisconsin Press, 1998. 3-56.

Stepto, Robert B. *From Behind the Veil*: *A Study of Afro-American Narrative*. Chicago: University of Illinois Press, 1979.

Stocking, George W., Jr., *Race, Culture, and Evolution*: *Essays in the History of Anthropology*. New York: Free Press, 1968.

Stocking, George W., Jr.. *The Shaping of American Anthropology, 1883-1911*: *A Franz Boas Reader*. Ed. George W. Stocking. New York: Basic Books, 1974.

Stone, Albert E., *Autobiographical Occasions and Original Acts*: *Versions of American Identity From Henry Adams to Nate Shaw*. Philadelphia:

University of Pennsylvania Press, 1982.

Tate, Claudia. Ed. *Black Women Writers at Work*. New York: The Continuum Publishing Company, 1983.

Tidwell, Joanne Campbell. *Politics and Aesthetics in The Diary of Virginia Woolf*. New York: Routledge, 2008.

Vermillion, Mary. "Reembodying the Self: Representations of Rape in *Incidents in the Life of a Slave Girl* and *I Know Why the Caged Bird Sings*." *Critical Insights*: *I Know Why the Caged Bird Sings*. Ed. Mildred R. Mickle. Pasadena: Salem Press, 2009. 128-48.

Walker, Alice, "Foreward: Zora Neale Hurston—A Cautionary Tale and A Partisan View." *Zora Neale Hurston—A Literary Biography*, by Robert E. Hemenway. Urbana: University of Illinois Press, 1977. xi—xx.

Walker, Pierre A. "Racial Protest, Identity, Words, and Form." *Critical Insights*: *I Know Why the Caged Bird Sings*. Ed. Mildred R. Mickle. Pasadena: Salem Press, 2009. 167-91.

—. "Zora Neale Hurston and the Post-Modern Self in *Dust Tracks on a Road*." *African American Review* 32(3) (Fall 1998): 387. From Literature Resource Center.

Williams, Roland L, Jr. *African American Autobiography and the Quest for Freedom*. CT: Greenwood Publishing Group, 2000.

Williams, Vernon J. Jr., *Rethinking Race*: *Franz Boas and His Contemporaries*, Lexington: University of Kentucky Press, 1996.

Willis, Susan, "Histories, Communities, and Sometimes Utopia", *Specifying— Black Women Writing the American Experience*. London: Routledge, 1987. 3-25.

Xu, Dejin. Towards a Contextualized Narratology of African American Autobiography. Doctoral Dissertation. Beijing: Peking University, 2003.

http://en.wikipedia.org/wiki/Zora_Neale_Hurston

http://en.wikipedia.org/wiki/Franz_Boas

http://en.wikipedia.org/wiki/Systems_theory_in_anthropolog

http://www.aframerican.net/Article/200812/83.html

Njuguna, Osman, "African Belief System Reveals Special Links With Land." *Africa News Service*. Aug. 31, 2012. <http://www.africaspeaks.com/ reasoning/index.php?topic=6825.0;wap2 Search_Date=08/31/2012>

Wikipedia, the free encyclopedia. "The Heart of a Woman." Oct. 7, 2012. http://en.wikipedia.org/wiki/The_Heart_of_a_Woman, Search_Date= 10/7/2012.

中文论文

Yang, Renjing. *The History of 20th-Century American Literature.* Qingdao: Qingdao Press, 1999.

［杨仁敬：《20 世纪美国文学史》，青岛：青岛出版社，1999.］

Wang, Shuqin. A Study of Black Feminist Literature Criticism in America. Doctoral Dissertation. Shangdong University, 2006.

［王淑芹：《美国黑人女性主义文学批评研究》，山东：山东大学博士论文，2006.］

Zhou, Chun. A Study on Black Feminist Literature Criticism in America. Doctoral Dissertation. Sichuan University, 2006.

［周春：《美国黑人女性主义：批评研究》，四川：四川大学博士学位论文，2006.］

Liu, Jiang. "The Unreliable Narration in Autobiography" *Foreign Literature.* 1 (2012).

［刘江：自传不可靠叙述：类别模式与文本标识，《外国文学》，2012 年第 1 期.］

Acknowledgements

I wish to express my gratitude to those who have contributed to the fulfillment of my book. My first and foremost gratitude goes to my advisor, Professor Yang Renjing. Without the warm encouragement and support of Professor Yang, this book could not have been completed. In the process of writing this book, Professor Yang not only kept encouraging me whenever I felt frustrated, but also gave me a lot of enlightening and instructive suggestions concerning all aspects of the book: selecting the topic, improving the outline, giving useful guidance on how to improve the book, etc. My heartfelt gratitude also goes to Ms. Xu Baorui, wife of Prof. Yang, who always shows great concern for both of my life and study.

I am deeply grateful to Professor Zhao Yifan, Professor Chen Shidan, Professor Zhan Shukui, Professor Zhang Longhai, Professor Zhou Yubei, Professor Li Meihua and Professor Liu Wensong for their patience in reading the book and their insightful comments.

I am indebted to my friends Sun Jian, Fan Xiaomei, Xiao Biao and Zhang Shufen for their friendship and help. I wish to show my deep gratitude to Sun Jian, who, when staying in the U.S., would devote himself to the collection of the books and articles I needed whenever I asked him for help. Fan Xiaomei and Zhang Shufen also spent much time collecting materials for me, which are very helpful to me in the writing of the book. My friends Lu Suzhen, Xiao Biao and Huang Jinna also kept encouraging me to carry on.

Besides, I wish to show my gratitude to my husband for his reassurance, patience and tolerance. I also want to thank the other members of my family, including my father-in-law, my grandmother, my parents and my sisters, who helped me take good care of my two-year-old son when I was writing the book last year. Here, I especially like to show my deep gratitude and love to my beloved 89-year-old grandmother, who helped to look after my son last summer. And it is such a pity that she passed away last month.

Finally, I am also indebted to my beloved son. Each time I telephoned him when he stayed at my mother's home, he would say to me: "Mummy, come to pick me up after you finish your homework."

图书在版编目(CIP)数据

赫斯顿、安吉洛和凯莉自传的新突破/江春兰著. 一厦门：厦门大学出版社，
2015.5
ISBN 978-7-5615-5429-6

Ⅰ. ①赫…　Ⅱ. ①江…　Ⅲ. ①赫斯顿,Z. N. (1891～1960)-自传-研究　②安吉洛,Z. N. (1928～2014)-自传-研究　Ⅳ. ①K837.125.6

中国版本图书馆 CIP 数据核字(2015)第 108355 号

官方合作网络销售商：　dangdang.com　亚马逊 amazon.cn　JD.COM 京东

厦门大学出版社出版发行

(地址:厦门市软件园二期望海路 39 号　邮编:361008)
总 编 办 电 话:0592-2182177　传真:0592-2181253
营销中心电话:0592-2184458　传真:0592-2181365
网址:http://www.xmupress.com
邮箱:xmup @ xmupress.com
厦门集大印刷厂印刷
2015 年 5 月第 1 版　2015 年 5 月第 1 次印刷
开本:720×1000　1/16　印张:14.5　插页:2
字数:285 千字
定价:45.00 元
本书如有印装质量问题请直接寄承印厂调换